Industrial Espionage: Intelligence Techniques and Countermeasures

Industrial Espionage: Intelligence Techniques and Countermeasures

Norman R. Bottom, Jr.
Robert R.J. Gallati

BUTTERWORTH PUBLISHERS
Boston • London
Sydney • Wellington • Durban • Toronto

Library of Congress Cataloging in Publication Data

Bottom, Norman R.
     Industrial espionage.

     Bibliography: p.
     Includes index.
     1. Business intelligence. I. Gallati, Robert R. J. II. Title.
HD38.7.B67   1983   658.4'72   83-7861
ISBN 0-409-95108-0

Butterworth Publishers
80 Montvale Avenue
Stoneham, MA 02180

10 9 8 7 6 5 4 3 2 1

Printed in the United States of America

To our beloved America. May it always be strong and vigilant. May its enemies within and without never prevail, so that this nation, under God, shall survive and prosper.

Contents

Foreword

The information age which has exploded around us in recent years has brought new attention to the discipline of intelligence to cope with the flood of facts and the need to protect ourselves from damaging exposure. Nowhere is this more true than in business and industry, where accumulating accurate information well analyzed can bring profit while allowing products and plans to be compromised can cause losses. But to benefit from this discipline, it must be fully understood and the techniques carefully adopted to the world of business and industry. Mistaken and ill-advised attempts to apply intelligence techniques can only produce more damage than ever.

Doctors Bottom and Gallati have undertaken this task of interpretation, and have performed it well. They have called attention to the real dangers of industrial intelligence conducted by foreign governments as well as unscrupulous competitors in the business world. The Soviet Union's successes in stealing our atomic secrets in the late 1940s are matched today by their—and the Japanese-manufacturers'—operations against American high technology. The authors have gone beyond this alarm to point out the lessons of central intelligence: that the patient gathering of publicly available information followed by its careful collation and analysis can often bring important and unnoticed conclusions to decision makers. They have also outlined the important roles of security and counterintelligence in protecting an industry or business from the leakage or willful diversion of its private and proprietary information into hostile hands. In so doing, they have discussed the contributions which effective technology can make to these processes, and have applied to the private sector some of the successful methods of our intelligence profession. The serious businessman, industrial leader, and security professional will gain greatly from a careful study of the material Doctors Bottom and Gallati have gathered and analyzed. They will find much of direct value and application as they develop their plans for protecting their companies against industrial espionage while, at the same time, improving their capabilities to wrestle with their own information flow in a fully lawful manner.

William E. Colby

Preface and Acknowledgments

During World War II the people of the United States were very conscious of all types of espionage. Industrial espionage was of grave concern both to the government and to the general public. This sensitivity prevailed up to and including the hostilities in Korea. Since the end of the Korean conflict, concern for industrial espionage has waned and our economy has been devasted by an onslaught of espionage agents, both domestic and foreign.

It is the authors' hope that this book will stimulate a new awareness of the necessity of counterintelligence to combat spies and saboteurs. Never before has U.S. industry—the arsenal of democracy—been under such a sophisticated espionage attack. Just as at dawn we slept in Pearl Harbor, so today we dream of peace while our technological defense is eroded by illegal foreign technology transfer. Many well-trained, dedicated espionage agents are infesting our businesses, our commercial establishments, our research facilities, and our high-technology industries. If this book serves no other purpose than to revive our dormant concern about espionage, it will have been justified.

We address this book to corporate and company security directors and to the American public. We plead for a reawakening, a new awareness, and a new resolve to counter the spymasters of the KGB and the Soviet bloc as well as other espionage practitioners.

We examine the past, the present, and the future. Industrial espionage is as ancient as biblical times and as modern as the latest high-technology surveillance device. While espionage runs rampant today, the future threat of industrial espionage becomes more enormous with each passing year. Each technological advance creates more powerful tools for the secret agent and the spymaster.

Attempting to cope with the threat of espionage is fraught with philosophical, ethical, and legal constraints in a democratic society.

In a totalitarian society, however, whatever is required, regardless of its immorality, illegality, or inhumanity, is allowed. In this one-sided minefield, we need to develop our counterintelligence with the tools that are available to us, but we need to double our zeal to compensate for our constraints.

In this book we discuss the defenses against espionage; planning, organizing, directing, and controlling the counterintelligence thrust are dealt with in detail, as well as research activity and investigative methods for counterintelligence. Scientific and technical aids are discussed from the standpoint of developing intelligence, and also from the perspective of defeating the hostile use of these powerful tools of espionage by our adversaries.

We devote several chapters to the steps involved in producing and using the intelligence product. These are both fascinating and frightening in their implications. Security professionals should seize the opportunity to develop their own counterintelligence capabilities by following the comprehensive treatment of the subject in this book.

We outline countermeasures to cope with the known threat. The dangers and hazards of hostile espionage in the industrial world may be checked by physical and electronic security measures. A final chapter on surveillance sensitivity will assist targets to recognize the onslaught of espionage and to be specifically sensitive to surveillance. Being aware of surveillance makes it possible to invoke countermeasures and can prevent successful penetration or compromise.

We wish to express our profound gratitude to all who so generously contributed to the concept, structure, research, and development of this volume, especially:

Mari Bottom, M.A., C.S.T., wife, friend, and assistant to the co-author of the same name;

George S. Blair, Ph.D., Elizabeth Helms Rosecrans Professor of Social Science, Claremont Graduate School;

The Honorable William Colby, former Director, Central Intelligence Agency;

Robert Croatti, Associate Dean, College of Criminal Justice, Northeastern University;

Romine Deming, Professor of Security, College of Criminal Justice, Northeastern University;

The Faculty of the College of Criminal Justice, Northeastern University;

Greg Franklin, our Editor and friend;

Robert Hair, Professor, John Jay College of Criminal Justice, City University of New York;

Colonel Henry Henn (USA-Ret.), formerly of the Defense Intelligence Agency;

Gerald Lunt, M.A., an able researcher;

Timothy F. Moran, Associate Dean, University College, Northeastern University;

Lewis Nelson, Ed.D., East Tennessee State University;

Steven M. Powers, dedicated student of industrial espionage while an undergraduate at the College of Criminal Justice, Northeastern University;

Norman Rosenblatt, Dean, College of Criminal Justice, Northeastern University;

Dave Shatraw, Special Agent (retired), Federal Bureau of Investigation;

Krishnan Subramanian, graduate student at the College of Criminal Justice, Northeastern University;

S. Subramanian, Deputy Director, National Police Academy, Hyderabad, India (formerly a graduate student at the College of Criminal Justice, Northeastern University);

John J. Sullivan, Dean, Mercy College, Dobbs Ferry, N.Y.; and

Charlie Woolhouse, Correspondence Secretary, Association of Former OSI Special Agents.

To all of these wonderful people and others just too numerous to mention, we express our heartfelt thanks.

N.R.B.
R.R.J.G.

I. INTRODUCING ESPIONAGE

1. Introduction and History of Espionage

TAKE, v.t.—To acquire, frequently by force but preferably by stealth.
—Ambrose Bierce,
The Devil's Dictionary

Espionage enjoys a romantic history. Glamorous ladies practicing ball-room seduction and handsome male agents braving danger thrill us when they spy for a good cause in the pages of a novel or on the screen. But espionage also has a disreputable history. There are weaklings blackmailed to commit unjustified acts of betrayal, ruined lives, and bankrupted employers in the picture too. Romance and dirty hands are not contradictory, however, as any fan of the historical novel or soap opera knows well. Espionage is a complex activity, indeed.

Espionage includes theft of secrets and invasion of privacy. In addition, it is often linked to such covert action as sabotage, assassination, and disinformation. Espionage performed by our government to protect national security may be praiseworthy; espionage by our enemies or competitors is always wrong.

The justifications put forth for espionage have not changed over the years. It is authorized for the purposes of deception or to locate hidden information or because information otherwise obtainable is considered to be incomplete or untrustworthy.

In wartime, espionage is granted far more latitude than in peace-time. The fact that no formal declaration of war exists between hostile nations or competitors does not eliminate the fact that some nations and some competitors use espionage. Organized crime and terrorists use espionage; society is at war with both at all times.

Industrial espionage agents are often traitors to their nations. These agents are associates or employees who have determined to compromise company secrets either voluntarily or under duress. A traitor's behavior is often based on a lack of character due to weakness in regard to sexual habits or greed. Less frequently, treason is based on intellectual conviction or revenge.

Those who betray secrets serve two types of masters. One type of master is a hostile government or terrorist cell and presumably motivated by some misguided idealism. The second type of master works solely for the compensation espionage offers to successful practitioners. Espionage threats are increased by cooperation among and between espionage practitioners. All supplement their efforts by using dupes or informers to help steal corporate data.

TRADECRAFT

Most occupational groups have developed their own complex jargon over the years. Espionage is no different. A partial list of espionage tradecraft terms follows.

- *Agent handler*: Spy supervisor, spy master, also known as *control*.
- *Agent-in-place*: Sometimes known as a mole or deep-cover agent, this individual has a legitimate reason to be in the environment but is secretly a spy.
- *Burned*: An espionage agent or counterintelligence agent who cannot maintain a cover story or fallback and is therefore exposed.
- *Code or cypher*: Audible or visible signals used to disguise transmitted information.
- *Control*: Agent supervisor, also known as *agent handler*.
- *Cut-out*: An intermediary who serves to screen the connection between agents; the cut-out may be witting or unwitting about his or her role.
- *Cover story*: Plausible rationale for any activity; also, false personal history data.
- *Dangle*: Offer a decoy to attract espionage agents.
- *Dead drop*: A place where secret messages or materials are deposited for pickup by another. Also known as a post box.
- *Double agent*: An espionage agent who has been turned to work against previous spy masters. *Doubling* is the process of creating a double agent.
- *Fallback*: Secondary rendezvous location; secondary cover story; any preparation of alternatives based on the possibility that the original plan cannot be used.

- *Mole*: A highly placed agent-in-place pretending loyalty but secretly committing espionage for some outside interest. Most dangerous of all spies. Also known as *agent-in-place.*
- *Safe house*: A sterile (safe) location where meetings can be held or individuals protected without fear of discovery or monitoring.
- *Sleepers*: Enemy agents who have been infiltrated into the target camp and ordered to maintain a low profile until activated. Also known as *illegals.*
- *Surveillance*: Monitoring someone and his or her activities. Surveillance can be performed by people or technical devices, such as microphones, or by both working in concert.
- *Turning*: The process of creating a *double agent*. Also known as *doubling.*
- *Walk-in*: Unexpected appearance of an enemy agent who offers to defect.

ESPIONAGE COLLECTION

This is a form of secrets theft characterized by the use of spies and/or their agents. All espionage depends on access to the desired information. Spies use sophisticated equipment to collect their information, as well as such traditional measures as blackmail, burglary, and subversion. They use false pretenses or other clandestine means. The information they seek is destined for the use of other parties. That ultimate use may be for financial, ideological, military, or competitive purposes. Employers of espionage agents directed against corporations include hostile nations, competitors, terrorists, and organized crime families. Often it is difficult, if not impossible, to discover the real employer of an espionage agent, who may not even know this information because the agent handler has used deception as to that identity.

The corporate information that spies seek appears in a number of forms, including computer-stored data, blueprints, letters or memoranda, files, formulas, charts and diagrams, production models, and prototypes. Espionage also profits from visual observations and the interception of verbal communications. In effect, anything of corporate informational value becomes a potential industrial espionage target. It must be protected by counterespionage, more often known as counterintelligence.

Deceit is at the heart of espionage collection. Much as the magician seeks to mystify his audience, the espionage agent uses misdirection, disguise, and other cover methods in attempts to remove sensitive corporate data without a trace or at least without correct attribution.

TECHNICAL ESPIONAGE

Technicians offer sophisticated, miniaturized eavesdropping equipment unavailable until recently. The fact that penalties for electronic eavesdropping are low in many countries has helped sales of such equipment considerably. The United States has strict laws about intercepting and recording conversations; the United Kingdom, France, Italy, and West Germany presently do not.

Microtransmitters are the most common type of eavesdropping device. They operate by battery or from house current, broadcasting conversations to a remote location. Tape recorders, often voice-activated, are used. Telephones may be tapped to record conversations or turned into microphones to pick up nearby sounds. Parabolic and laser microphones can be focused on a group or a window to eavesdrop on conversations.

The early history of technical espionage is slight because the technology is mostly recent. Telescopes and binoculars used with lip readers have long proved effective. Motion pictures have the advantage of leisurely analysis. All children have put a glass against a door or wall to eavesdrop and found it more or less effective. So have espionage agents.

Postal communications have always been a subject of espionage. Former U.S. Secretary of State Henry Stimson is alleged to have remarked, "Gentlemen do not read other peoples' mail." Perhaps not, but spies do. Under the elizabethan spy master, Sir Francis Walsingham, the British Secret Service regularly opened, read, resealed, and sent on mail of interest. Walsingham's Department of Intelligence employed Thomas Philippes to invent and break codes. It should be noted that all major European powers have used *black chambers* in order to censor mail. Modern U.S. government *mail covers* is one type of mail censorship. It involves the recording of external information, and sometimes the internal information as well.

Codes and cyphers, an integral part of the history of espionage, are as old as communication. Early attempts to encrypt messages were ingenious if uncomplicated. For instance, the rulers of Sparta wrote messages on leather wrapped around a staff. When the leather was unwound, the letters became jumbled. The recipient of the leather strip had to wind it around a similar staff to decode the message. Julius Caesar used a transposition code, replacing each letter with another letter three places down the alphabet.

Code breakers realize that the most common letter used in English correspondence is *E*. The next most common is *T*. The letter *H* often precedes vowels. The most common pair of letters is *TH*. Vowels are often followed by *N*. Commonsense knowledge like this enabled early code breakers to get the message.

Cryptographers progressed to develop book codes. Numbers are used to transmit a message. They indicate a page. The first (unrepeated) 26 letters on that page are to be substituted for the alphabet. Book codes rely on the difficulty in determining the book chosen by the agents, each of whom has a copy of the same book.

One-time pads, first developed in Germany, are mathematical keys never repeated and never reused. Both the sender and recipient must know the proper key, often based on a particular day. The random nature of one-time code pads makes them virtually unbreakable. The most recent development in cryptography is the electronic cypher machine. These embody complex formulas virtually impossible to break even by computer and are a type of electronic one-time pad.

COVERT ACTION

Espionage activities sometimes extend beyond the theft of valuable secrets. Covert action refers to radical, often violent, attempts to harm an individual, organization, or political structure. It is called covert action because the perpetrators attempt to disguise their motives, identities, or both. Covert action, unlike espionage collection, cannot occur without attention from the media and the target of the activity.

The agent provocateur is someone employed by espionage masters and ordered to infiltrate a social group, business, organization, or labor movement. Pretending to be sympathetic, the agent provocateur secretly works to lead or prod associates to commit illegal or troublesome activity. Frequently they would not have committed the acts without this push.

Another type of covert action is disinformation, a propaganda attack based on lies, false accusations, and doctored facts. Users of disinformation disguise their true bias. They promote demonstrations, riots, public outcry, legal action, and media coverage, all designed to harm the corporation chosen for attack.

Covert action includes sabotage. Spies seeking to damage production may cause explosions, fires, breakdowns, or other accidents. Usually an inside spy is responsible for covert action sabotage. (*Sabotage* is a word stemming from the early years of the industrial revolution in France. Workers who wanted to stop factory production lines used their wooden shoes, *sabots*, to jam the mechanism.)

Terrorist groups frequently use an inside source to assist the planning and carrying out of assassination and kidnapping, as well as other violent activity. This type of covert action is the most dangerous to the corporation, its executives, their families, and the stockholders. Terrorists are known as meticulous planners. Captured safe-house documents have verified their ongoing use of espionage. Terrorists here are defined as violent political activitists who routinely attack noncombatants and interfere with legitimate business in the pursuit of political ends. Their methods include sabotage, bombing, maiming, kidnapping, hostage taking, extortion, and assassination.

ROOTS OF INDUSTRIAL ESPIONAGE

Intelligence is the parent of espionage and its foe, counterintelligence. Intelligence is a method of providing the most accurate data available to decision makers, those who control organizations, corporations, or nations. It involves the collection of information for later analysis.

Publicly available information often is a mixture of lies, distortions, half-truths, and occasional facts. Such information represents a poor basis for crucial decisions. Espionage activity seeks to uncover facts (unavailable from open sources) that are vital to the success of an organization, corporation, or nation-state. Such facts are, or should be, carefully protected. Industrial espionage seeks to penetrate the corporate protective shell.

Industrial spies may try to blackmail employees who control or have access to sensitive information. They may covertly penetrate a corporation in order to steal or photograph data or install electronic eavesdropping devices. External espionage activity includes surveillance, lip reading, the use of parabolic (long-range) microphones, and other electronic devices.

Espionage agents, national and corporate, first try to compromise individuals by exploiting the common human weaknesses of greed and sex. Should this tactic not work, undercover agents or a clandestine penetration (burglary) of the facility are used.

Espionage represents the dark side of information collection. The history of espionage proves that both the good guys and the bad guys have enjoyed the services of espionage agents on a regular basis.

In all cases of competitive espionage, the basic motive is profit. Some business competitors use espionage as an alternative to paying for their own research and development. Other corporations favor espionage to destroy the profit base of competitors. Another reason for corporate-controlled industrial espionage is simply curiosity about the opposition, a form of self-protection.

Of course, espionage is a form of laziness as well as greed. Corporations that practice industrial espionage are incapable of competing in a straightforward, normal manner. They must have an edge, however illegal or unethical.

Political terrorists are not concerned merely with data; they want the blood and money of governments and commercial enterprises. The fruits of terrorist crimes are said by the foolish to advance some revolutionary cause. Noted as careful planners, terrorists seek intelligence information for each strike (hit). Most of this information comes through espionage activities of terrorist gang members of their informants.

Organized crime, another element of the industrial espionage picture, has a money problem. Their illegal gains must be laundered through legitimate business operations. Legitimate business is subject to takeover bids, which depend on inside information. Such information is usually generated through espionage methods, however crude. Corruption of corporate officers into *moles* is a usual tactic. The threat involved in organized crime espionage is loss of corporate control. This threat should be considered second only to that of terrorism, which seeks death for its enemies.

Nation-states, business competitors, political terrorists, and organized crime families represent intelligence users and potent espionage threats to modern corporations. Any combination among these interests doubles or triples the industrial espionage threat. This sort of cooperation has taken place. For example, terrorists have cooperated with organized crime, principally in Europe. Business has cooperated with organized crime, principally in Europe and Asia. Nation-states have cooperated with terrorists; Libya is an example. And nation-states have cooperated with organized crime throughout the world in respect to espionage.

Any understanding of espionage must follow from an understanding of intelligence. Intelligence is simply a method or process for refining raw information of varying reliability. Traditional steps in this process are usually referred to as the essential elements of intelligence (EEIs). These include direction of data-collection efforts, collection of data, interpretation of data, evaluation of data for utility, collation of similar data materials, analysis of these materials, and the reporting of conclusions. (The EEIs are discussed further in Chapter 8.)

For the purpose of this discussion, it is necessary to focus on collection of data. Espionage is one method used to collect data. It represents a secret, usually illegal, collection activity. Other collection methods are *open*; they range from studying newspapers and magazines to debriefing departing employees. Most information is collected by such open methods, known as overt collection.

Intelligence has long been deemed necessary for government agencies as well as for corporate enterprises that require up-to-date, accurate data. The need for true intelligence has become increasingly crucial because of the information explosion. Too much information is available, and too much is contradictory; it cannot be accepted on face value. Intelligence processing turns information into usable data, and this knowledge is power. As an example, consider the British role in World War II. Rather recently it has been learned that the British decrypted many German code messages, sent through the German Enigma code machine, that pinpointed U-boat positions, announced ground assault plans, and identified Luftwaffe aerial targets. This intelligence allowed Allied victories. Undoubtedly the breaking of the Enigma codes hastened the end of World War II if it did not actually prevent the Allies' defeat by the Axis powers. Code breaking is an intelligence activity.

Harold L. Wilensky has commented, "Failures in intelligence . . . can be more fatal than lapses in control."[1] He means that organizations that neglect intelligence risk ruin. Wilensky points out, correctly, that the Edsel automobile, introduced by Ford in the 1960s, was the result of a colossal error in judgment due to faulty consumer intelligence.

Conversely, but just as correctly, it can be maintained that counterintelligence failure—the failure to prevent industrial espionage— can bankrupt a corporation or gravely interfere with profits.

The overall world of intelligence can be subdivided into four basic sections: strategic intelligence, tactical intelligence, counter-intelligence, and security. Strategic and tactical intelligence are much the same but with one crucial difference: time available for collection of information and its study. Counterintelligence and security are defensive efforts to protect an organization from attempts to commit illegal acts. Such acts collectively are called espionage. Espionage can be committed in a variety of ways. Counterintelligence seeks to foil each method in a timely fashion. Security in this context is an internal guarding function concerned with safeguarding data at their source or place of storage. Counterintelligence focuses on the external sphere, serving as a first line of defense for corporate secrets.

This book is largely concerned with counterintelligence and the intelligence techniques and countermeasures used in counterintelligence. Since counterintelligence cannot exist in a vacuum, strategic and tactical intelligence production, as well as security, cannot be neglected. Many intelligence techniques, such as the EEIs, are shared

---

[1] Harold L. Wilensky, *Organizational Intelligence* (New York: Basic Books, 1967), p. 7

functions. Others, such as turning an agent, are strictly counterintelligence methods.

SHORT ACCOUNT OF ESPIONAGE

The following section should convince even the most optimistic reader that industrial espionage is not a recent threat nor one likely to disappear as long as humans inhabit this planet.

The authors debated on where to start the unending history of espionage. There is no intention here to bore the reader with too numerous examples or overemphasize the longevity of espionage. Examples provided are meant to be illustrative, not all inclusive. Chronology takes second place to other organizational considerations.

Foreign Technology Transfer through the Ages

Foreign technology transfer refers to the illegal exportation of data and/or materials, parts, or equipment. It is often, although not always, due to industrial espionage. At other times foreign technology transfer occurs as a result of lax export controls or illegal transshipping, often to or through a false nominee. Hostile nations and unethical foreign competitors benefit from foreign technology transfer. Nations victimized through their private sectors suffer economic losses, as well as loss of military superiority in many cases. Examples highlight successful espionage, old and new, that resulted in the illegal transfer of technology to a foreign nation.

SILK. Silk was highly prized in the ancient world. The only source of silk was China and it exercised a tight monopoly. The results were high prices for silk and control of cloth supplies. Dangers, expense, and time delays made the silk caravan routes unpleasant. The situation changed when Persian monks visited the Roman Emperor Justinian.

The monks revealed the secret of silk. They explained that silkworms, fed on mulberry leaves, spun cocoons that were later woven into silks. Justinian became convinced that the climate in certain parts of Greece were suitable for cultivating the vital mulberry leaves. He could obtain the mulberry trees, but needed the silkworms. These Persian monks, presumably for ample reward, reentered China and were successful in smuggling silkworms to Rome in hollow canes. Justinian became wealthier, and China lost millions in foreign trade.

TEXTILES. Early American colonists depended on England for factory-produced goods. In return, the colonists furnished vital raw materials, including wood and agricultural products as well as cotton and tobacco. But these colonies suffered from the exchange because England controlled the market. The prices for imported goods, especially textile goods, seemed excessive to the Americans. England refused to allow textile craftsmen to immigrate to the New World and prohibited export of factory machinery and plans to the colonies. The situation looked hopeless until Samuel Slater did something about it.

The American industrial revolution is often dated from 1789 when Slater founded a textile mill bearing his name in Pawtucket, Rhode Island. As an apprentice in England, he had memorized textile mill plans and was able to slip out of England (perhaps assisted by an American financier) and make his way to the colonies where he used his knowledge to break the British monopoly.

RUBBER. Brazil enjoyed a virtual monopoly on rubber up to the early years of the twentieth century. Its economy was heavily dependent on the rubber industry, which ensured reasonable national prosperity and full employment. But many other nations were anxious to break the monopoly and share the profits because the uses for rubber were increasing steadily. The situation looked hopeless until a British firm took action.

Although the exportation of rubber plants was strongly forbidden by the Brazilian government, a plant or two was illegally taken from Brazil to England. British horticulturists studied and cultivated the rubber plant in a greenhouse until they had confidence in their abilities. They decided to cultivate the plant in Malaya because of its climate and because it was part of the British Empire. Malayan rubber soon took over much of Brazil's former market, and Brazil suffered severe economic decline as a result. Great Britain enjoyed a rubber boom until the Japanese took over Malaya during World War II and substitutes for rubber were developed.

BANKING. European banking houses have a long history of espionage activities to keep abreast of anything that could affect their loans or reserves. The banking house of the Rothschilds (in Frankfurt, London, Paris, Vienna, and Naples) is believed to have created one of the greatest intelligence systems of its time. The Rothschild's secret communications network at the time of World War I was faster than those of the belligerents; in fact, the Rothschild bank in England received battle reports before the prime minister heard through official channels.

In addition to wartime communications, the Rothschilds kept close watch on government and private activity through overt means and the use of espionage. A favorite method of keeping the transfer of money under surveillance was the *fiche*. Attached to records of an account, the *fiche* consisted of instructions to notify someone, often in another country, of account transactions. The account holder usually knew nothing of the *fiche*, which was as efficient in its own way as a modern electronic transmitter covertly attached to someone's vehicle.

Modern Foreign Technology Transfer

The Federal Bureau of Investigation (FBI) in the 1970s reported that American corporate secrets and technology increasingly are diverted to the Soviet Union through illegal means. Top CIA officials later termed the problem as *acute* hemorrhaging of our know-how.

Of course, not all the Soviets' information gathering is by means of espionage; technical journals and scientific conference proceedings provide a great deal of information, for example. But there have been numerous cases of outright spying.

William Webster, FBI director, stated in 1981 that a "representative of an Eastern European intelligence service offered an American automotive engineer at a large U.S. firm approximately $200,000 to assist with the theft of a patented glass production process which had cost the company millions of dollars to put into production."[2] In another instance that Webster reported, agents of the U.S.S.R. hired a foreign national to acquire sophisticated computer software technology. He reportedly attempted to pay half a million dollars to an undercover FBI agent. Arrested, the spy pled guilty to violating the Export Administration Act.

Speaking in 1981, Attorney General William Smith noted the Soviet espionage threat is composed not only of agents dispatched to the United States with false identities and diplomats believed to be intelligence officers but also trading company representatives. Often students, scientists, and reporters from the Societ Union are spies. Some immigrants and refugees from Cuba are espionage agents.

In December 1981, a Polish trading company executive living in California who had been buying secret defense information was sentenced to life in prison. This man was a deep-cover agent who had

---

[2] *FBI Bulletin* (August 1981).

used the Polamco trading company as a screen for his espionage activity. He used greed to compromise a Hughes engineer. That engineer, William Bell, had already passed over secrets worth millions jeopardizing several weapons systems, including the TOW missile antitank technology, F-15 radar technology, and quiet radar of the B-1 stealth bomber.

In 1982, FBI agents set up a sting operation that resulted in the indictment of Japanese businessmen who allegedly paid for secret IBM data. Years earlier Japanese business interests were discovered committing espionage in North Carolina to learn clothing mill production secrets. The Japanese have a history of pirating and copying American technology going back at least to the 1930s.

Political Espionage

Little recorded information is available on espionage practiced by corporate interests, terrorists, or organized crime, but there is a wealth of information on the practice of national espionage, often for both political and economic advantages as well as military superiority.

According to the Bible, Joshua dispatched spies into Egypt. Queen Esther's secret agents told her of a planned pogrom against the Jewish people. And Moses sent agents into Canaan:

> In sending them to reconnoiter the land of Canaan, Moses said to them, "Go up here in the Negeb, up into the highlands, and see what kind of land it is. Are the people living there strong or weak, few or many? Is the country in which they live good or bad? Are the towns in which they dwell open or fortified? Is the soil fertile or barren, wooded or clear? And do your best to get some fruit of the land."[3]

Sun Tzu, in *The Art of War* written more than two thousand years ago, devoted a chapter to the employment of secret agents. His description of five types of secret agents is often quoted today as an example of how espionage has changed little. The five types are native, inside, doubled, expendable, and living espionage agents:

- Native agents: Citizens of the enemy but not having any official authority.
- Inside agents: Citizens of the enemy with official (governmental) status. (Today we refer to both native and inside agents as agents-in-place.)

---

[3] Numbers 13.

- Doubled agents: Spies of the enemy who now work for us due to coercion, conviction, or greed.
- Expendable agents: The dirtiest type of espionage popularized by many recent books and films highlighting betrayal of the agent. An expendable agent is sacrificed to the enemy after having been primed with false information.
- Living agents: Professional spies expected to return alive with the information.

Francis Dvornik has established that recorded political espionage can be traced to some of the earliest national states.[4] The ancient cultural states of the Nile and the Middle East practiced espionage. For example, in the Eighteenth Dynasty of Egypt, which existed over 3,500 years ago, royal messengers, the eyes and ears of the pharaoh, were supplemented by secret signaling by fire beacons.

Carthaginians employed concealed writing by marking a wooden tablet later covered with wax. Hannibal employed what we would call disinformation; false information was allowed to fall into enemy hands in the form of spurious official letters. Both Rome and Carthage used merchants as spies.

Roman financial speculators and merchants actually financed the Roman intelligence service at one time. Not only did they finance espionage, they performed it, at the risk of their lives. The Arab Muslim Empire, originating in sixth century A.D. expansion, relied heavily on espionage through a carefully controlled postal establishment that carried no private correspondence. Carrier pigeons were used as a means of transmitting Arab intelligence. This form of message transmission perhaps preceded the use of carrier pigeons by the Chinese beginning about 700 A.D.

Alexander the Great used a spy force to gather intelligence before his attacks. Julius Caesar used a squadron of *exploratores* to learn the weaknesses of his opponents on the battlefield, as well as in the political sector of Rome itself.

Medieval Europe saw the rise of the Venetian Republic. It employed the *sbirri*, a group of spies, to keep tabs on rival Italian city-states. England developed the beginnings of its modern secret service during the reign of Queen Elizabeth I. She employed Sir Francis Walsingham as her spy master during the time of the Spanish Armada.

---

[4] Francis Dvornik, *Origins of Intelligence Services* (New Brunswick, N.J.: Rutgers University Press, 1974). Much of the information on the ancient world is adapted from this important text.

John Thurloe, Sir Oliver Cromwell's intelligence chief, is said to have spent the equivalent of millions of dollars a year to buy the best spies and informants in England and on the Continent.

Joseph Fouché served under Napoleon as head of the secret police and state counterintelligence agency. He was perhaps the first to establish thousands of extensive background files on suspects.

George Washington also recognized the need for intelligence. The names of Benedict Arnold (British spy and American traitor), Nathan Hale (executed American spy) and John André (executed British spy) are familiar to all American school children.

Wilhelm Stieber of Prussia was in charge of both military intelligence and the secret police. The secret police later became the Gestapo under first Field Marshal Goering and later the Reichsführer-SS, Heinrich Himmler. Stieber developed mass espionage by flooding an area with his agents. This tactic was practiced later by the U.S.S.R. after World War II.

Russia began surveillance of foreigners inside its borders in the sixteenth century. Agents called *pristan* were assigned to spy on visitors. In the seventeenth century, Russia began sending spies to guard and monitor Russian citizens traveling abroad, a practice that still continues.

Domestic Industrial Espionage

Many acts of industrial espionage have gone unreported by victimized American corporations. There are a variety of reasons for failing to report all types of crimes, as recent victimization studies have shown. In the case of unexpected industrial espionage, laws have often failed to provide remedy for the theft of trade secrets (see Chapter 4). There has been a reasonable fear that discovery proceedings and witness testimony in open court could cause further exposure of trade secrets. Additionally, corporations do not like the public embarrassment that could come from revelations of successful espionage. Also industrial espionage may be unrecognized or attributed to the wrong cause.

In late 1981, police in northern California charged an accountant, previously fired from Oakland-based Mother's Cake & Cookie Company, with trying to sell twelve of Mother's cookie recipes to the rival firm of Pepperidge Farms, Inc. Pepperidge Farms pretended to cooperate with the accountant but turned the offer of the recipes over to the authorities.

In 1981, the C-E Cast Equipment division of Combustion Engineering in Cleveland, Ohio, noticed that orders for replacement parts had slowed, and officials hired private detectives to look into the reasons. They discovered that ex-employees had gone into the parts business for themselves with blueprints stolen from Combustion Engineering. Four former employees were indicted for theft of trade secrets and other charges

In a 1978 decision, Michigan Judge Hunter Stair dismissed a lawsuit brought by a Detroit-area armored-car maker, the Cadillac Gage Company, that alleged the theft of valuable plans by a rival concern. But Judge Stair noted that Cadillac Gage often left plant site gates unlocked and valuable blueprints on the plant floor. During the trial a defense attorney was successful in entering a Florida plant of Cadillac Gage without challenge. He took extensive photographs without complaint from Cadillac Gage personnel.

Mobile Oil confronted Superior Oil in U.S. District Court in September 1978 charging personnel raiding and trade secret loss. Mobil was concerned that former employees would divulge sensitive information concerning Mobil's lease-evaluation and exploration-bidding techniques. The raid of key personnel was said to have taken place over a two-year period. (Such complaints are not infrequent in the oil industry or other industries with a high turnover of skilled and scientific personnel.)

Francis Thomas Dunlap met with Peter K. Gopal in September 1978. Dunlap was pretending to be an officer of National Semiconductor while actually serving as an employee of Intel Corporation. Both companies are high-technology manufacturers in the Silicon Valley area of Santa Clara county, California. Gopal offered what he called Intel designs to Dunlap who agreed to buy plans of a best-selling computer memory chip for $100,000 in unsigned traveler's checks. Their conversation was recorded by Dunlap, Intel Security, and the Santa Clara Police Department. Several days later when Dunlap and Gobal met to complete the transaction, Gopal was arrested. He was later convicted.

Kenneth Brehnan is a Canadian who was taking graduate courses at the University of Miami and working for Coulter Electronics in Hialeah, Florida, during the early 1970s. Coulter is one of the leading manufacturers of electronic blood analysis machines. Coulter even financed some of Brehnan's college research. But Brehnan wanted to go to dental school and considered his salary insufficient so he decided to steal plans for one of Coulter's most important projects, the Model S Plus, a highly advanced blood-cell counter.

With the help of Robert E. Lamb, he offered the plans, which cost several million dollars to develop, to competitors.

Writing to Lamb, Brehnan explained which corporations might want the stolen plans. "We can do two things," he wrote. "Sell information about the project I am working on. I can get all the schematics . . . or gather information requested by the other companies. Ask them what they'd like me to collect and what it's worth." Lamb got a response from Technicon Corporation, which had notified the police of the offer. Lamb flew to New York City to deliver the plans and was arrested. Brehnan was arrested in Florida a few days later. The pair had priced the plans at $40,000, offering to sabotage Coulter's manufacturing for an additional $60,000. Lamb pleaded guilty to a New York charge of possessing stolen property. Brehnan was convicted of mail fraud and fined $1,000.

Personnel at corporate headquarters of Chesebrough-Ponds, Inc., were accused of designing a scheme to pirate a product invented and patented by Laurie Visual Etudes, Inc., a small music company. This conspiracy was said to have taken place during 1974 and 1975. The center of the dispute was a small device assembled from a tube, a plastic cage, and a Ping-Pong ball. Blowing into the tube causes the ball to hang suspended. Laurie marketed the product to music students as a breathing exercise, but the product had other uses; bedridden patients, for example, often need lung exercise. Laurie began negotiating with Chesebrough, a corporation with a strong hospital supply unit.

Documents filed by Laurie in New York State Supreme Court alleged that Chesebrough began a deliberate program to pirate Laurie's patent. Office memoranda in Chesebrough files located by Laurie's lawyers called the piracy project "Project Knockoff." Chesebrough broke off talks with Laurie and began to sell a breathing exercise product of its own making, nearly identical to the Laurie design. Sales of $13.5 million were realized in the first three years. The trial judge ruled that Chesebrough had stolen Laurie's trade secret and awarded Laurie $1.5 million. But the judgment was later overturned. An appellate panel found that Laurie had disclosed the design in a patent application; therefore the invention was not a trade secret. The two companies later reached an out-of-court settlement.

The FBI claimed in 1982 that it broke up a plot to sell the bidding plans of an Arlington, Virginia, computer firm to a competitor. The FBI said the suspects were trying to sell detailed information about Computer Sciences' bid on a $40 million Defense Department contract to a competitor for $150,000. Undercover FBI agents made the buy, and two persons were arrested.

A 1965 case ended in a men's room at New York's Kennedy Airport. It involved the marketing plan for Crest toothpaste. Eugene Mayfield, a former Procter & Gamble employee, offered the plan to Colgate-Palmolive Co., the manufacturers of Colgate toothpaste, for $20,000. (Procter & Gamble executives later placed the value of the plan at $1 million.)

Colgate called in the FBI, which monitored a meeting between a Colgate employee and Mayfield. The money was exchanged and the document passed between two adjoining men's room stalls. The buyer handed over his trousers on Mayfield's instructions so he could not pursue Mayfield out of the restroom. FBI agents were waiting outside to arrest Mayfield as he left the men's room. He later pled guilty to a federal charge of interstate shipment of stolen goods.

A construction crew engaged in building a Texas methanol plant for E.I. du Pont de Nemour's Company in 1968 noticed a small airplane flying overhead. Officials at du Pont became concerned that a secret manufacturing process for methanol could be learned from the layout of equipment inside the partially completed plant. The roof was not installed yet because interior equipment had to be lowered by a crane. Du Pont traced the plane's registration to brothers who operated a private flying service. The pilots admitted photographing the plant and under court order identified a local industrial consultant as their client. He apparently wanted to know when the plant would be in production because it was likely to ruin the market price for his own client's methanol.

A letter to *Locksmith Ledger* (September 1982) complained that rivals had persisted in photographing safe displays despite being denied permission on multiple occasions. (Such overt espionage is rare but a clear danger at trade shows.)

Several industries, especially the chemical industry, have complained that the 1966 Freedom of Information Act, amended in 1974, allows legal industrial espionage. Business is required to share much sensitive information with the U.S. government due to federal regulation. This information includes trade secrets, research development, design, and other proprietary data otherwise protected from disclosure. A high percentage of Freedom of Information requests come from rival business interests seeking competitors' data. Information allegedly sought improperly includes competitive bid information and marketing data. It is well known that the act has inhibited intelligence sharing at the national level. Friendly nations hesitate to release sensitive files to the United States fearing the data will be subject to release on a routine freedom of information request.

The late Allan Dulles wrote, "Americans are inclined to talk too much about matters which should be classified. I feel that we hand out too many of our secrets, particularly in the field of military 'hardware' and weaponry."[1]

Common Threads

Epionage is always theft. The users of espionage share common tactics. Damage to corporate interests is the same no matter who the spy or to whom the spymaster may report. Espionage has been used throughout recorded history without interruption.

The economy ties all citizens, their institutions, and their private enterprises tightly together. We have noted, as early as Roman times, that merchants shared with government a concern for espionage as a part of the need for intelligence. Today's FBI and CIA echo the ancient concerns of Rome in relation to modern technology. Indeed, while many say that death and taxes are the only sure things, we may be able to insist successfully that espionage will always be part of corporate and governmental life.

Recognizing the threat of espionage and doing something about it seems a difficult combination to put together. Everyone seems willing to recognize that espionage is a constant threat. But almost no one in the corporate sector can boast of an effective counterespionage-counterintelligence program. A common fear is that any form of intelligence is repugnant to corporate America. But this concern seems to be moderating as more and more voices call for increased attention to intelligence concerns. Thus the climate now seems right for taking action against industrial spies.

The increased concern for ethical behavior in corporate transactions actually augments the argument for counterintelligence against industrial spies. Corruption is the most common tool of all espionage masters and their agents. Organized crime uses kickbacks, bribes, discounted stolen goods, free contraband, prostitution, and loans to corrupt officials in both the public and private sectors. In these ways, organized crime acquires informants, if not actual agents-in-place or moles. Terrorists corrupt by fear and bribe to alienate the allegiance of secretarial help, domestic help, and other workers who then become informants or agents-in-place. Hostile governments favor compromise of individuals selected to become agents-in-place. They corrupt by greed and sex. Competitor espionage usually corrupts with money,

---

[1] Allan Dulles, *The Craft of Intelligence* (New York: Harper & Row, 1963), p. 8.

good jobs, and various monetary benefits. All employers of industrial espionage, then, serve to corrupt people in order to damage corporations through successful espionage.

Successful espionage often goes unnoticed and has no history except in someone's files. Professionals rarely boast of their exploits and then cannot be believed. Good spies are like the stage handlers in a Japanese play, where there is no curtain. Those assigned as stage hands wear dark clothing and move as silently as possible. The audience takes no notice of their activities because they are invisible.

Invisible people are all around us; some live next door, others ride the train or bus to work with us or silently stand beside us in elevators. Invisible people are those we take no notice of because they do not attract our attention. And so it is with the history of espionage. Good agents are generally *grey* men, hard to pick out in a crowd and hard to remember.

That is successful espionage: quiet work done without fanfare or notice. Good spies, not necessarily working for a good cause, stay out of the light and work in the shadows. Nonetheless, espionage can affect war and peace, prosperity and bankruptcy. To ignore the espionage threat is to risk disaster. It is as simple as that.

SUMMARY

This chapter gave some information on the who, what, where, when, why, and how of industrial espionage. There was no attempt to answer the "to what extent" question. The users of industrial espionage are hostile nations, competitors, terrorists, and organized crime families. The victims are individuals, government, the corporate sector, the economic, and the military and political strength of a nation.

Espionage is part of intelligence, an effort to supply decision makers with the information they need. Espionage is a method of collecting information; it may be illegal or unethical, usually both. Most information is collected openly. While pure espionage involves theft of secrets and invasion of privacy, certain covert acts often accompany or are served by espionage. These include acts of terrorism, such as assassination and kidnapping.

All types of information can attract the attention of a spy. Virtually all documents, computer data, and conversations have potential as an espionage target. No matter how espionage proceeds to gather secret data, deceit is involved, making it all the harder to recognize.

Technical espionage takes many forms, including optical as well as audible eavesdropping. Ancient code methods have given way to the one-time cypher pad and the electronic cypher machine.

Covert action allied with espionage includes more than terrorism. Sabotage is often committed by the spy to cover up other illegal acts. Agent provocateurs serve to sow discord and to foment violent activity. Disinformation is another covert action tactic.

Intelligence encompasses strategic intelligence, tactical intelligence, counterintelligence, and security. Counterintelligence is designed to prevent and control industrial espionage from whatever source. Counterintelligence failures can be catastrophic to the corporation.

The Short Account of Espionage began with examples of foreign technology transfer by hostile nations and competitors. Political espionage has ancient roots. Sun Tzu wrote of espionage in *The Art of War* 2,000 years ago. The Pharoahs of the Eighteenth Dynasty practiced espionage over 3,500 years ago. The tradition continued through medieval times up to today. Domestic industrial espionage examples come from all types of industries including cookies, repair parts, armored cars, oil companies, electronics, chemicals, and medical technology.

There are many common threads woven throughout the world of espionage. Aims, methods, and tactics are shared; the effect on the victims is the same. Worrisome is the apparent inability of the private and public sectors to control the espionage threat. The most damaging effect of espionage may be the major corruption that surrounds the activity.

2. Espionage Today

The fox changes his skin but not his habits. —Suetonius

NATIONAL AGENCIES AND FOREIGN ESPIONAGE

The role of industrial espionage has assumed great importance in the modern world, largely due to the changing nature of national power. Today the success of foreign policy rests to a significant extent on industrial power, and industrial power in turn is dependent on science and technology. The lessons of 1982—the war in the Falklands and the incursions of Israel into Lebanon—have demonstrated that the might of any nation is based on its possession of advanced products of the arsenals of industrial innovation.

In the past, the power of nations was measured by the size of armies, the quantity of ships, the proliferation of planes, the availability of nuclear weapons. In that environment military espionage to determine the capability of countries to implement hostility with armed strength was of paramount importance. Politcal espionage designed to discover the intentions of hostile, or potentially hostile, powers surpassed even military espionage in its contribution to national survival. Today new priorities are becoming recognized by the international community. A better appreciation of the criticality of industrial espionage is beginning to emerge. The enormous importance of economic power in terms of international relations is better understood than ever before, and economic wealth is seen as having a decisive influence on a nation's foreign affairs.

There are several reasons why industrial espionage is of such overwhelming importance to the economy of nations. Historically, theft of industrial secrets has bolstered the economies of some nations. Their spies have successfully purloined the fruit of expensive and

time-consuming research and development by the industrial companies
of other powers. A corollary is that it creates a kind of guerrilla warfare in industry. When it is found to be more profitable to pirate
the industrial efforts of other nations rather than to improve one's
economy through original research, innovation, and long-term development, industrial espionage is likely to emerge.

As industrial espionage undermines the economic foundations of a
victim country, it also may have direct bearing on the military might
of that nation. One has but to reflect on the worldwide effect of the
treason of Julius and Ethel Rosenberg and more recently on the activities of foreign agents in the Silicon Valley of California to recognize
the thin line that separates industrial and military espionage in their
effects on the economy and on national power.

More and more, economic sanctions are used as weapons of
international diplomacy. To the extent that industrial espionage
has weakened the impact of these sanctions, national survival has
been compromised.

The economic viability of a nation depends to a large extent on
its ability to compete in world markets. U.S. economic strength has
weakened in recent years due to foreign competition in autos, steel,
and electronics. At least some part of this economic decline has been
due to industrial espionage. FBI Director William H. Webster stated
in 1981:

> United States technology, whether it is military or purely industrial, is spy
> target No. 1 for foreign intelligence operations. I don't think there has
> been another time in our history when America's business has been under
> such a sophisticated espionage attack.

Recent arrests have certainly sustained his allegation.[1]

Even purely domestic industrial espionage, such as that between
and among American-owned companies, can threaten the thrust of
research and development. It inhibits the willingness to take risks in
expending time and resources in creating new products when the
potential for piracy is so great that the risks may no longer be
cost-effective.

To the extent that innovation and creativity are dampened, a
nation's economy is hurt, and those companies that might otherwise
have had high earnings have much less profit and pay much less tax.
Thus the entire economic fabric of a nation is jeopardized even when
the industrial espionage takes a home-grown and home-consumed form.

---

[1] "IBM Data Plot Tied to Hitachi and Mitsubishi," *Wall Street Journal*, June
23, 1982, p. 4.

The appropriate response to espionage is counterintelligence, which is a division of Intelligence. The United States has numerous intelligence agencies, including those of the various branches of the military. For our purposes the Central Intelligence Agency (CIA), the FBI, the National Security Agency (NSA), the Defense Investigative Service (DIS), and the Defense Intelligence Agency (DIA) are probably the most important intelligence resources for industrial counterespionage. To the extent that the United States may engage in foreign espionage, this role is the responsibility of the CIA.

Other nations have central intelligence organizations. The U.S.S.R. has the KGB (State Security Committee), which, "combines positive foreign intelligence with domestic counterintelligence and internal security functions."[2] Its Directorate T has the role of "intensifying the theft of western data concerning nuclear, missile, space research, strategic sciences, cybernetics and industrial processes."[3] It coordinates the scientific, industrial, and technical espionage of all KGB divisions. Members of Directorate T serve as specialists in each major Soviet embassy abroad.

The United Kingdom has no central intelligence agency such as the CIA or KGB. It maintains the British Secret Service (D.I.6), which is the principal arm for secret foreign operations, including espionage and covert political interventions. The Security Service (D.I.5) handles counterintelligence and is concerned primarily with domestic internal security. The Defense Ministry Intelligence Staff integrates the intelligence operations of the military service.

In France, foreign espionage and domestic counterespionage are carried on through the Service de Documentation Extérieure et de Contra-Espionage (SDECE). China maintains the Foreign Intelligence Department for these same purposes. Israel's Central Institute for Intelligence and Security engages in foreign intelligence gathering and seems to be modeled after the CIA. Counterespionage is handled by the General Security Services (SHIN BET).

COMPETITIVE INTELLIGENCE

Competitive intelligence (intelligence efforts by American and other nations' industries directed against American industries) may involve clandestine and covert operations related to corporate and financial

---

[2] *International Encyclopedia of Social Sciences* (New York: Crowell, Collier and Macmillan, 1968), 7:414–421.

[3] John Barron, *KGB The Secret Work of Soviet Secret Agents* (New York: Bantam Books, 1974), p. 107.

data, production data, marketing information, research and technical data, and legal matters. The objectives are:

1. To ensure the availability on a timely basis of credible and comprehensive information about the capabilities of and options of key competitors.
2. To determine the manner in which actions of key competitors might affect current organizational interests.
3. To monitor continuously and provide credible and comprehensive information on situations and contingencies in the competitive and environmental systems in the marketplace that might affect the interests of an organization.
4. To maintain comprehensive and reliable information on political, economic, legal, social, and technological systems affecting the competitive posture of the organization.
5. To achieve efficiency and eliminate duplication of efforts in the collection, analysis, and dissemination of complete intelligence for the organization.[4]

Theoretically these objectives can be achieved without resorting to unethical or illegal methods. Indeed many corporations have set up extensive competitive business intelligence systems that could rely entirely on open data that might be obtained from a variety of sources: field sales forces, the treasury department, research and development, business literature, professional associations, customers, distributors and suppliers, local chambers of commerce, the press, annual reports, stockholders' meetings, investment bankers, purchasing departments, key executives, government publications, license agreements, trade associations, and so on.[5] But these open sources are not adequate to provide the competitive edge. Also technology is advancing so rapidly that industry has difficulty keeping up with the pace. The temptation to engage in industrial espionage is overwhelming, and many otherwise circumspect companies have responded by forming industrial espionage task forces.

Richard Austin Smith has put it this way:

> Industrial espionage makes it possible for unscrupulous management to get million-dollar information at bargain-basement prices. Instead of developing their own market data, industrial processes and contract-bid figures, they

---

[4] David I. Cleland and William R. King. "Competitive Business Intelligence Systems," *Business Horizons* (December 1975):19–26. Copyright, 1975, by the Foundation for the School of Business at Indiana University. Reprinted by permission.

[5] Ibid.

find it profitable, and relatively safe, to steal from their competitors. Thus, practitioners of industrial espionage not only get information at nominal cost, but acquire with it the invaluable knowledge that the information is the basis of their competitor's strategy.[6]

There are a number of questions that immediately come to mind. When is industrial espionage likely to occur? Where can one anticipate its occurrence? Who is likely to be involved? How is industrial espionage carried on? Why is this a special concern in society today?

WHEN IS INDUSTRIAL ESPIONAGE LIKELY TO HAPPEN?

Industrial espionage is organized and continuing. There are espionage persons who sell their services for specific assignments and espionage gangs who conduct ongoing espionage activities across the entire spectrum of industry. There are also groups of spies who operate in specific areas as specialists. These groups, usually operating with fronts, maintain a market for stolen trade secrets, know-how, formulas, designs, processes, financial information, and so on within a particular industrial field, such as:

1. Designer clothes
2. Perfumes and cosmetics
3. Chemical processes
4. Electronics
5. Automobiles
6. Food products
7. Pharmaceuticals and drugs
8. Computer software
9. Defense manufacturing, research, and development

Therefore, the best answer to the question of when espionage is likely to happen is to respond that it is happening all the time on a continuing basis across the entire spectrum of industry. At various times it may be more prolific and pervasive in one field or another, but it is most likely to be operating all the time in every industry to a greater or lesser extent. Only a small number of actual espionage successes are ever detected, and many that are detected are never disclosed to authorities or the general public. Most often the first that the public hears about industrial espionage is when a lawsuit

---

[6] Richard Austin Smith, "Business Espionage," *Fortune* (May 1956):118-121, 190, 192, 194.

for damages is brought against the spy and/or the competitor company that commissioned the espionage. In rare instances there is a sensational arrest, such as that of the Japanese businessmen who tried to steal computer secrets from IBM in June 1982.

Although espionage is continuing in all fields, it may be more pronounced at various times in particular areas. Currently, the field of electronics is experiencing a special boom in industrial espionage. Also, efforts to penetrate the defense weapons industry have been accelerated, and special attention is being accorded to gene splicing and other advanced biological developments.

Societal changes have contributed to the rise of industrial espionage. Moral strictures have been seriously weakened, and the stability of community life has been shaken. In today's environment, corruption is simply a matter of playing it smart and not getting caught.

Two types of people become involved in dealing with espionage agents: the caught and uncaught. The caught are seldom dealt with harshly by the courts; the uncaught achieve wealth with a minimum of risk, thereby setting the stage for the corruption of more and more of their colleagues. During periods of recession and high inflation, individuals are subject to even greater stress and temptations, and they will be more likely to deal with agents who to all appearances, are working only for domestic competition. Cooperating employees may find it easy to rationalize greed, thinking they are doing nothing to harm their country. They may harbor a grudge against their own company and obtain perverse satisfaction feeding secrets to competitors.

Thus penetration today is facilitated by a condition of acute anomie. When we consider the professionalism of the industrial espionage agent with his or her years of experience, know-how, and corruptive skills, it is not unlikely that success will be obtained by the agent at the expense of the company penetrated, and possibly at the cost of harming the nation.

WHERE ARE WE MOST LIKELY TO ENCOUNTER INDUSTRIAL ESPIONAGE?

If we are to structure security and counterintelligence efforts, it is essential to spend resources wisely. Cost-effective measures depend on careful planning and assessment. Mounting a security scheme based on extra protection of realistic target areas should assist in frustrating some portion of the total espionage offensive.

The first question to answer is whether a particular operation is a likely target for industrial espionage. While an industry should not overestimate its attractiveness to spies, it should not fail to be alert to possibilities. In 1959 the *Harvard Business Review* conducted a survey of 1,558 businesses and determined that the most-sought-after data in industrial espionage operations were highly prized processes and the know-how that gave the company some marketing advantage over competitors.[7]

A subsequent study reported in 1974 revealed a number of other facts about industrial espionage.[8]

1. Most executives assumed industrial espionage had increased. Asked whether they felt espionage or spying activities had changed, 12 percent of the respondents in 1959 and 34 percent of the respondents in 1973 felt that they had increased. Thirty-four percent in 1959 and 39 percent in 1973 felt that the position remained the same. Thirty-seven percent in 1959 and 7 percent in 1973 felt that espionage never existed.

2. The level of interest in all kinds of competitive information had increased. Asked about the kinds of information management needed to know about competitors, responses revealed a number of changes since 1959.

| Kind of Information | 1973 | | 1959 | |
	Rank	Percentage of All Respondents	Rank	Percentage of All Respondents
Pricing	1	79	1	67
Expansion plans	2	54	7	20
Competitive plans	3	52	8	18
Promotional strategy	4	49	2	41
Cost data	5	47	6	24
Sales statistics	6	46	4	27
R&D	7	41	3	36

Between 1959 and 1973, pricing continued to hold the place of importance, but expansion plans gained importance, moving from the

---

[7] Edward E. Furash, "Industrial Espionage: Problems in Review," *Harvard Business Review* (November–December 1959):6–12, 148–156, 161.

[8] Jerry L. Wall, "What the Competition Is Doing: Your Need to Know: Probing Opinions," *Harvard Business Review* (November–December 1974):22–38, 162.

seventh place in 1959 to second place in 1973. Similarly, competitive plans advanced from the eighth position to the third position. Promotional strategy became less important in 1973. There was no significant difference in respect of the importance of cost data and sales statistics. R&D declined from the third to seventh position.

3. There was no movement toward more formal intelligence collection systems, although many executives felt that their systems should be improved. Asked whether their company should have a more systematic method of gathering, processing, analyzing, and reporting information, 37 percent of respondents in 1973 and 57 percent of respondents in 1959 felt that there was a definite need. Thirty-five percent of the respondents in 1973 felt that there was probably a need. Twenty-eight percent of the responses were negative in 1973 and 43 percent in 1959.

4. Hiring a competitor's key employee as a source of gathering competitive information increased in popularity among the respondents. Similarly, use of published sources and the company's own sales representatives for collection of information increased in popularity. The significance of this finding is that many executives believed that the competitor's key employee would provide the required information if hired by them.

5. Contrary to their beliefs, executives in general in 1973 did not experience more espionage activities than did those questioned in 1959. Those in defense and space industries appeared to be more aware of the espionage.

6. Larger companies were using more security measures as a defense against espionage.

7. In 1973 a higher percentage of younger executives than the older ones appeared to condone all forms of information-gathering techniques, including the more questionable ones.

8. In the opinion of the executives, the following factors had led to an increase in industrial espionage: tougher competition, decline in ethical standards, survival of the company at stake, self-defense, and higher executive stake in the company.

The *Harvard Business Review* articles reported surveys of business executives. They did not ascertain the views of private security practitioners, which also, have been reported.[9] One study reports the inquiries of five security experts employed as corporate security directors concerning these matters. The questions and answers were summarized as follows:

---

[9] S. Subramanian," Industrial Espionage Causes and Prevention" (Master's thesis, Northeastern University, 1982).

1. Do you think that there is an increase in Industrial Espionage in the U.S.A.?

   Yes. Not only from business competitors but also from foreign sources, particularly in matters involving high technology data.

2. If so, are the top managements conscious and aware of the threat?

   Yes, The sheer economics of the situation demands such awareness. But such awareness is not universally encountered. Even where there is awareness, there are degrees of consciousness impeding prompt approval of defensive measures.

3. Has private security played or is it not playing a significant part in reducing the magnitude of the threat?

   Yes, but to a limited extent. This frequently depends on the nature of the business or industry, the professionalism and communication skills of the security director and the extent to which senior management supports the security effort.

4. Do you feel existing safeguards in the Law are adequate?

   The majority felt that the laws are not adequate and opined that effective legal measures are called for to curb industrial espionage.

5. On the basis of your personal knowledge and experience, what are the areas of Private Security which deserve special attention from the point of view of industrial espionage?

   High technology, scientific, highly specialized industrial fields, all aspects of proprietary information security require special attention.

6. Prevention is better than cure: what specific steps would you like to take to prevent Industrial Espionage?

   Identification and realization of the value of the proprietary information. Positive thinking on the issue by all concerned; improved employee orientation and awareness programs in order to elicit a higher degree of understanding of the seriousness of the problem, and the need for employee cooperation in dealing with it; better screening of applicants, particularly those being considered for sensitive positions, or positions that will provide access to sensitive data; more realistic and improved measures for disposing of sensitive waste materials; expansion of the legal avenues available for dealing with industrial espionage matters that do not necessarily involve patent or copyright violations.

7. Are the measures prescribed by public sector, like Department of Defense (DOD), adequate to meet the threat in private sector handling of defense contracts and the like?

The opinion of the experts was divided on this issue. The majority felt that the DOD requirements do a pretty good job of protecting classified information. Breaches are mainly due to attitudinal and other personality problems. However, for purely private sector concerns, an attempt to adopt a modified version of DOD requirements would be too restrictive. The minority view is that the DOD requirements are too complex and cumbersome. They are unwieldy and needlessly expensive. They concern themselves with trivia. One of the reasons top managements fight shy of security precautions is the "spectre" created by DOD requirements. Overclassification is the hallmark of DOD methods. For effective implementation, the private sector should have a simpler, and more easily understood, and readily enforceable system.

8. Are existing training and academic facilities adequate to deal with and prepare private security operatives to face the threat?

No. They are not only inadequate but they are antequated and more theoretically oriented. Candidates coming out of these academic institutions were found wanting in appreciating the magnitude of security problems as their comprehension was found to be limited.

It is instructive to note the differences and similarities between the views of business executives and security practitioners with responsibilities for countering espionage. It is also instructive to note that there appear to be many business executives who are innocent of the need for intelligence systems and some, albeit a very small minority, who in 1973 believed industrial espionage never existed.

Clearly there are differential needs for counterintelligence. Some businesses probably have little need and do not perceive the threat; other businesses must be concerned for a variety of reasons and see a real need to be prepared to deal with industrial espionage. It would also appear that corporate security directors are especially alert to the potential or existing problems of espionage in an industrial society.

To answer the question, Where are we most likely to encounter industrial espionage? it appears that it might be encountered in any competitive business where pricing is a concern of management or where expansion plans and competitive plans are involved. The perceived need of a substantial number of executives for acquiring information of competitive promotional strategy, cost data, and sales statistics indicates also that there may well be a threat of industrial espionage wherever such matters are held to be confidential. Finally, although business executives appear to be less sensitive than corporate security directors to the threat of industrial espionage in high-technology, scientific, and highly specialized industrial fields, there appears to be little question that these areas are also where we are most likely to encounter industrial espionage.

In summary, the threat of industrial espionage is most likely to exist wherever, for business or other reasons, personal or proprietary, information is kept secret or confidential. If there are data, information, or other matters not readily available to competitors through open sources, espionage efforts are likely to be mounted to obtain them through covert sources.

WHO IS LIKELY TO BE INVOLVED IN INDUSTRIAL ESPIONAGE?

Although it is possible for virtually any employee, vendor, visitor, trespasser, maintenance person, or contract security person to be involved in industrial espionage, it is most probable that the spy is a person with access to inside expert knowledge. This would seem to indicate that persons in the area of middle management whose job brings them into regular contact with confidential materials might be most suspect.[10] Such an individual may be the key person involved in espionage, but he or she may not be the person directing the enterprise. Others may be involved—indeed they may be the principals—and the person with inside expert knowledge may be merely a pawn. Perhaps the person needed money and was bribed or seduced into corruption by the promise of funds. The person may have been blackmailed or otherwise intimidated. On the other hand he or she could have false loyalties or ideological quirks. If he or she is vulnerable in any way, professionals will exploit that weakness.

There is, in fact, an espionage boom going on, and identifying possible corruptees is a key part of the business of counterintelligence. Industrial espionage has burgeoned to the point where it is no longer a concern of the government only. Any high-technology enterprise that is working at or near the state of the art in almost any field is vulnerable to the loss of trade secrets, know-how, technical data, sensitive instruments, and special processes. There exists a thriving underground economy in the products of espionage.

The agents and informers engaged in espionage will not appear to be spies. Those who are working for the Soviets will not appear to be Russians; those who are working for the Japanese will not necessarily

---

[10] Paul I. Slee Smith, *Industrial Intelligence and Espionage* (London:Business Books, 1970), p. 75.

be Japanese; those who are working for domestic competitors will not look like persons out of a James Bond movie. Chances are great that the best spies are those whom one would least suspect of being engaged in industrial espionage. The dupes and the corrupted who convey sought-after secrets to espionage agents are most likely ordinary people who have gone astray. They may have agreed to compromise their integrity for a variety of reasons: the lure of easy money and personal greed; a true need for additional funds, perhaps because of family circumstances or unemployment; a personal grudge against the employer and the company; seduction by the promise or provision of sex, drugs, expensive holidays, motor cars, boats, or other material pleasures; intimidation of the individual or members of the person's family; blackmail based on compromising evidence of sexual entanglements or other embarrassments the subject cannot afford to have exposed; or false ideology.

The professionals, however, are a different breed. In the area of California known as Silicon Valley, for example, there exists an electronics underground, sometimes called a gray market in electronic components. Some of the trading may be legal, but to a very large extent it is now a true black market that is rapidly becoming organized. Today it is the main source of silicon chips, microprocessors, and other state-of-the-art materials for the unscrupulous. They include domestic competitors and foreign industries in Japan and West Germany, as well as the Soviet Union and other hostile, or potentially hostile, countries. It is alleged that the many brokers in the valley deal with foreign brokers who serve as way-stations for East bloc countries, thereby damaging U.S. economic and military security.

It would seem, therefore, that almost anybody is likely to be involved. Those who have ready access to secret materials or who have knowledge of target processes, plans, procedures, and techniques are prime targets and therefore likely to be suborned. Agents of foreign governments, investigators hired by competitors, or organized spy rings are likely to be the source of corruption. They prey on otherwise decent Americans and sometimes, too often, succeed in enlisting them in this dark business, often for paltry sums. They have studied their pigeons well and know all about their problems, their grudges against their companies, their weaknesses, and their vulnerabilities.

HOW IS INDUSTRIAL ESPIONAGE CARRIED ON?

The operations and methods used in industrial espionage are many and varied. We could consider the threats to be both internal and external. Probably the greatest threat is internal, although the internal threat may be caused or stimulated by outside forces. The entire range of employees from top executives down to the mailcarrier or the cleaning staff are potential spies given the right price. Employees may be disloyal, disenchanted, anxious to improve themselves with another company to which they can bring proprietary information from their prior employment, or they may just want more money and not care how they get it.

Our present way of life with its mobility of employers and employees and its general lack of stability spawns espionage. Marketing personnel, purchasing personnel, scientists, researchers, technicians, and executives all are prime targets for espionage agents. In many cases it is necessary for a company to share proprietary information with vendors and subcontractors whose security should be, but is not, as tight as that of the parent company. This provides the espionage agent with excellent opportunities to develop information in an indirect fashion about the parent contractor. Seminars, conventions, trade shows, and various publications and news releases are ready sources of bits and pieces of data that may be fitted into a picture or pattern. A word or two here and another word or two there can create a mosiac that begins to emerge, even though insiders do not believe they have revealed anything important.

External threats and subversion usually are directed by professional agents and experienced industrial spies. They may assume a number of typologies:[11]

1. The setup agent, the smooth-talking con artist who assumes many guises to entrap the innocent or ignorant insider.
2. The undercover agent, who may assume a false identity and enter an organization to achieve specific goals.
3. The trespasser, who gains access to the facility by ruse or by actual physical breaking and entering. The trespasser may actually burglarize files, documents, processes, and computer tapes or may establish false credentials that permit access to target personnel and objects.
4. The listener, the eavesdropper who uses the range of sophisticated wiretap and bugging devices currently available or just is always around employee hangouts.
5. The lookout, who maintains physical surveillance of personnel of interest, looking always for the hook—a documented indiscretion, a contact of questionable character, or any

---

[11] Some of the material in this section is adapted from "A Study of Industrial Espionage—Parts I and II" by Edward J. Anderson, *Security Management.* January and March 1977.

shortcoming of targeted individuals that may be exploited to extort information or recruit an accomplice.

6. The trash collector. Perhaps the most dangerous instrument in espionage is the telephone. Certainly the second most dangerous artifact is the waste bin. Many valuable trade secrets have been reconstructed from bits and pieces of trash. There are devices available that pulverize documents, which should be more potent in frustrating scavenger espionage than the current shredding and burning techniques. However, many employees are careless about shredding and burning, and they may still be careless when pulverization becomes available.

7. The pollster, with questionnaires asking apparently innocuous questions ostensibly to obtain public opinion. Many employees reveal far more than is discreet.

8. The financial wizard, who approaches executives with attractive propositions and offers and in the process elicits sensitive proprietary information purportedly essential to the successful fruition of the deal. Once the desired data are disclosed, the venture is abandoned.

9. The blind advertiser, who advertises widely for resumes to be forwarded to a post office box. If the resumes themselves do not disclose the desired information, the advertiser interviews enticing prospects and wheedles the applicant into disclosing proprietary information from the present employment. Occasionally the applicant may actually be hired by a competitor in an effort to gain the applicant's information.

10. The reverse engineer, who analyzes the proprietary product or process into its component parts and tries to synthesize a clone of that trade secret, protected product, or process.

11. The solicitor, who recruits legitimate visitors, customers, subcontractors and their employees, and others who may have access to the targeted facility as operatives.

Industrial espionage is carried on by domestic businesses against competitive domestic industries. It is also carried on by foreign businesses against domestic businesses, and, most likely, by some U.S. concerns against foreign companies. Perhaps the most significant fact that has raised the level, intensity, and criticality of espionage in recent years has been the involvement of nations in industrial espionage. Under its total-espionage concept, the U.S.S.R. and the Soviet bloc nations are as interested in trade secrets, military and nonmilitary, as they are in political espionage. In order to cope with the Soviets' total espionage, the CIA presumably has expanded its role in foreign counterintelligence.

There is little difference among political, military, and industrial espionage regarding tools, techniques, and skills. Indeed, the distinctions are becoming blurred in terms of results as well. Given the nuclear stalemate, a secret war to bolster economic power is being waged. One aspect of this was the resignation of Alexander Haig as President Reagan's Secretary of State and his replacement with George Shultz. The new secretary is expected to put an economic emphasis on foreign policy. It is no longer possible to take U.S. economic supremacy for granted; we need to protect our economy in the future to the same extent we protected ourselves with political and military intelligence in the past.

WHY IS INDUSTRIAL ESPIONAGE A SPECIAL CONCERN TODAY?

Industrial espionage is a special concern today largely because we failed to recognize the scope of the problem in the past. In 1979 Nat Wood stated "Industrial espionage is as widespread, sophisticated, and lucrative as ever. And it has taken on an international flavor what with growing multi-national corporations and the expansion of international trade in competitive world markets."[12] Herchell Britton of Burns International Security Services, Inc. states, "It is a multi-million dollar business and has led to a complete sell-out of American superior technology to our enemies. It strikes at the very economic lifeline of America. The objective of industrial espionage is information. The best defense against spying is solid research and marketing on your own part."[13] *Market research* is a shadowy term for industrial intelligence that relies on published information, company sales representatives' reports, personal and professional contacts, suppliers, and advertising agencies for sources of information. Covertly it may involve actual industrial spies and undercover agents hired to seek employment with competitors or corrupting and buying off competitors' employees to get information illegally; often the material sought is that which could not be obtained in any other way, such as trade secrets.

Perhaps the most pervasive reason for the current importance of industrial espionage is its impact on national economic power. We are face-to-face with the totalitarian pragmatism of the Soviets who will zealously steal every possible industrial secret we may possess. The day when industrial espionage was a question only of profit and loss is over. It is now a question of national survival. Just as there is no

---

[12] Nat Wood, "Security with No 'Strings' Attached," *Security World* 16 (April 1979):22, 23, 74–80.

[13] Herchell Britton, "U.S. Technological Superiority is Threatened," *Security Management* 25 (November 1981):15–18.

place to hide in nuclear war, there seems to be almost no place to hide our technological and scientific secrets from the merciless pursuit of Soviet spies and the spies of its satellites.

Governments have always spied on each other. One's own activities are viewed as necessary and benign, and those of other nations unnecessary and evil. Governmental spying inevitably includes commercial spying too. Each government seeks to keep abreast of or acquire the industrial secrets of the others. The KGB's Active Measures apparatus pursues this effort relentlessly. Communist countries do not have independent companies. The state owns all industrial concerns, and if those concerns want to steal trade secrets from their foreign rivals, they have behind them the resources of a powerful state that does not have to account to its populace. Peter A. Heims has put it in this way:

> The world has been geared for war for thirty-seven years—ever since the nominal end of the Second World War—the reality of the matter is that 1945 saw a world divided by different frontiers and a totally changed balance of power. In the new grouping, no great power trusted any other. Each watched the other with increasingly efficient surveillance including, in due course, the detailed "outer-space" spying from satellites encircling the earth. Each sought hard to keep abreast of or acquire the industrial secrets of the others.
>
> "Industrial" secrets, in this sense, are the secrets of agression, defence, or survival.[14]

CONCLUSION

Some social forces in the United States contribute to the virulence of domestic and foreign competitive intelligence gathering and to the success of industrial espionage by foreign agents.

Some terrorists and terrorist organizations are geared for sabotage and/or espionage. They cooperate to assist foreign technology transfer in order to advance their own ideologies. Closely allied with terrorists are various subversive groups and organizations dedicated to the destruction of democratic society. Our society accommodates them.

Organized crime is another facet of our society. Organized criminals have wealth and political power, and they have mastered the arts of corruption and the application of force. If they cannot corrupt a victim, they threaten physical harm. Organized criminal activities such as drugs, gambling, prostitution, and loan sharking are used

---

[14] Peter A. Heims, *Countering Industrial Espionage* (Leatherhead, Surrey, England: 20th Century Security Education, 1982), p. 29.

to soften up the target facility or industry and make it easy to turn targeted individuals into spies. Organized crime, on its own to obtain profits or working with foreign agents for fees, can often readily turn otherwise honorable persons into spies.

A less obvious but pernicious threat to the integrity of industry is the social phenomenon of white-collar crime. Although some of this type of crime may be committed as a result of coercion from terrorists or organized criminals or threats of exposure from foreign agents, much of it results from greed.

Espionage professionals are expert in the practice of their trade craft. They may pursue their strategies and tactics on their own or may employ terrorists and organized criminals. However they proceed, they seem to be eminently successful. There are forces in our society that have operated to soften up their targets. It is little wonder that our industrial leadership is being lost and our advanced technology is being drained away.

SUMMARY

This chapter demonstrated the environment in which industrial espionage exists today. The relationship between industrial espionage and national survival, and political and military strength was noted. We discussed the roles of various national agencies in combating industrial espionage. The intelligence services of the United Kingdom, France, China, Israel, and the U.S.S.R. were cited as examples of both espionage and counterespionage agencies.

Since competitive industrial intelligence may be domestic as well as foreign-directed, it was discussed in its broadest context. We distinguished between open sources and covert, or clandestine, sources in the development of industrial intelligence. Although there are vast sources that are readily available on an open basis, the competitive edge tempts many otherwise legitimate industrialists to become involved in espionage.

We looked into the "when" of industrial espionage. It is a continuing and organized operation that at various times may be more prolific and pervasive in one field or another, but is most likely to be operating to some extent all the time in every industry. The current climate in America is most favorable for the success of industrial espionage.

We also looked into the "where" of industrial espionage. What are the most likely targets of the spy? The *Harvard Business Review* articles of 1959 and 1974 were cited to help us understand the target areas of industry and the perceptions of business executives concerning their vulnerabilities. Significantly, the 1974 article indicated that most executives assume that industrial espionage had increased since 1959. The report also indicates a greater tolerance for unethical practices. A very recent survey (1982) of five major security experts, employed as corporate security directors, indicated an awareness of increasing espionage from both domestic and foreign sources.

In response to the question, "Who is likely to be involved in espionage?" we noted that it is most probable that the spy, or the spymaster's dupe, would be a person with access to inside expert knowledge. Almost anyone may be involved, including white collar criminals, terrorists, criminals in organized crime, and agents of foreign governments.

How is industrial espionage carried on? Threats may be external and internal. Probably the greatest threat comes from insiders, although such threats may be caused by outside forces. Spymasters and foreign agents are prepared to pay whatever the essential person's price may be. Seminars, conventions, trade shows, and various publications and news releases may be ready sources of bits and pieces of data that contribute to the agent's intelligence.

Why is industrial espionage a special concern today? The most pervasive reason for its enormous importance in our modern world is its impact on national economic power. Governments, as well as individual companies, seek to keep abreast of, or acquire the industrial secrets of, others. Hostile nations want international trade for the sake of the foreign currency they need. If they can capture an increased proportion of world trade by stealing their competitor's secrets they will do so. Spying is, today, part of a power game that makes industrial espionage on a vast scale inevitable.

3. Future Problems

A penny for your thought.—John Lyly

MANY CHALLENGES AHEAD

We live in an age of information. More and more facts are available to all. Some persons and some institutions would rather steal another's secrets than use their own resources to develop similar information. That is espionage. A variety of current circumstances favor expanded opportunity for successful industrial espionage. Today's threat is greater than yesterday's. The business world and the world of technology continue in growth and partnership, suggesting that tomorrow's threat of industrial espionage will be very great indeed.

Information is more plentiful today and becoming more important than ever before. Along with information dependence has come increased value of many types of information. Bits and pieces of personal, corporate, and political data once considered insignificant by themselves have become vital when considered together with other bits brought together using high-technology data processing. That processing takes place in seconds and can be shared almost instantaneously through microwave links and satellite transmissions worldwide.

The FBI reported in 1981, "Foreign intelligence [espionage] efforts within the United States . . . have a strong interest in technological secrets, especially computers, micro-electronics, fiber optics, and lasers."[1] This technology itself will make future espionage even easier. Those four classes of communications equipment are useful to spies!

Scientists are vulnerable to the argument that all science must be international and therefore that exchange of scientific information should be unrestricted. KGB agents represent themselves as members of the international scientific community. When U.S. scientists are asked to be more circumspect about what they publish, they often resent suggestions to be prudent, crying thought control. Voluntary censorship among scientists is not likely in the future. (Corporations *can* control the activities of their own scientific personnel in respect to the disclosure of trade secrets or proprietary data. Prior review of all articles authored by scientific and technical personnel is a sensible procedure.)

KGB overtures to scientists often take place in seemingly neutral sites. Conferences and conventions, especially those held outside the United States, are favored points of contact between the espionage agent masquerading as a congenial scientist and the politically unsophisticated American researcher. The increase in conferences and the ease of travel heightens such threats for the future.

American corporations employ a large number of people who have relatives living overseas. Depending on the country in which the relatives reside, a hostage situation can occur. The employee may be told that these relatives will suffer if he or she does not supply the requested information. The influx of refugees into the United States in recent years suggests an increase to come in such espionage pressure.

The person making the contact may be a native-born American or a foreigner from a third country. The agent need not be a native of the country where the relatives reside. Espionage agents are skilled in choosing potential weak links in a corporation. Security and loss-control departments must be equally mindful of employee vulnerabilities and alert to unusual relationships. The current decline in background investigation capabilities is sure to bring espionage costs in this regard.

Hiring away a key employee has long been a technique of industrial espionage. Such a technique has an increased value in an age of job mobility, an uncertain business climate, and a decline in moral values. The new employee is expected to bring all knowledge gained while at the previous job. Sometimes the new employee is expected to bring copies of data that could be useful to the new employer.

---

[1] William H. Webster, "Director's Message," *FBI Bulletin*, August 1, 1981.

Due to the miniaturization in data storage and the expansion in micro-chip usage, this illicit transfer will be harder to prevent as time goes by.

THE COST IN DOLLARS AND LIVES

No one has made an accurate estimate of the business loss resulting annually from industrial espionage. We do know that few cases are prosecuted. Corporations tend to hide business loss, not wanting to admit they have been bested by spies. Also, allegations of espionage may fail a court test. Failure makes the corporation open to civil actions. Corporations with defense contracts may fail to report espionage for fear their facility security clearance may be lost, barring them from lucrative government contracts.

More important, most corporations simply cannot determine exactly how their losses occur. There is extensive use of the word *shrinkage*, a catch-all category that includes all unexplained losses.

Human life as well as property can suffer from industrial espionage. Corporations may be embarrassed when information is wrongfully diverted. They can lose millions if a competitor benefits from stolen research data. Individuals have even more to lose from industrial espionage. Terrorist spies may gather information leading to the assassination or kidnapping of corporate officers. Death or years in an underground people's prison or tiger cage is a stiff price to pay for careless handling of information.

The cost in dollars and lives can be expected to increase unless corporate counterintelligence is emphasized.

EXAMPLES OF FUTURISTIC THREATS

Friendly nations may judge industrial espionage to be an acceptable activity in their efforts to improve their own economic or military posture. Take the case of stolen nuclear technology.

Israel joined the nuclear club in the late 1960s. Many authorities believe their achievement was due to industrial espionage and covert action. The Nuclear Materials and Equipment Corporation (NUMEC) was located near Pittsburgh, Pennsylvania. Contracts were signed between Israel and NUMEC. Many Israeli scientists had occasion to visit the Pennsylvania facility.

After some investigation, it was determined by the Atomic Energy Commission that enough weapons-grade uranium was missing to construct nine nuclear bombs. The Atomic Energy Commission found that NUMEC was careless in data security. The missing metal was found to total 206 pounds with a value of $929,000. NUMEC had to reimburse that amount to the federal government.

Various theories have been offered to explain this nuclear loss. In the case of radioactive materials, little likelihood exists that they went out with the trash. The best bet is Israeli espionage with later covert action to remove the material to the Near East. That is reasonably probable.

Additional nations hope to join the nuclear club. Their best bet is espionage directed toward the nuclear industry.

Competitors are only one type of private agency that may benefit from stolen secrets. Social action groups and the media relish sensational exposures and the disclosure of sensitive materials taken from corporate or government files. The emphasis on more and more news programming may fuel much future espionage of this type.

Organized crime has a strong interest in legitimate business. Past takeover methods include not only violence but also theft of secrets through the subversion of corporate personnel. Organized crime elements have been taking over legitimate businesses for many years. In 1981 the Pennsylvania Crime Commission released results of a three-year investigation linking organized crime to unions and prepaid health care services.[2]

Earlier the commission linked organized crime in Pennsylvania to a variety of business interests: vending machines, pizza, beer distribution, cheese, coal companies, cable television, trucking firms, food stores, and furniture stores. As part of their conclusions and recommendations, the Pennsylvania Crime Commission noted:

- Literally thousands upon thousands of Pennsylvanians are engaged in either managing or assisting the licit and illicit businesses of organized crime.

- Hundreds of businesses in the state have been influenced by organized criminals. Their involvement reflects a varying degree of influence ranging from minimal and hidden control to blatant ownership.[3]

The situation in Pennsylvania is little different from that of the other states. Can anyone doubt that organized crime activity, including espionage, will continue long into the future?

---

[2] Pennsylvania Crime Commission, *Health Care Fraud: A Rising Threat* (St. Davids, PA; Commonwealth of Pennsylvania, December 1981).

[3] Pennsylvania Crime Commission. *A Decade of Organized Crime, 1980 Report*, (St. Davids, PA; Commonwealth of Pennsylvania, September, 1980), p. x.

THE OPEN SOCIETY BRINGS RISKS

Information is easy to come by today. Scores of specialist journals are springing up; cable television is offering more and more channels for sports, news, and other purposes; satellite transmissions offer immediate and constant information flow. The office and home computer market is expanding rapidly.

As long as the Freedom of Information Act remains valid, there is a potential for abuse. The 1966 act and its 1974 amendments were written primarily to allow citizens to learn more about the activities of their government and to see what was included in government files.

Federal regulations compel corporations to report a wide variety of information. This includes oil and gas lease data and chemical formulas used by the cosmetic industry. Such information has high value to the owner and may be of much interest to competitors. The Food and Drug Administration (FDA), for example, maintains records of fragrance formulas. The manufacturer that submits the information has no way of learning when a competitor petitions to see the formula listing. The FDA keeps a log of requests, but private research groups do not disclose the name of their clients. Most of the requests come from attorneys who may be working for competitors or future competitors.

The Manufacturing Chemists Association claimed that the Environmental Protection Agency (EPA) placed sensitive Monsanto Chemical information in an EPA public reading room. The EPA admitted the lapse, blaming a clerical error. Chemical producers raised strong objections to certain provisions of the Toxic Substances Control Act of 1977, which requires companies to submit information on chemical structure, production volume, plant locations, and other data the industry believes should be held confidential. The producers fear that other government agencies may receive EPA-held data without enforcing proper safeguards for confidentiality.

Unless the legal climate changes, these federal acts will serve as future espionage threats to the private sector.

ESPIONAGE AND PROPAGANDA CAN BE COMBINED

As far as the Soviet Union is concerned, both espionage and propaganda are closely associated.[4] Foreign technology transfer bears a double hazard: loss of secrets and defamation. The KGB specializes in

---

[4] James L. Tyson, *Target America: The Influence of Communist Propaganda on U.S. Media* (Chicago: Regnery Gateway, 1981), p. 8.

disinformation, or black propaganda. Its Directorate A is in charge of propaganda attacks. In one case a company discovered a set of costly blueprints was missing and presumed in the hands of a competitor, domestic or foreign. Later it became obvious that copies of internal memoranda dealing with an overseas subsidiary went with the blueprints. Corporate management was horrified to see damaging out-of-context paragraphs of these memoranda headlined in the overseas press.

In addition, the Soviets often set up research front organizations to do much of their work. Corporations that remain ignorant of the true ownership of think tanks and front organizations may find themselves victimized by this industrial espionage technique. Many corporations are overeager to cooperate with nonprofit researchers and educators or students in order to boost the corporate image. The Gulf Oil building in Pittsburgh has very sophisticated internal security today. It was not always so. In the 1970s a young man, purportedly a student, was allowed to use the Gulf corporate library after hours. One night he left behind a bomb.

A knowledgeable commentator hypothesized in 1981 that "there are probably a few thousand Communist propaganda agents working within the United States today, and that over $240 million is being spent annually on such efforts."[5]

Industrial espionage may be identical to political espionage in respect to threats to corporate America. Some political and industrial espionage agents report to the same masters. Their goal is to destroy the United States by any means. Efforts are bound to continue since past espionage has proven so successful.

ELECTRONIC DANGERS

Electronic eavesdropping devices are available through the mail. And competent electricians or electronics practitioners can make their own. Anyone who has ever had a crossed telephone line or heard a CB transmission through the television recognizes the impossibility of privacy. Microwave transmissions handle long-distance calls. These are routinely monitored, we are told, by the Soviets, and no doubt by others.

Computers, becoming the major data repository for both government and business, are often described as safes without any doors. Even school-age children have been able to enter and manipulate computer data. With the expanded availability of remote terminals, it

---

[5] Ibid.

becomes likely that any corporation may have its data looted wherever a remote terminal may be located.

A 1977 presidential panel warned Americans that threats to privacy were on the increase. Few recognized that a corporation, legally a person, is vulnerable to the same threats. Technology is one villain. Electronic banking and computers are repositories of sensitive corporate data. Files in governmental and private hands contain information about corporate finances, trade secrets, projected activity and building, corporate executives, and more. These data may flow from agency to agency, acquiring more meaning as bits and pieces are assembled.

Electronic mailing is a recent threat insufficiently studied as to the ease of interception. Some experts feel that these systems may become more important as time goes on, eventually displacing the first-class letter as the primary form of written communication. That will mean a decrease in communication privacy, of course.

A developing industry could mean further assaults on privacy. Information specialists using computers in a dozen American cities vie to answer any question a business person raises, and quickly too. These requests may concern market data, analysis of competitors, new products, and other sensitive data.

One information specialist commented anonymously in early 1982, "There has never been a greater need for commercial intelligence or information retrieval than there is today." A New York firm has a staff of seventy and is said to answer about 4,000 requests for information each month. The corporation maintains files on thousands of companies. Another company, located in Pittsburgh, has advertised that it analyzes as well as collects information. How do such services determine the legitimacy of information requests? And what limits do they put on their own collection activity? As their files expand, the risk of espionage grows.

BEHIND THE SPY MASK

Cloak and dagger is a common expression used to refer to espionage activity. Unfortunately for the victim of the spy, no such uniform is common to espionage agents. They are hard to identify. Their work may never be discovered. The future results of industrial espionage may be blamed on poor business practices or carelessness.

The users of espionage agents attempt to hide their identity and their intent, confusing those who must counter industrial espionage. A suitable pretext remains the working tool of undercover investigators and espionage agents. That pretext presents a plausible, common-sense front to the observer which is meant to put the victim off guard. If a false sense of security results, the industrial spy can more easily steal the information desired by those who direct the espionage activity.

Recognizing who ordered an espionage activity is as important as identifying an espionage agent or detecting an electronic eavesdropping device. But the espionage agent may be unaware of whom his or her employer actually represents. For example, a Soviet espionage master may hire an agent under the pretext that the spying is on behalf of a competitor from a friendly or neutral nation. Indeed a gullible employee may be talked into supplying proprietary data on the pretext that a security exercise is taking place designed to gauge the strength of corporate loss control. The on-going struggle for a share of the world's markets brings more and more nations to the brink of bankruptcy. Espionage easily becomes attractive in such a situation.

The espionage agent may be witting or unwitting. Even if the agent knows the activity is illegal, he or she may be unaware of who will benefit from the theft. All employees and outsiders must be regarded as potential spies. Therefore corporations must pay serious and constant attention to ferreting out espionage agents and locating electronic eavesdropping devices.

Penetration attempts by future industrial spies may be internal, external or electronic. Each possibility creates a different type of threat equally dangerous to business. Internal espionage threats usually come from employees. They come also from contract personnel who work a few hours, days, or months inside the company. Vendors or suppliers must be considered internal threats since they have legitimate access to the corporate premises.

Some attention must be given to management as well as to lower-level personnel. Management personnel routinely have complete facility access and often possess master keys or the equivalent. Seldom are these employees searched on departure. In fact, we believe that management personnel pose the biggest industrial espionage threat. They certainly pose the greatest overall loss and unethical-practice threats for the future.

Janitorial, maintenance, and engineering staffs also have master keys. They work by day and by night, often roaming the facility without challenge. The sloppy janitor could be an electronics expert whose real mission is not to empty wastebaskets but to examine lab notes and prototypes. The trend toward use of part-time personnel and independent contractors for these tasks will raise the likelihood of espionage.

Vendors are a particular internal threat because their vehicles are parked at critical junctures, such as shipping and receiving docks.

Privileged parking spaces near building entrances are usually allotted to vendors who service machinery. Vendors are expected to bring things in and to take things out. Their visits may easily be a useful pretext to install electronic eavesdropping devices or to change tapes on recording devices previously installed.

The ultimate vendor threat may come from computer service personnel. The computer provides industrial espionage agents a single target to penetrate. The presence of computer service personnel, as is the case with most other vendors, is taken for granted.

External espionage threats will come from legitimate visitors, customers, unauthorized visitors, and outsiders. Electronic technology enables spies to focus microphones on office windows or to tap telephone lines from a remote point. They need not actually be on the property.

Visitors can bring eavesdropping devices to install or may have disguised cameras to assist their espionage attempts. Visitors can hide in a facility in order to pursue their espionage activities after the facility has closed for the day. Visitors may wander into sensitive areas where they hope to learn something useful. If their presence in the area is challenged, they will claim to have lost their way. If they are not challenged, they will proceed into the area of their interest.

A visit may be a pretext to examine titles and names on offices. This information makes it possible to concentrate attempts to subvert, blackmail, or intimidate a particular person.

Visitor conversations with key employees are an espionage threat. Employees in their familiar work environment are often careless in conversation, unnecessarily revealing proprietary data. Their enthusiasm can lead them to display materials or documents that ought to be kept secret. A visitor who casually asks for a photocopy of a document may be given it without question. (One of the authors was given a photocopy of the architectural plans of a U.S. senator's home without a question of his purposes.)

Customers and potential customers are seldom viewed with suspicion. Often they receive a tour of the premises, and their questions are freely answered in an attempt to procure sales or production orders. The customer, however, may pass this information to competitors or other unfriendly interests. Again, economic pressures point to future espionage acceleration from that source.

The purchase of a sample, which seems a natural transaction, can have a sinister meaning. The sample may be desired for the purpose of copyright infringement in another country or for the purpose of sabotage and resale of defective merchandise in order to create an unfavorable public image for the manufacturer.

Espionage penetration can take the form of burglary. This crime may not be apparent or it may be disguised. The espionage burglar who compromises a security system may simply photograph blueprints or documents, leaving no evidence of theft. If the spy is sufficiently skilled, the evidence of intrusion will be minimal or even overlooked. For example, examine any business desk. No doubt you will find scratches around the lock. How did they occur? When? Perhaps someone has jimmied the desk open at some time in the far past—or only yesterday.

Should the espionage burglar desire to remove items certain to be missed, a deception—perhaps arson—may be used to cover up the theft. Arson investigators frequently discover that fires have been set to disguise fraud, burglary, or murder. The damage from the fire and the actions of firefighters make subsequent investigation for espionage difficult.

Outsiders frequently prey on dissatisfied employees or those in financial or other difficulties. Should these conditions not be present, attempts to compromise employees may take place.

Espionage agents use various means to motivate employees to betray their trust, often greed and sex. The price paid may be in the form of money, vacations, or material goods. Espionage agents are proficient at learning what the targeted employee wants the most. If the employee accepts what could be viewed as a bribe, compromise has taken place. The espionage agent will proceed to demand more and more by threatening the employee with public disgrace and loss of livelihood, potent and usually successful threats.

Sex is often viewed as a quicker method for compromising the targeted employee. The act may take the form of a perversion recorded on sound film or, less frequently, by telephoto lens on a 35mm camera. The employee is threatened with legal, social, and work penalties resulting from exposure of the act. If the employee is married, he or she is threatened with results of exposure to the employee's spouse.

Most employees compromised by espionage agents eventually break down under the strain. This eventual action in no way diminishes the damage caused. All too often, signs of nervousness or despair in an employee are passed off by other employees as personal strain such as is caused by marital difficulties. No one wants to pry into another's personal life. Most employers do not recognize the problems of an employee until productivity diminishes too far to escape notice. Each troubled employee must be recognized as a potential espionage target or threat for the future.

ABSENCE OF COUNTERMEASURES BRINGS TROUBLE

Vulnerability to industrial espionage is due in part to a general lack of corporate resources dedicated to deal with this threat. Most corporate security departments are busy with less sophisticated crimes, such as theft of products or materials. Other activities may include safety-related responsibilities such as ensuring compliance with applicable occupational safety and health legislation and dealing with fire suppression.

The only successful method of dealing with espionage agents is through counterintelligence. Unless the corporate security department understands this activity and has the resources to perform it, the corporation is easy prey for secret agents. It takes time to set up a useful counterintelligence unit.

A common espionage threat in both government and business concerns the failure to classify sensitive information appropriately so that safeguards can be designed and implemented. Neglect to establish a system of classification can be as dangerous as any lapse in following prescribed security procedures. Classification is an espionage countermeasure.

High technology and scientific specialization hamper the establishment of a unified classification system. For example, the security department is unlikely to contain the expertise necessary to recognize a chemical or mathematical formula that must not be released. Only cooperation from research and development personnel can make classification a workable concept.

Categories of information that may require classification leading to appropriate safeguards include board memoranda, personnel and payroll data, marketing and production information, security and crisis-management plans, research and development files, and expansion and retrenchment schedules. All businesses, even the smallest, have information that requires protection from unauthorized access or disclosure.

Security personnel have learned to rue the status afforded certain corporate employees insofar as such status causes disdain of security procedures. Any lack of cooperation in industrial security countermeasures will radically increase the threat of successful espionage.

Top management must support security in its counterintelligence activities. They must also abide by and follow security procedures, setting an example for other employees. Top management's priorities may minimize attention to security policy; if this is the case, the possibility of successful industrial espionage is increased.

Telephone communications are difficult to protect. The use of microwave transmission exposes most corporate calls to interception. The situation is even worse as to preventing direct tapping of hard-wire lines. A federal study considered commonly available electronic communications equipment on sale in the country. It concluded in 1976 that persons with subprofessional electronics training could successfully wiretap a suburban residential telephone; professional engineers schooled in communications and data processing could eavesdrop on computer data transmissions; and telephone network engineers could eavesdrop on specific conversations in the switched telephone network.

President Reagan stimulated what had been a very weak *national* counterintelligence posture in late 1981 when he allowed the CIA to collect significant foreign intelligence inside the United States. The Ford and Carter administrations had severely restrained intelligence activities. They did much mischief, especially with regard to the detection of industrial espionage practiced by terrorists and hostile nations. Reagan's orders were aimed principally at stopping the accelerated hostile espionage within our borders.

Speaking before the Los Angeles World Affairs Council in December 1981, Attorney General William French Smith noted serious problems in dealing with the threat of Soviet espionage. His warning included the following statements:

- First, as diplomats. About one-third of the Soviet bloc personnel in the United States assigned to embassies, consulates, and the U.N. or other international organizations are believed to be full-time intelligence officers. And over the last dozen years the number of official representatives of governments with hostile intelligence activities in our country has increased by 400 percent.

- Second, as trading company representatives. There are dozens of corporations in the United States that are largely or exclusively owned by the Soviet bloc countries. Earlier this week in Los Angeles, a Polish trading company official who had been purchasing classified documents from an employee of one major defense contractor, was sentenced to life in prison.

- Third, as students, scientists, and reporters. Soviet bloc exchanges with the United States have increased dramatically over the past decade. And their ranks have been packed with full-time or part-time intelligence operatives.

- Fourth, as immigrants and refugees. Although virtually non-existent prior to 1973, Soviet immigration here has since then amounted to some 150,000. More recently, there has been a vast influx of Cuban refugees—who last year alone exceeded 100,000. We believe that a small but significant fraction of these recent refugees have been agents of Soviet and Cuban intelligence.

- Finally, we know that hostile intelligence services continue to infiltrate agents under assumed identities. In 1980 the FBI disclosed that Colonel Rudolph Hermann of the KGB had entered this country through Canada with his wife and son a dozen years earlier and had thereafter posed as a free-lance photographer living in a suburb of New York City.

- The likely number of foreign spies in our country in those guises has increased sharply over the last decade. Unfortunately, our resources have not increased. At one time the FBI could match suspected hostile intelligence agents in the United States on a one-to-one basis. Now, the number of hostile agents has grown so much that our FBI counter-intelligence agents are greatly outnumbered.

- The costs to national security are incalculable because we depend upon our superior technology as a defense against Soviet military advantages in manpower and sheer volume of weaponry. A television documentary on the KGB shown by the Canadian Broadcasting Company a few months ago, for example, concluded that the theft of inertial guidance technology by Soviet intelligence improved the accuracy of Soviet ICBM's and made U.S. fixed, land-based missiles vulnerable—and argued that the theft created the need to build a costly MX missile basing system. The multi-billion dollar cost of the proposed MX missile basing system may thus illustrate the effectiveness of Soviet intelligence.

- Perhaps even more insidious is the threat posed by hostile "active measures" in this country, which are aimed at influencing public opinion and the political process through "disinformation" and "agents of influence." Most serious of all, however, is the threat of international terrorism. Although we have been fortunate as a country to have been spared the degree of terrorism experienced by many of our Western European allies, we cannot permit our relative good luck to engender complacency. A small number of well-trained fanatics could change our fortunes overnight. As all of you know from press reports, the threat is real today. Libya's capability of sponsoring an effort to assassinate high U.S. government officials provides a sobering example. As members of an open society that is the target of aggressive foreign powers, we must all recognize the grave threat from hostile intelligence and the need for more effective U.S. intelligence and counterintelligence.

The authors hope the business community takes note of Smith's remarks because the threats he talks about will affect business in the years ahead.

INFORMATION GATHERING AND RETENTION

Decision making requires information. All organizations continually gather information, which they screen for accuracy and possible utility to the corporation. There are times when accurate information is critical, particularly in a weak economy.

Within the corporation, a number of groups seek and process information: research and design, marketing, estimation, industrial relations, and security or loss control. External information gatherers funded by the corporation include contact personnel, lobbyists, external counsel, and public relations.[6]

Gathering information is a necessary part of corporate activity. How the information is gathered raises questions of propriety and legality. Corporate information is gathered mostly through overt or open sources—publications, conversations, the media, and the like. Even national intelligence agencies spend most of their resources in overt collection of data. But corporate information is also gathered through covert or clandestine means. Industrial espionage is a covert collection method that makes use of blackmail, undercover agents, burglars, tapped telephones, hidden microphones, illegal access to computer data, theft of documents, and similar tactics.

Industrial spies seek the easy route to their goal. Corporations that lack effective security and loss-control programs often allow espionage agents to gather vital facts simply by asking for them.

Legitimate information gathering and production requires safeguards. Absence of any of the following loss-control measures may lead to industrial espionage: access control, document control, personnel screening, visitor control, espionage awareness, and customer screening. Incomplete or ineffective application of these measures negates their value.

Access control implies all that is necessary to allow the right people, equipment, and material to enter while barring the wrong people, equipment, and material. Document control includes classification of documents, safeguarding them and preparing backup copies, and controlling dissemination. Personnel screening involves background investigations, both preemployment and prepromotional. Visitor control means monitoring all authorized visitors while on site and logging their movements and contacts. Espionage awareness is an educational program that emphasizes the necessity of preventing opportunities for industrial espionage and reporting attempts. Customer screening secures the true identity of purchasers of sensitive products to prevent foreign technology transfer.

ESPIONAGE TARGETS AHEAD

The facts of espionage currently available make it difficult to pin-point areas of the world that have little to fear from this threat. Industrial espionage targets are informational, not the geographical settings sought by the military commander.

---

[6] Harold L. Wilensky, *Organizational Intelligence* (Philadelphia: Basic Books, 1967), chap. 2

Concentrations of valuable information often draw spies. The Silicon Valley, a thirty-mile section between Menlo Park and San José in northern California, is a major target for the activities of industrial spies. This region has over 1,500 corporations engaged in electronics and computer chip research. The military value of such technology is enormous and so is the economic value.

Switzerland is a target because of its political neutrality, technological achievement, and central location in Europe. The Swiss Federal Ministry of Justice reported in 1982 that 240 cases of espionage have been uncovered since 1948. In over two-thirds of those cases, agents of the Soviet Union or their allies were involved. Geneva seems to host the most espionage activity in Switzerland, probably because it is the European home of the United Nations and has 122 diplomatic missions and 14 major international organizations. Although much of the espionage is political, there have been many incidents that the Swiss call economic espionage.

Certain industries are everywhere particularly vulnerable. Fashions are an attractive target. Spies go to Paris to steal from the designers. They also frequent New York to determine what the manufacturers are doing. The perfume industry, whether located in Texas or Great Britain, attracts espionage. The list is endless. Whatever information has value on the open or black market is subject to espionage. In years to come, the concentration of industrial espionage will undoubtedly shift with the political and economic changes around the world.

ACCELERATING FORCES

Forces that can accelerate the industrial espionage threat are personal, technological, political, and cultural. The directions currently taken by these forces continue to make industrial espionage profitable. Corporations that ignore these forces will suffer losses as a consequence.

Personal

The ethics and morality of earlier generations are no longer followed so strictly. Until the trend is reversed (and there are signs that it will be), personal advantage remains the major consideration.

All employees look to improve their personal situations. Certain professionals, such as computer specialists, university professors, and engineers, accelerate income and promotion by changing jobs. Obviously they carry information from each job to the new employer.

As economic conditions deteriorate, business persons face the prospect of salary cuts, layoffs, and termination. When the survival of a corporation is at stake, its employees may try to use any tactics, even illegal ones, to secure their positions. With so much riding on the outcome, no holds barred easily becomes the order of the day. Industrial espionage may be practiced with glee. It will certainly be condoned by employees whose jobs may hinge on the results of such activity.

Technological

Technology is important not only in and of itself but also in respect to obsolescence. Each corporation must offer up-to-date products if it is to capture a reasonable market segment. Creative abilities being unequal, someone will forge ahead, and competitors will try to close the gap, perhaps even with industrial espionage. The life cycle of products seems shorter as technology advances; increased pressure is the result. Should a corporation lack the funds to satisfy the priority for change through massive research, an alternative is to acquire others' research in some fashion, legal or illegal.

Pressures to keep up with technology are strong. Each division and profit center needs to show profit. The alternative is bankruptcy or a merger unfavorable to existing management. Thus an industrial espionage effort may be localized and unknown to headquarters' corporate management. This activity is often justified as due to an emergency. Apologists tend to argue that unethical behavior of this sort does not reflect business character but is merely a temporary aberration.

Political

Political forces have long been recognized as motivating political espionage. Economic espionage is also a tool of governments as they seek to equalize or gain advantage over rival nations. The need for economic espionage rises as world tensions among nation-states increase. The superpowers spend a large portion of their budget on military research and development. In America most of this research is performed by private enterprise under government contract. Government spies may try to get this information from the private sector.

Cultural

The business environment has its own culture. All cultures have certain taboos that influence behavior. Modern man has substituted laws for tribal prohibitions. Business thrives on the loophole concept in relation to taxes. Headlines throughout the 1970s and into the 1980s alerted the public to business misdeeds in respect to price fixing, bribery, and corruption. Consumer activitists were able to convince the public and the Congress that consumers needed protection from American business and citizens needed protection from government, the latter under constant pressure from business lobby groups. As a result, much legislation was enacted in occupational health, privacy, freedom of information, and credit investigations. The Federal Trade Commission, the Environmental Protection Agency and other government bodies became active on consumers' behalf during the same period. For instance, tens of thousands of motor vehicles were recalled to correct defects. Other products were taken off the market entirely. The message of these actions is that business is not self-regulating in the ethical area.

Ethics, or rather the lack of ethics, play a great part in respect to the level and intensity of industrial espionage practiced by competing interests. Corporations with low ethical standards can be expected to practice industrial espionage at every opportunity though publicly condemning the activity. Corporations with high ethical standards may fall victim to the espionage unless they support an adequate counterintelligence unit.

Looking back to the consumer activist movement of the 1970s, it seems strange that during the same period business journals published articles on how to beat the competition by practicing thinly disguised espionage, labeled as something else. This is the last thing one might expect to see at a time when business ethics were coming into serious question.

Certain professional groups have ethical standards; for example, doctors, lawyers, certified public accountants, ministers, dentists, and members of the American Society for Industrial Security (ASIS). Businessmen are not organized as a profession. Competition, fair or foul, is their method; too often it is foul. Unless the moral climate of business improves significantly, more industrial espionage will be practiced in the years ahead. To the extent that industrial espionage is simply a function of standard business procedure that is internally rewarded, the climate of business is corrupt.

SUMMARY

Many factors compound the future problems of industrial espionage. More information is available, and it is available to more people. Technology in the form of computerized data storage is not able to protect the facts it contains.

Legislation designed to make government more open has instead led to exposure of corporate secrets. The expansion of the media has created a hunger for news material from any source. Electronic eavesdropping devices are better than ever and smaller.

Almost anyone could be a spy. Employees are subject to exploitation after being compromised. Dupes may be persuaded to turn over corporate secrets. Visitors, vendors, customers, and part-time employees have engaged in industrial espionage. Other crimes are used to cover up espionage. Counterintelligence to control espionage is weak at both national and corporate levels.

Espionage is a type of crime. Any effort to control espionage must consider all espionage possibilities. Espionage and propaganda are closely allied. The Western media are a target of the KGB. Scientists are another KGB target. They often fail to exercise caution in their publications.

Information gathering is a common corporate function. Both inside and outside personnel are involved. If a corporation lacks scruples, this collection often includes espionage.

Industrial espionage is not restricted to any geographical setting, although the Silicon Valley of northern California and Geneva, Switzerland, seem to experience more espionage than many other places. Accelerating forces for espionage include personal, technological, political, and cultural influences. Ethics is a problem at the individual and corporate levels.

4. Philosophical, Ethical, and Legal Issues

To be moral is to be realistic. —A.C. Germann

ESPIONAGE IN A DEMOCRATIC SOCIETY

In 1965, President Lyndon Johnson established the Commission on Law Enforcement and Administration of Justice by Executive Order 11236. After two years of investigation and examination of "every facet of crime and law enforcement in America," the commission submitted its report.[1] This massive report was supported by a lengthy series of nine contributing subreports, each of which was a stand-alone volume that contained an examination of some function of the criminal-justice system or some aspect of crime.

The final report contained a volume on organized crime, which almost did not see the light of day. Last-minute pressure by the members of the Task Force on Organized Crime kept it alive and it was published both as a stand-alone volume and as Chapter 7 of the master document, *The Challenge of Crime In a Free Society.* Why this portion of the President's Commission Report was sought to be suppressed is anybody's guess. Importantly, however, it was saved from the dust bin, and it did make a strong case for legalized wiretapping and eavesdropping to combat organized crime. In the course of the discussion of legal wiretaps by the police we find this statement, ". . . numerous

---

[1] Attorney General Nicholas de B. Katzenback, "Foreword," *The Challenge of Crime in a Free Society: A Report by the President's Commission on Law Enforcement and Administration of Justice* (Washington, D.C.: U.S. Government Printing Office, 1967).

private persons are using these techniques. They are employed to acquire evidence for domestic relations cases, to carry on industrial espionage and counterespionage."[2]

Further discussion of these matters under the subheading of The Threat of Privacy clearly indicates the distaste of the Commission for this type of employment of various technologies, including the electronic cocktail olive, parabolic microphones, laser beam listening devices, microminiaturized electronic surveillance components, and the general assault on privacy of these and all other bugging activities. No discussion of industrial espionage and counterintelligence occurs in the President's Crime Commission Report other than this passing reference. Apparently, the crime of espionage did not trigger any concern on the part of the Commission except a knee-jerk revulsion to the very idea of electronic surveillance without court supervision.

The National Advisory Committee on Criminal Justice Standards and Goals published in 1976 seems to have taken a more realistic approach to espionage in Standard 7.5, entitled Electronic Surveillance:

> Every state should have a wiretap and microphonic surveillance statute permitting the use of nonconsensual procedures in cases involving organized crime and related corruption. States should also provide for rigorous enforcement of laws against the illegal use of wiretap and microphonic surveillance.[3]

But the commentary accompanying the standard did not address the problems of nonofficial electronic surveillance except to point out that the "public and the media [should] have a clear idea of the difference between the misuse of wiretap and microphonic surveillance by nonofficial groups and its legal use as a tactic to enforce the law."[4] Indeed, the entire discussion centered on the need for legalization of official surveillance and again ignored the illegal use of these powerful weapons for espionage.

Clearly the President's Crime Commission and the National Advisory Committee on Criminal Justice Standards and Goals, the two most prestigious bodies to have dealt with crime problems in the last forty years, ignored the crime of espionage. But is this surprising? Despite the fact that spy stories—internationally oriented stories or those that deal with local snooping by private detectives—seem to titillate the public, most people look upon espionage as something

---

[2] Ibid., p. 202.

[3] U.S. Department of Justice, Law Enforcement Assistance Administration, National Advisory Committee on Criminal Justice Standards and Goals: *Report of the Task Force on Organized Crime: Organized Crime* (Washington, D.C.: Government Printing Office, 1976).

[4] Ibid., p. 149.

apart; something not real, like the robber or the burglar whom they fear to the point of paranoia!

The fact is, although industrial espionage is widespread, it commands little attention by the police, the public, or even industry itself. There have been some isolated instances of law enforcement initiatives to deal with the problem, but for the most part industry is on its own. This is true even though the object of industrial espionage may be to supply a hostile foreign nation with valuable information. Of course, if we are engaged in classified government operations there will be greater official concern. Yet much of the data and information that industry protects in its own interests is grist for the mill of foreign espionage.

Thus, while espionage in the United States is illegal under many statutes, it lacks consistent enforcement unless a very clear and unmistakable national interest is involved. It almost seems that we have gone out of our way to make espionage a simple matter. In our open society spies do not even have to resort to covert operations or clandestine tactics in order to obtain a very sizeable portion of the data that is sought. Our democratic society is so open that leaks are easy to come by. Even the more protected information may be obtained with little effort by a competitor in industry or by a hostile foreign nation. Industrial espionage has spawned a whole new breed of domestic spies who can obtain almost any secret for a client. They are not selective in choosing their clients, some of whom are foreign agents or stand-ins for foreign agents.

In most countries, industrial espionage is a crime and may be a prison offense, but not so in the United Kingdom.[5] One of the rules of the Association of British Investigators is that, although industrial espionage is quite legal in England, it is unethical. Such blindness to reality is unethical in a perverse sense, for it exposes industry to the searching glare of espionage. Many American corporations operate in the United Kingdom. In the very highly competitive world we live in, every large industry should be very concerned and develop its own industrial counterintelligence capability.

It is impossible to know how much industrial espionage exists and what the dollar cost may be. Good spies generally do not get caught. Why so many top executives are oblivious to the threat is difficult to understand since they have been aware for years of the industrial spying and the piracy that has flourished in the worlds of

---

[5] Peter A. Heims, "Unethical, But Legal," *Security Management* (December 1981), pp. 10-15.

fashion, cosmetics, perfumes, automobiles, and other consumer goods. The same top executive who will not accept the threat to himself, his family, and his company, knows full well that his alma mater spies on prospective opponents of good, old Ivy College whenever the football season rolls around. Business is certainly more sensitive than the yearning of old grads for victory on the gridiron.

When any business is in a competitive situation (and what business is not?) there is in fact, or there is likely to be, industrial espionage. This is true even though the business may not be a high-technology firm or seek government contracts. Objects of espionage include customer lists, credit ratings, special processes, pricing plans, new designs of everything from cars to product packaging, marketing plans, financial data, stock purchases and sales, takeovers, mergers, anticipated court decisions and legislation, advance information concerning the rulings of government bureaus, and, of course, trade secrets of all kinds. Espionage involves the theft of classified information, whether government classified or industry-restricted and sensitive data. It includes the purloining of protected industrial processes or products, piracy of industrial blueprints, record albums, motion pictures—the list is endless.

ETHICAL DISTINCTIONS

Industrial espionage is a crime. But some people may vacillate about how bad this industrial espionage activity is. If we call it market research and are only trying to protect our own flanks so that we will not be competitively disadvantaged, is that unethical? Some business people hire private investigators who may engage in some unethical practices in order to obtain this data.

The ultimate deception is to engage in espionage and call it counterintelligence. Who would say that it is unethical to prevent others from penetrating our secrets and our privacies? Do we not have the right of self-defense? If competitors will not play the game above board, we must counter with defensive tactics. In this case, counterintelligence is proper, right and ethical, is it not? Is it ethical to think like a spy to catch a spy? Is it ethical to act like a spy to catch a spy? These are difficult questions. Most of us would say that industrial counterintelligence is quite proper and ethical, while industrial espionage is unethical and unlawful. This conclusion would be in tune with community perceptions and accepted standards. However, some of the agents of counterintelligence employ much the same tactics to achieve their objectives as do espionage agents themselves. Some persons employ defensive tactics that are as reprenhensible as the spying that we abhor and clamor against.

Let us remember, however, that most business people are ethical, and they would not personally engage in industrial espionage or hire anyone to do this work. Some industrialists will remain uninvolved in this contest except to make certain that their vulnerabilities are protected by standard defensive security practices. They assume and maintain a true defensive position and will not be lured into questionable tactics. Their subordinates may not be so ethical, however.

There exists at least a presumptive difference in the philosophical, ethical, and legal sense between espionage and counterintelligence. Is there a similar distinction to be found between industrial espionage that is strictly for domestic competitive purposes and that which serves the best interests of a foreign power, possibly a hostile foreign power?

The danger in trying to compare spying for domestic competitive purposes and spying for a hostile foreign nation is that the lines between the two are not easily drawn. Legally, of course, there is a world of difference between being a spy and being a traitor. Industrial espionage that involves covert operations to obtain a competitive edge is one thing; spying in the service of a hostile power is quite another matter. Clandestine spying is reprehensible whatever the reason. However, if the purpose of such espionage is treason, an entirely new set of philosophical, ethical, and legal sanctions is involved. Few could argue that treason is ethical or that traitorous espionage is ethical; however, many do not perceive domestic industrial espionage as serious. There are the caught and the uncaught. If the domestic competitive industrial spy, through error, indiscretion, or lack of skill, is trapped, he is on his own. Penalties are not excessively harsh, and the spy looks forward to inevitable release. He is not in total disgrace as he would be if he had been a foreign agent.

The danger with this type of loose philosophical, ethical, and legal perspectives involved in industrial espionage is that our lack of outrage at the home-grown industrial spy may be our nation's undoing. The number of spies is increasing; they propose to sell their special services to industries that want to find out about the activities, processes, practices, and secrets of their competitors in order to survive. Government reaction to this unnerving development is much less than vigorous. As the number of spies increases and their skills become sharpened, they obtain more and more sensitive data, information that may be of more value to a hostile foreign power than to any domestic industrialist. Since the spy is in an unethical occupation, it is hard to imagine that he or she would not sell information to the highest bidder, who may be a hostile foreign power operating through a carefully cultivated intermediary who appears to be anything but a foreign agent.

It is obvious, therefore, that many of the ethical distinctions we have discussed are, in fact, distinctions without a difference.

ETHICS OF POLITICAL ESPIONAGE

Politicians and political parties have used espionage in order to keep apprised of the intent, motives, and plans of the opposition. It is somewhat puzzling to observe the national shock and outrage that was occasioned by Watergate and the events surrounding the public exposure of those dirty tricks. Most of the sophisticated among us knew they were going on all the time in virtually all political contests. It is somewhat analogous to the media hype that was generated by Serpico and the New York City Knapp Commission on police corruption. Serpico told us nothing that law enforcement officials did not already know or suspect. Likewise, the Nixon cover-up and later disclosure did not reveal any deep, dark secrets previously unsuspected of the political enterprise in our nation. This is not to say that such conduct is ethical; Watergate was not a one-time aberration. Political espionage at the domestic level is part of the charade that characterizes the entire process of spying in our society.

It is certainly ironic that politicians will fault business and industry for using the espionage tactics that political parties have used for many years. Political espionage is unethical but usually not prosecuted unless there is public outcry. Since both major parties have the same skeleton in their closets, there exists an implicit conspiracy to keep the public ignorant about political espionage. It takes a major upheaval to pierce the veil of mutual self-protection.

ETHICS OF INDUSTRIAL ESPIONAGE

Many industrialists are innocent of industrial espionage. But general technology is advancing so quickly that industrial espionage is becoming almost a necessary adjunct to the business scene. Is it possible to be part of that scene and avoid compromising one's ethical and moral scruples?

One answer may be that it is theoretically possible to engage in a sterile counterintelligence position and not engage in questionable tactics. For example, market research theoretically could develop intelligence from open sources and avoid any covert or clandestine access to secret sources. The ultimate question is whether it is possible to survive in this less-than-perfect world with such uncompromising ideals concerning competitors who have probably already screwed on the silencers and are out there gunning for confidential and secret data any way they can get it.

Perhaps there are ways in which society and government could protect the innocent. Perhaps we could do a better job in the white-collar atmosphere of corporate operations and attempt to make industrial espionage a less attractive vocation. William H. Webster has committed the FBI to the priority of combating white-collar crime, organized crime, and foreign espionage. He has not specifically mentioned domestic industrial espionage, but it may be implied as a component of white-collar crime and as a component of foreign espionage. As noted previously, it is a very fine line that separates domestic competitive and foreign espionage and that line has a tendency to become blurred. Director Webster has stated that the Communist bloc countries have initiated a massive effort to steal business technology. He recommends tightening of internal controls by businessmen. Let us hope that the FBI may come to the rescue of our ethical business people by giving support of a controlled counter-intelligence effort to tighten internal controls without industrialists' falling into the trap of suborning spies themselves.

ETHICAL AND LEGAL ROLE OF PRIVATE
SECURITY IN ESPIONAGE

The private security profession is bound to become involved in counter-intelligence and probably also in espionage. The Code of Ethics promulgated by the American Society for Industrial Security (ASIS) states, among other canons,

    I. A member shall perform professional duties in accordance with the law and the highest moral principles.

    II. A member shall observe the precepts of truthfulness, honesty, and integrity. [In further comment on this canon of the Code it is stated that a member shall not knowingly release misleading information.] . . .

    V. A member shall safeguard confidential information and exercise due care to prevent its unauthorized disclosure.

In the pursuit of counterintelligence, ASIS members may have difficulty living up to this code. To the extent that private security personnel become involved in carrying out industrial espionage, it will be virtually impossible, raising the question as to whether the security profession should become involved in any way with industrial counterintelligence and/or industrial espionage. On the other hand, if private security is not available to assist the members of industry in counterintelligence, where will they turn?

Despite the ASIS Code of Ethics, it is likely there will be some few people in the field of private security who may be hired for espionage purposes. In this connection we should be aware that the key man of the Watergate fiasco has formed his own security business. (Undoubtedly, there are a few other private security persons and concerns that share the same ethical standards that have caused such notoriety.)

One does not have to proceed farther than his autobiography in order to fathom the ethical standards of G. Gordon Liddy.[6] He tells how he volunteered in Washington to be an authorized assassin. (He also volunteered to be assassinated.) His autobiography is replete with a recounting of all the dirty tricks one could possibly imagine.

The U.S. government has not stepped in to provide greater assistance to industry in dealing with the threat of industrial espionage. (In the U.S.S.R. and its satellites, industrial espionage and counterintelligence are conducted by the state for the economic welfare of the country. Of course, industry in such countries is controlled by the government, so it is an economic extension of political and military intelligence.) One may question whether it could be conducted more ethically in this country if it were the responsibility of the government, rather than the individual businesses involved. That is, would government agencies do a more edifying job than private security?

It is difficult to answer that question, except to note that the government would have access to its own manifold covert sources, and, therefore, there would be fewer gaps in information that might seem to require direct espionage techniques. Also, industrial espionage and counterintelligence conducted by private security could attract some of the more "kinky" contract security companies, as opposed to the more ethical and more professional firms. This would be unfortunate because industrial counterintelligence is so vital to our economic health and national survival that only the very best should be involved.

Nor is future legislation likely to provide for a federal industrial counterintelligence campaign, even though ASIS has recommended that government efforts should be increased with respect to counterintelligence. Thus, at present it appears that American industry, for the most part, must provide its own resources to deal with industrial espionage. There are a number of consultant and contract security

---

[6] G. Gordon Liddy, *WILL* (New York: St. Martin's Press, Inc., 1980).

agencies currently specializing in this area, and more may be expected in the future. Hopefully, these will ultimately include many of our highly reputable security experts. (ASIS has also recommended that monies be appropriated for better training of local, state, and federal law enforcement agencies, specifically targeted in the industrial espionage area.)[7] However, for the most part, we must expect little legal support from the federal government unless there is involved a clear and present danger to the nation in the particular industrial espionage situation.

Generally there are no legal impediments to private security's performing a counterintelligence role for industry. On the other hand, there are serious legal questions when counterintelligence becomes outright industrial espionage. The line is hazy and somewhat obscure, so private security agencies must be meticulous in ensuring that their tradecraft is practiced in a legal manner. Government agencies have greater flexibility in this area because they are involved for the benefit of the nation, whereas private security is in the hire of private individuals and groups concerned about their business. The net effect, however, of successful industrial espionage, particularly if the data ultimately are acquired by a hostile power, is the same whether the information was protected by private security or by a government agency. The espionage may weaken the United States in the secret war for economic power, or it may have direct political and military implications.

Senator Sam Nunn, former chairman of the Senate's Permanent Subcommittee on Investigations, summarized the subcommittee's objectives as follows:

> (1) a determination of whether remedial action is necessary with regard to the espionage laws, (2) to serve in an oversight capacity to determine the effectiveness of federal intelligence and law enforcement agencies whose jurisdiction includes the protection of data with potential value to our adversaries, and (3) to determine whether these agencies have been handicapped by recent laws and regulations, such as the Privacy Act and the Freedom of Information Act in dealing with private industry in the protection of data.[8]

The United States seems to be awakening to the threat of industrial espionage and realizing that what appears to be a strictly competitive business affair may have serious implications for the survival of the

---

[7] ASIS Speaks Out, "Theft and Diversion of U.S. High Technology," *Security Management* 26 (July 1982):32.

[8] Senator Nunn to ASIS, in ASIS, "Theft and Diversion of U.S. High Technology," *Security Management* (July 1982):25.

nation. The Japanese attempts to steal IBM secrets may not be atypical. "Suspicion grows that Japanese companies may be selling U.S. technology to Russia. Commerce Department officials are preparing to ask Japanese firms for proof that they have agreed in writing, as required, not to transfer American-supplied technology to a third party. Aides believe Tokyo may be a hotbed of Soviet industrial intelligence-gathering."[9] This is no doubt part of the major thrust of the Soviet Union to obtain Western technology through legal and illegal channels. Using agents, co-opting citizens, preying on gullible business people, moving goods through other nations, and exploiting the weaknesses in our control system, they are gaining access to Western technology on an unprecedented scale. The Japanese connection is truly not unique; it is symptomatic of a rapidly spreading practice.

CONSTITUTIONAL AND LEGAL CONSTRAINTS

There are constraints on espionage just as there are constraints on intelligence and counterintelligence and on surveillance and counter-surveillance. Industrial espionage is a criminal offense in most states, and while counterintelligence is justifiable, it may easily become espionage and can be criminal. There are serious problems of privacy involved in intelligence gathering, and in terms of counterintelligence there are constraints on the government to disclose matters that may not be in the best interests of the United States. There are constraints against surveillance on the ground that it has a chilling effect on freedom of public assembly and political association. Surveillance of the spies who are conducting their own surveillance is constrained by considerations of domestic versus foreign espionage. Thus the CIA is constrained to limit itself to nondomestic espionage, subversion, and sabotage.

U.S. counterintelligence and intelligence services have been fairly effective under tremendous handicaps such as judicial decisions based on interpretations of personal civil rights, liberties, and freedoms, hostile legislation, and various politically inspired executive orders. Since the administration of Gerald Ford, executive orders have attempted to regulate the American intelligence community. An executive order signed by President Jimmy Carter in 1978 reshaped the intelligence structure and provided explicit guidance on all facets of intelligence operations. President Nixon earlier, by executive order, narrowed the

---

[9] *Wall Street Journal*, July 9, 1982, p. 1.

scope of material that the government could classify. The intelligence community has fared better under President Reagan, although he was careful to assure the public that no U.S. intelligence agency will be given authority to violate the rights and liberties guaranteed to all Americans by our Constitution. As a result of these constraints, America has become disadvantaged competitively in the international market, and its former military superiority has been degraded. While we may still be #1 in high technology, if industrial espionage continues to suck us dry we will lose this superiority as well.

Industrial America is much on its own in counterintelligence. It does not need restrictions and constraints put on its already beleaguered attempts to stay competitive through self-defense. Private security, as the surrogate for American industry in these matters, needs to be better understood by the judiciary, have supportive legislation enacted regarding its flexibility and prerogatives, and be protected in its efforts to collect, store, analyze, and disseminate intelligence information to support its counterintelligence thrust. If there are moles in government agencies, one can be sure there are moles in private industry. Private security needs official backing in its efforts to rid private industry of spies, saboteurs, and subversives. The bloodletting of our trade secrets and high technology advantage must be staunched. The secret war for economic superiority calls for realism and hard-headed decisions that reject legal niceties in favor of the equity of having our liberties and freedoms preserved from destruction by foes.

SOCIETAL PRESSURES AND TABOOS

There is probably more industrial espionage going on today than ever before, and attempts to steal corporate secrets are growing tremendously. In fact, some executives believe it is not only ethical to steal secrets, it is required for continued success in business. Most executives appear to believe that their companies need more systematic methods for gathering, processing, analyzing, and reporting data concerning competitors.

Foreign espionage of all three types—political, military, and industrial—is spurred on by world tensions that exist in the cold war and the nuclear stalemate. Also industrial espionage is exacerbated by the secret war for international economic power and superiority. It is not nearly so apparent that there needs to be an escalation of domestic spying of one American firm against another. Many theories have been advanced: the new morality, stronger competition, fighting fire with fire. There is also a new interest by executives in the company's profitability due to the dangers of bankruptcy on the one hand, and the value enhancement of stock options on the other.

It is ironic that the escalation of domestic industrial espionage should occur at this time in history. During the past ten to twelve years, there has been a public revulsion against government-sponsored *domestic* intelligence efforts and *domestic* spying. Until recently, the Privacy Act and the Freedom of Information Act seemed to represent the position of the great majority of Americans. There were societal pressures against excessive secrecy in government, spurred on by the Watergate scandals. Officials and the general public affirmed the right to privacy—the right most valued by civilized man—and protections were legislated to ensure maximum safeguards for individual privacy.

Espionage and its parent, intelligence, are generally believed to be the antithesis of all that freedom of information and privacy stand for. Are not the usual methods and operations of the spy to penetrate privacy and ferret out personal information and guarded secrets? Does not intelligence involve the compilation of dossiers on individuals and their companies to create data prisons that cannot be readily breached by the citizen-victim? For more than a decade, intelligence has been held in low regard. Many intelligence files have been destroyed, and the limitations placed on surviving intelligence operations made them vulnerable and often ineffective.

Watergate and the realization of the enormous capacity of computer information storage and its capability for rapid retrieval of computer contents has had a chilling effect, causing political figures and the general public to rally around the thrust toward protections for personal privacy. Yet within these kinds of societal pressures and the taboos associated with them, industrial espionage apparently has reached epidemic proportions. Because of these pressures and taboos, the FBI has been unable to realize its goals of a computerized criminal-history record system. The application of these pressures and taboos has prevented the full development of organized crime intelligence.

These pressures and taboos have prevented private security from having access to criminal-offender record information. However, like legalized guns, legalized wiretaps and bugs, and other restrictions on those who are not likely to abuse these privileges, they leave wide open the devastating employment of these powerful instruments in the hands of the unscrupulous. For every handgun covered by a permit, there are hundreds in the hands of potential abusers. For every court-approved wiretap or eavesdropping installation, there are scores of surreptitious, illegal, and privacy-threatening electronic surveillance operations.

This is the irony of the current situation. In the face of strict controls on those who are working in behalf of the best interests of society, there is a failure of control over the pirates, renegades, and criminals who exploit the limitations on lawful endeavors. Organized crime, for example, has used the Freedom of Information Act to identify informers and dispose of them summarily. With all the noble intent of the act, it has probably been the proximate cause of hundreds of gangland hits. Organized crime, and criminals generally heartily endorse their own rights to privacy and have perverted this high-minded social thrust to serve their own nefarious goals. It is within this context that one can understand the proliferation of industrial espionage. On the one hand, ethical counterintelligence is crippled by restrictions and limitations; but on the other hand, unethical, illegal, criminal, and subversive forces appear to operate freely. They are difficult to identify, apprehend, and convict and even on conviction are all too frequently the objects of judicial leniency. Espionage is a highly profitable, low-risk enterprise that attracts many otherwise reputable citizens to its ranks.

ETHICS OF INFORMATION COLLECTION:
THE INDUSTRIAL PERCEPTION

In the nineteenth century, the robber barons were not inhibited by ethical or legal limitations. It is probably true that most industrial leaders today are more circumspect, if only because they have discovered that the reputation for fair dealing is a business asset. It is also probably true that although at the higher levels of business and industry there is a display of commitment to ethical practices, that lip-service may not filter down to the intermediate and lower echelons. As a result we still discover price fixing, bribery, and other foreign and domestic corrupt practices, including industrial espionage.

Business ethics in reference to information collection was surveyed by the *Harvard Business Review* in 1959.[10] This survey relied on the

---

[10] Edward F. Furash, "Problems in Review—Industrial Espionage," *Harvard Business Review* (November–December 1959).

perceptions of the respondents rather than on empirical investigation. Thus, the survey gives some idea as to how business executives say they feel about data collection. The report based on responses from 1,558 business and industrial leaders, found that the majority of those questioned would use ethical means to collect data. Equally to be expected, most said they received information from only open or non-clandestine sources. As pointed out by Walsh and Healy, a sizable minority, however, did admit to getting data from undercover activities, the hiring of competitors' employees, and formal marketing research. The large majority did not approve of wiretapping competitors, planting confederates in a competitor's organization, or rewarding a competitor's employee for certain process information. Also only a small minority approved of a company president's instructing an aide to record conversations secretly in a competitor's office or a design engineer's stealing plans of a competitor's new model. A sizable number and percentage approved, however, the following:

- A vice-president hires a detective agency to watch the proving grounds of a competitor, 16 percent.
- A company representative poses as a prospective customer to get information from a competitor, 32 percent.
- A sales manager wines and dines his competitive counterpart, pumping him for information, 47 percent.
- A key employee is hired away from a competitor, 59 percent.
- A company, learning of a competitor's test market, quickly puts on a special sale in the same location, 64 percent.
- An oil company establishes a scout department to watch the drilling activities of competitors, 71 percent.
- A retailer sends someone to shop in a competitor's store to get product and pricing data, 96 percent.[11]

A similar kind of survey among practicing managers of business and industry in 1977, conducted to ascertain what type of information they felt they needed and that they considered ethical in terms of the information itself and/or the method by which it was obtained, was conducted by *Industry Week*. It found the following:[12]

---

[11] Timothy J. Walsh and Richard J. Healy, *Protecting Your Business Against Espionage* (New York: AMACOM Division of American Management Associations, 1973, p. 166. Excerpted by permission of the publisher. All rights reserved.

[12] S. Brian Moskal, "Sleuthing the Opposition: Does Anything Go?" *Industry Week*, November 21, 1977, pp. 52. Reprinted by permission.

		Ethical	*Not ethical*
1.	Published material and public documents, such as court records	98%	2%
2.	Camouflaged questioning and drawing out of competitors' employees at technical meetings	50	50
3.	Financial reports and brokers' research studies	98	2
4.	Acquisition and analysis of competitors' products	99	1
5.	Legitimate employment interviews with people who worked for a competitor	84	16
6.	Direct observation under secret conditions	9	91
7.	Disclosures made by competitors' employees and obtained without subterfuge	72	28
8.	Job interview with competitor's employee when there is no real interest in hiring him	3	97
9.	Hiring a professional investigator to obtain a specific piece of information	9	91
10.	Market surveys and consultants' reports	99	1
11.	False negotiations with competitor for license	2	98
12.	Trade fairs, exhibits, and competitor's brochures	100	0
13.	Hiring an employee away from a competitor to get specific know-how	31	69
14.	Reports of own salesmen and purchasing agents	99	1
16.	Trespassing on competitors' property	0	100
16.	Bribing competitors' suppliers or employees	0	100
17.	Planting an agent on the competitor's payroll	0	100
18.	Eavesdropping on competitors via bugging	0	100

The results of this survey, similar to the Furash survey, tell us not what business and industrial leaders and practicing managers actually do but rather their perception of what is ethical in information collection. There appears to be a hidden agenda here. If 100 percent of these practicing managers deem unethical such surveillance techniques as bugging, planting an agent on a competitor's payroll, bribing competitors' suppliers or employees, and trespassing on competitors' property; if almost 100 percent deem unethical false negotiations with a competitor for a license, a job interview with a competitor's employees when there is no real interest in hiring the person, hiring a professional investigator to obtain a specific piece of information, and direct observation under secret conditions, then one has to wonder why we are plagued with just kinds of industrial espionage.

Perhaps one answer to that question is that although executives speak of moral principles and probably would want their subordinates to be guided accordingly, in the absence of real leadership, methods used at lower levels may be directly contradictory. We may take the position that most industrial espionage is conducted in such a way that it insulates people at the top, so that one never knows whether the activities were condoned, or even encouraged, by the chief executive officers. In any event, it is often perceived by those, such as salesmen, as a magic password or royal road to success. The Japanese have long recognized the importance of salesmen and field representatives and have schooled them in American customs and methods. One would have to be very naive not to draw logical conclusions concerning information collection from these circumstances. Our executives are not nearly so obvious, but many of their subordinates still believe they receive a loud and clear signal that loyalty to the company may be demonstrated through information collection concerning competitors. If executives look the other way or appear to condone unethical practices, tacit approval will be the message.

There are, indeed, philosophical, ethical, and legal issues permeating every phase of private security. These issues are far from being settled. It appears that our best hope is to ensure that enforcement officials, courts, and legislators understand the counterintelligence imperatives of the 1980s. We can suffer a withering away of innovation, research and development, and the know-how that have made our nation so economically powerful unless we protect industry from domestic and foreign espionage. We have already suffered crippling blows to our economy from unfair foreign competition based on espionage. How much domestic industrial espionage do we have to suffer before industry says, "What is the use?" If we wind up with an industrial base that provides no incentives for initiative, enterprise, or clean competition, we will have suffered a weakened economy and thus become prey for the predatory powers that seek our downfall. Philosophically, espionage, both foreign and domestic, must be brought under control. Industry needs new tools, official support, and public understanding to mount an effective counterintelligence offensive.

LEGAL RESPONSIBILITIES

The extent of competitive spying can only be a matter of conjecture, for it is the bungler that gets caught. The superbly trained spymaster and control agents of the U.S.S.R.'s KGB pass among us undetected. Wherever there are industrial secrets, high technology processes, confidential commercial data, and advanced prototypes, one may be sure there are spymasters swarming around.

President Reagan has said, "The balance between the United States and the Soviet Union cannot be measured in weapons and bombers alone. To a large degree the strength of each nation is also based on economic strength."[13] The economic strength of the United States is threatened by industrial espionage. Yet laws have not been updated to deal with the enormity of this threat to national survival. Restrictions on private security and weak enforcement of existing criminal statutes play into the hands of domestic and foreign industrial espionage. New laws need to be fashioned and old laws revised and reaffirmed. Let us consider some of the anomalies of our present legal position.

The purpose of the Freedom of Information Act (FOIA) was to make information in the government's possession available to public interest groups, scholars, the media, and other citizens.[14] It is estimated, however, that some two-thirds of the requests for information under the act come from industry or its representatives. Businesses have obtained sensitive, proprietary information concerning their competitors from the government files. It is, in effect, a statute that legalizes industrial espionage. The act has also been used to determine the identity of government informers. Spy masters, espionage agents, and organized crime syndicates have been able to locate informers with legal assistance provided by FOIA.

Consider the restrictions placed on private security in the name of the Privacy Act of 1974 (Public Law 93-579). Access to arrest

---

[13] Radio address by President Reagan, November 13, 1982.

[14] FOIA of 1966, P.L. 89-487, 80 Stat. 250 (1966). (Codified at 5 U.S.C. §552) (1976).

records has been denied even though they are needed for personnel screening and legitimate investigations to defend against industrial espionage. Time-honored surveillance practices have been denied to private security even though we have tasked the private sector to fend for itself in dealing with industrial espionage. At the same time that we have tied the hands of private security, technological advances in eavesdropping have created an open season on company secrets. Limited legal sanctions and ineffective enforcement have brought aid and comfort to the enemy. We are, indeed, a very soft target.

To add to the ineffectiveness of the war on industrial espionage, the FBI is limited in its opportunity to identify persons involved in industrial espionage. The CIA, unlike the KGB, is restricted in its jurisdiction and its role in domestic industrial espionage. State and local agencies are often ill equipped legally and functionally to provide necessary enforcement. Many state criminal statutes do not take cognizance of the sophisticated types of crimes involved. Only when a common crime is committed do the police swing into action. This is usually after the fact and after the damage has been done.

Traditional legal remedies against industrial espionage have been found wanting in virtually every respect. Criminal and civil remedies need to be revised and restructured. Legal defenses against espionage are largely dependent on a patchwork of civil remedies that reflect commercial crimes of the past. The law has yet to catch up with the advent of the computer as henchman in technological raids on technology.

Consider the legal obstacles of the distinction between tangible and intangible property. This distinction must be abolished in order to eliminate key defenses available to legally adroit industrial spies. Another serious problem has been the failure to include procedural safeguards against trade secret disclosure during criminal prosecution. A theft conviction is often obtained at the expense of public disclosure of business secrets. Combating industrial espionage requires precisely drafted legislation and judicial understanding. But courts generally have been naive about industrial spies and find reasons for assessing fines instead of jail sentences in the rare event a conviction is obtained.

ETHICAL AND LEGAL TACTICS

Given the inadequacy of the legal response to the threat of industrial espionage, what can we do?

Our response should be holistic. A number of thrusts are available:

1. Working within the present legal environment, attempt to use legal tactics to combat espionage.
2. Mount campaigns to provide new and improved legislation, executive orders, and judicial interpretations.
3. Strive to develop legally supported counterintelligence systems, including legally structured controls on access and dissemination.
4. Work toward the elimination of legal and constitutional constraints on the role of private security in coping with industrial espionage.
5. Use available legal sanctions to bring identified spies to justice.

Let us look in detail at each of these potentially effective categories of legal tactics. No single category is likely to meet the entire problem, yet the discreet application of some or all of these types of possible tactics may be of value. Individual situations and circumstances will need to be considered.

Some legal tactics we may employ within the present legal environment include the following:

- General policy statement by management to communicate and educate all personnel to the need to protect the organization from espionage.
- Communicate the reasons for security and the hazards to the survival of the organization.
- Afford a full explanation of the total program of defense against espionage threats.
- Provide individual explanations of specific responsibilities.
- Draft legal agreements to hold information in confidence and not divulge it improperly. These agreements may be with employees, visitors, vendors, contractors to whom the information is given for needed processing by another outside organization, and information discussed at any meetings with outsiders.
- Publish procedures and distribute a security manual to employees and appropriate others.
- Sign noncompetitive covenants with employees who resign or retire. The objective of these contracts is to circumscribe the types of employment such employees engage in after leaving the company. These contracts should identify specific proscriptions on the kinds of employment and the types of competitors; they must indicate the geographical limits and

the duration of the restrictions. They should also set out the compensation given the employee as legal consideration for the agreement.

- Sign covenants with nonemployees, which include lists of security precautions, provisions for the nonemployee to be responsible for his or her own employee's secrecy, and assurances that all sensitive materials (and any copies) will be returned inviolate.

The courts generally have strictly construed these types of restrictive covenants, so they must be fashioned with care. Since these tactics include an employee's knowledge[15] and the right of a former employee to seek employment in his or her area of competence, there must be specific consideration to make the contract legally binding. Satisfactory consideration must be more than some token award or reward; it should be some form of continuing compensation for the duration of the restrictive agreement.

We need to plan campaigns to revamp present legislation. Instead of restricting inordinately our efforts to protect our technology advantage, legislation should be directed at strengthening our defenses. Specifically, those provisions of the Freedom of Information Act and the Privacy Act that have proven treacherous should be stricken. Criminal sanctions against illegal wiretapping and bugging and all types of espionage surveillance should be bolstered and zealously prosecuted.

We need to ensure that future Executive Orders from the president continue the Reagan initiative to restore public confidence in and provide respectability for the intelligence community. Former Executive Orders demeaned the role of counterintelligence to the extent that it became ineffective. To a significant extent the present disarray of our efforts to cope with industrial espionage stems from misguided Executive Orders.

We should be vigilant to ensure that prosecutors understand the significance of industrial espionage and vigorously pursue these cases. Similarly, courts need to be educated in the implications for national interest that are inherent even in cases that appear to be purely domestic competitive espionage. Our economy is weakened by every successful espionage situation. The cases that come before the courts are but a small fraction of the multitude of industrial espionage attempts. For every spy caught and prosecuted, there are scores who are never discovered, hundreds who are never turned

---

[15] William Bowen, "Who Owns What's in Your Head," *Fortune* (July 1964):177.

over for prosecution, and thousands who would have succeeded except for the presence of counterintelligence and effective security.

It appears to be tempting for the judiciary to regard domestic espionage benignly and on conviction of these criminals to impose fines instead of jail sentences. Judges should be made to realize that there is no such thing as purely domestic spying. All industrial espionage cases have international ramifications, some more than others. Industrial espionage is most often foreign competitive espionage, which is all too readily converted into hostile power advantage, or it may be directly conducted by the spy masters and agents of the Soviet bloc. Also terrorists and organized crime syndicates are prominently involved in these criminal spy activities. We cannot ignore the larger picture; courts must be realistic. Bar associations, legislators, prosecutors, and the judiciary need to be targeted in the thrust to turn around the legal structure.

Counterintelligence systems require support from the legal fraternity. The success or failure of efforts to curb industrial espionage depends to a large extent on the quality (and quantity) of intelligence systems. Public agency intelligence systems provide only a partial answer, since many of these are unavailable to private security. The business world must develop its own counterintelligence components if it is to cope. It is little wonder that the U.S.S.R. and Japan have been so successful in illegal technology transfer when we see how much support their governments provide for their espionage efforts. Is it too much to ask that our government stop throwing legal roadblocks against efforts to develop necessary intelligence? We have to do the best we can with little or no government assistance. We must ask government to provide legal support for the development of meaningful and effective counterintelligence capabilities in the private sector.

In attempts to develop viable counterintelligence, we need to share with both public and private intelligence systems. To the extent that business and industry can legally have access to public counterintelligence data, we will be more effective. Strict legal and security controls can be instituted. We need to have liaison with those in private security so that we all maximize the utility of our information. This dissemination can best be controlled by enforceable legal covenants between and among ourselves. Such legal agreements need to be supported by the courts. Legally structured controls on access and dissemination of counterintelligence will serve to give greater credibility to our efforts.

It is to be hoped that we will be able to strive toward the elimination of legal and constitutional constraints in counterintelligence efforts. If we are to perform a service, we need the tools to carry

out the job. Among other responsibilities properly accorded to counterintelligence is to provide background checks of employees in a position
to disclose information to enemies. Barring private security from access
to arrest data in the files of the FBI's computerized criminal history
center is nonsense. Also, applicant and other personnel investigations
often require the use of technical surveillance. Private security is virtually
foreclosed from obtaining wiretap and/or eavesdropping orders. Much
can be accomplished through the use of polygraphs, psychological
stress evaluations, and pen and pencil integrity tests. In many states
private security is denied even these tools for counterintelligence.

It is truly unfortunate that our domestic competitors, our foreign
competitors, and nations that are our deadly enemies utilize these
technological devices against us. We cannot respond in kind. If the legal
constraints on private security become more rational, and legal tools to
combat espionage are strengthened, private security can defend us.
Without such support our counterintelligence effort is doomed to defeat.

Finally, if we are to succeed, we must have the understanding
support of prosecutors and the judiciary. Prosecutors must assist private
security as they do public agencies. We need the zealous assistance of
attorneys general, district attorneys, and all who have the legal obligation to bring espionage to heel. We need the full support of the judiciary
at every level of the system. Counterintelligence, no matter how
brilliantly operated, will have little effect on espionage and subversion
unless the courts share our goals and objectives. The best case possible
may result in the conviction of a spy, a mole, a spy master, or a foreign
agent, but if the sentence of the court is weak and vacillating, it will
turn out to be a license for the industrial espionage cabal. Intestinal
fortitude and rigorous sentencing is the proper legal response to the
heroic efforts of our counterintelligence community.

CONCLUSION

There are, indeed, philosophical, ethical, and legal issues permeating
every phase of private security. These issues are far from being
settled and will be with us for many years. It appears that our best
hope is to ensure that our enforcement officials, our courts, and our
legislators understand the counterintelligence imperatives of the 1980s.
We can suffer a withering away of innovation, research and development, and the know-how that has made our nation so economically
powerful, unless we are able to protect industry from domestic and
foreign espionage.

We have already suffered crippling blows to our economy from
unfair foreign competition based on espionage. How much domestic

industrial espionage do we have to suffer before industry says, "What is the use?" If we wind up with an industrial base that provides no incentives for initiative, enterprise, or clean competition, we will have suffered a weakened economy and thus become prey for the predatory powers that seek our downfall. Philosophically, espionage, both foreign and domestic, must be brought under control if it cannot be wiped out. Industry needs new tools, official support, and public understanding to mount an effective counterintelligence offensive. There is no other way out.

SUMMARY

This chapter has examined the philosophical, ethical, and legal issues that arise in connection with espionage activities in a democratic society. The President's Commission on Law Enforcement and Administration of Justice and the National Advisory Committee on Criminal Justice Standards and Goals ignored the crime of espionage. This is not surprising in view of the fact that industrial espionage has attracted little attention by the police, the public, and even industry itself. Although espionage in the United States is illegal, it lacks consistent enforcement. As a result, industrial espionage has spawned a whole new breed of domestic spies who will obtain almost any secret any client desires.

There are some ethical distinctions between espionage and counterintelligence and between domestic and foreign espionage. There exists at least a presumptive difference in the philosophical, ethical, and legal sense between espionage and counterintelligence. Does a similar distinction obtain between domestic and foreign espionage? Unfortunately the lines between the two are not easily drawn. Legally there is a vast difference between a spy and a traitor. Few would argue that treason is ethical; however, many do not perceive competitive domestic industrial espionage as inherently unethical. This ambivalence has encouraged the growth of industrial spies.

Political espionage at the domestic level is unethical and illegal yet common practice. Industrial espionage, while perhaps not as pervasive as political espionage, is advancing quickly. Today industrial espionage appears to be almost a necessary part of business. If one is a security officer and subscribes to the ASIS Code of Ethics, such adherence forecloses employment of the types of operations sometimes associated with counterintelligence and totally rules out engaging in espionage.

Legislation is not likely forthcoming to authorize and mount a federal industrial counterintelligence campaign, even though ASIS has recommended that such efforts should be undertaken. In the 1980s the Senate Permanent Subcommittee on Investigations began a comprehensive study of the need for remedial action with regard to the espionage laws. While this is a hopeful sign, actual legislation that will ameliorate the handicaps of the Privacy Act and the Freedom of Information Act is not likely to be passed soon.

Some constitutional and legal constraints plague the intelligence services. Executive orders by several presidents have hobbled the intelligence community. As a result of the weaknesses of our counterintelligence, competitive foreign espionage is rampant. Intelligence must also face the societal pressure and taboos generated by Watergate. As our counterintelligence has been rendered less potent, industrial espionage has flourished. Ethical counterintelligence is crippled by restrictions and limitations, yet unethical, illegal, criminal, and subversive espionage forces appear to operate freely.

We have examined in some detail industrialists' perceptions of industrial espionage. These perceptions do not seem to square with what is happening in our country in the domestic competitive arena. However, executives are becoming aware of the threats of foreign technology transfer and all that that entails.

Serious legal responsibilities are involved in our losses to foreign competitors and hostile nations. Laws need to be updated and strengthened to deal with the enormity of the threats. Criminal and civil remedies need to be revised and restructured.

Ethical legal tactics can provide some remedies. We can mount campaigns to provide new and improved legislation, executive orders, and judicial interpretation. We can strive to develop legally supported counterintelligence capabilities and share our intelligence within legally structured controls on access and dissemination. Prosecutors and courts must provide assistance. Espionage, both foreign and domestic, must be brought under control. Without the zealous coordination of all concerned, the United States will continue to be impotent against the industrial espionage threat.

II. COUNTER-INTELLIGENCE OPERATIONS

5. Planning and Organizing

Well begun is half done. —Horace

PLANNING

The first step in planning for counterintelligence is to assess the threat of industrial espionage. There are few companies of any size that do not have some form of industrial secrets and these precious confidential matters may well be the basis for the company's survival. Naturally, some industrial and business concerns will have a larger share of valuable industrial secrets than others. It is essential to determine precisely what the particular situation may be before any meaningful planning can begin. This process is not as simple as counting up the number of industrial secrets that need to be protected. Ideally, a formal survey that includes interviews, physical inspections, analysis, and risk determination should be conducted.

Interviews should be conducted with all major executives to determine their perceptions of matters vulnerable to espionage. The interviews should also probe their evaluations of the probability of penetration and the criticality of such an event if it were successfully carried out. The perception of the various executives is not an end in itself; it is merely a point of beginning. The interviews will show if any executives have a narrow view of the entire problem. They may have overlooked some obvious vulnerabilities. Indeed, unless the security director or an outside consultant under the security director's guidance is charged with responsibility for the survey, it may be wholly inadequate and skewed by the personal predilections of the various executives. Even the chief executive officer may not be able to provide the clearest picture of the situation because he or she may not be able to think as a spy does and see the full potential for espionage.

The second step in the process of preparing for planning is to conduct a physical inspection of the facility. Among other items that might suggest themselves in a particular environment, the following should be inspected:

1. Perimeter control with fences, walls, gates, barriers, protective lighting, and guard patrol.
2. Location, fencing, and lighting of parking areas.
3. Protective lighting systems.
4. Protective security dogs.
5. Burglar-resistant glazing and security coverings for windows.
6. Guards, patrol, closed circuit television, and visitor control.
7. Locking devices and key control.
8. Fire prevention and protection systems.
9. Establishment of restricted areas.
10. Use of safes, vaults, and other secure storage.
11. Review of the operations of the various functional departments to determine their potentials for loss, their target items for industrial spies, and other hazards that may be exploited by espionage, subversion, or terrorism.
12. Control of employee abuse areas such as photocopying machines, postage meters, fraudulent use of invoices and other company forms, and so on.
13. Attention to hiring, promotion, and assignment-to-sensitive-positions practices.
14. Review of all security operations conducted directly under the security manager, including radio dispatch procedures, monitoring by closed circuit television or other surveillance, eavesdropping, wiretapping, use of informants, undercover personnel, security files and records, fire and disaster plans, training, communications, guard activities, and available security resources in personnel and equipment.

In some cases it may be desirable to employ a professional survey company to conduct the inspection. This would be particularly suitable in high-technology facilities that are obvious targets for espionage. Marilyn Chase, a staff reporter for the *Wall Street Journal*, reports that computer makers are turning to security firms to help crack down on high-technology thefts. A partner in a security firm in the Silicon Valley, said, "Believe me, if a competitor or a foreign power wants what you have, they will find out who works for you and what their weakness is: liquor, narcotics, money problems, a spouse with cancer, or a taste for the ladies. They'll find out where they're vulnerable and compromise them." Chase further reported: "A senior counterintelligence consultant was once an intelligence officer with Delta Detachment, the Army anti-terrorist unit. 'We use contacts overseas, sources developed in our federal work, as well as low-level informants in Silicon Valley,' he reported. 'We often know what's gone down in the Valley before the companies do, and we can usually anticipate when they'll call. We do security surveys, which can cost up to $20,000, anticipating everything from plant sabotage to power failure—what happens to your fancy electronic locks when the lights go off?' says the consultant. 'We also look at information security, paper flow, who's got control of the Xerox machine. We can also do an electronic sweep to determine whether your office has been bugged, or your computer tampered with.' "[1]

In many cases, the security survey can be conducted adequately by the facility's security director and staff, but consultants should be hired to supplement in-house expertise wherever it may be deemed necessary. The important point is to conduct a comprehensive and conscientous survey before beginning the planning process.

The results of the security survey should be carefully analyzed. Where there appears to be a need for summary action, such should be taken immediately. However, to the extent that there is no emergency, it is better to integrate all action into the comprehensive plan, a method that should allow for better coordination and more functional and cost-effective security. Also it should afford the opportunity to perform rational planning in accordance with normative, strategic, and operational planning.

Normative planning responds to the question, What should we do and why? An analysis of strengths and weaknesses, the present rate and trend of industrial espionage, and forecasts of future environments will provide the framework for dealing with overall objectives and priorities, the identification of problem areas, and policies and guides to strategic planning (see Figure 5-1).

Strategic planning attempts to answer the question, What can we do and how? Using information from normative planning, problem analysis, and considering and evaluating alternatives, we can begin to set up programs and contingency plans and set out guidelines for operational planning.

Operational planning asks, What will we do and when? Using strategic and program guidelines, being conscious of operational constraints, and having available operational information, we can schedule projects, prepare budgets, and proceed to deal with personnel and organizational plans.

Thus, once the survey has been completed, projections and anticipations have been determined, and alternative futures have been

---

[1] Marilyn Chase, "How Safe Are Corporate Secrets Here in Silicon Valley?" *Wall Street Journal*, July 22, 1982, p. 1.

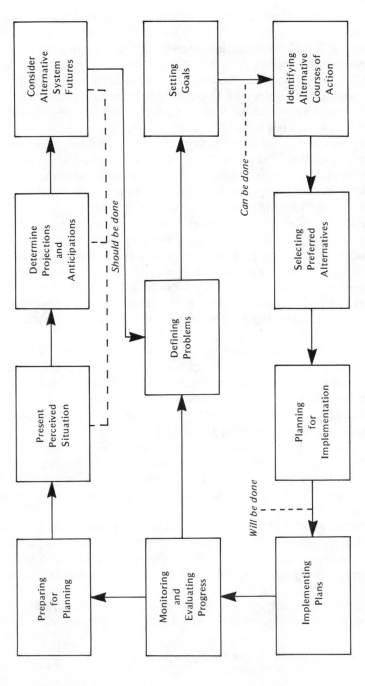

Source: This diagram of the planning process was formulated as a training aid by the Criminal Justice Planning Institute, University of Southern California, sponsored by the Law Enforcement Assistance Administration, U.S. Department of Justice, 1976.

Figure 5-1. General planning process model

considered, we know what should be done and can proceed to problem definition and goal setting in the light of normative planning.

The next step is to determine what can be done and perform strategic planning through goal setting, identifying alternative courses of action, and selecting preferred alternatives. Goal setting will be conditioned by the problem statement since the purpose of goals is to cope with the problems presented. Goal setting should be in the context of the overall goals of the facility and within its resources.

Before proceeding, the broad statements of desirable goals should be reduced to time-phased and measurable goals and objectives. These objectives should be challenging, feasible, desirable, and facilitate the accomplishment of the selected goal(s). Thus, objectives should propose to accomplish a measurable amount or degree of progress in a specific period of time. If the time element is twelve months, we can judge month by month or quarter by quarter whether the measurable target for the year will be met.

Summing up then, there are these major goal-setting steps:

1. Identifying alternative goals. Since one problem may generate many goals, we need to identify those that are reasonable, feasible, and within the realm of accomplishment—that is, what can be done, or strategic planning,

2. Selecting among alternatives. There may be overwhelming constraints on implementation of some of the alternative goals. We need to consider the advantages and disadvantages of each of the remaining goals and select the most rational ones.

3. Planning for implementation. The selection of a program or programs, which may include many individual projects. At this stage, we are deciding what will be done or operational planning.

4. Implementation of plans must be followed immediately by evaluation of progress. Evaluation is basically of two kinds. *Performance evaluation* usually relates to the projects undertaken and asks such questions as: Are we doing the things we planned to do to carry out the program? How many of those things are being done? In what time frame? How much does it cost to do these? Performance evaluation may be of individuals, groups, or the entire project. *Impact evaluation* usually relates to the program. It asks whether the projects undertaken support the program purpose and affect the goals and objectives. Evaluation should be continuous in order to feed information back into the planning

process so that the progress of goals, objectives, programs, and projects may be assessed and possibly adjusted in order to optimize the endeavors.

ORGANIZING

In order for selected goals to be met, an organization is needed to conduct programs and projects. The size of the security force and its counterintelligence effort will determine whether a formal organization or a less formal structure is needed. In any event, it is wise to be aware of the principles of organization that apply regardless of the size of the department or unit.

Organizing the security effort and its counterintelligence unit include the following steps:

1. Divide the necessary work into individual jobs, showing the flow of authority and responsibility.
2. Decide on line and staff functions and relationships and hierarchical levels.
3. Ensure the functioning and flow of channels of communication.
4. Regulate the interrelationships of the various functioning units.

Usually the organization is depicted in an organization chart (see Figure 5-2), and the accompanying manuals of regulations and procedures provide for continuity and consistency. These charts and regulations depict the approved organizational status of individual jobs and the authorized hierarchical structure within the organization. These charts graphically illustrate the chain of command and support the concepts of unity of command. They also call attention to the span of control at various levels of the organization. In the security counterintelligence environment, we are likely to find organization by time, since security generally and counterintelligence in particular are not a 9 A.M. to 5 P.M. operation. We are also likely to structure organization by special needs. Interpreters must be readily available, and certain specialists must be on call at all times. The organization must be developed to ensure control and maintain feedback. Although much of the counterintelligence effort will be shared with general security operations, there is an organizational need for a special division or unit specifically charged with responsibility for combating espionage. This special squad should be organizationally an integral part of the security department yet an entity of its own. It should have its own leadership, which, though responding to the security director, must

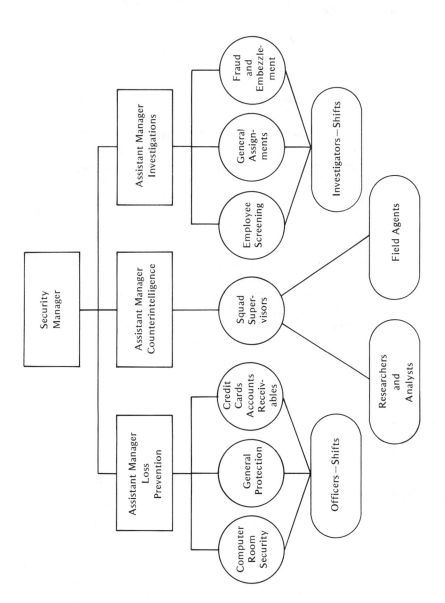

Figure 5-2. Organization chart

have autonomy because of its specialized responsibility. It is suggested that the head of the squad be immediately subordinate to the security director.

STAFFING

The counterintelligence squad must be staffed by carefully selected personnel. Ideally its members should have high educational qualifications and special talents. It could use intelligence expertise as well as investigative skills. Members should have diverse backgrounds and linguistic abilities. Prior experience in engineering, electronics, undercover work, interviewing and interrogating, and government counterintelligence would be desirable. Special attention should be given to the loyalty of squad members to the United States and its institutions, including the vital industrial base. Thorough background checks must be conducted with special emphasis on personal integrity, professional dedication, and trustworthiness. Selectees must demonstrate initiative, ability to subordinate self to team play and discipline, and a stable personality. Some of the members will be slated for "white" positions as researchers and analysts. Others will serve in "black" positions, which may require dissimulation, identity changes, boring from within, eavesdropping, con jobs, and disinformation—indeed, virtually all of the tradecraft of espionage itself, but for a better cause!

TRAINING

The counterintelligence group will need to be particularly concerned with its special training needs. Given the rigorous screening procedure conducted, it is not likely that there will be disciplinary problems; it is possible, however, that some selectees may not measure up to the nature of the tasks assigned them. The training period also provides an excellent opportunity to evaluate personnel in terms of their abilities to adjust to a difficult and unusual aspect of security employment. The training experience and the probationary period will enable the unit director to weed out those who cannot meet expectations.

Some training may be suitable for all members of the counterintelligence squad; other training is directed to persons designated duties in white or black positions. All members should receive the basic security training that is given to members of the security department, including firearms training. On this foundation should be built a special training program for counterintelligence personnel. Squad members should be schooled in classification and clearances, the nature of intelligence, the elements of subversion, the threats of terrorism and sabotage, the prevention and detection of espionage activities, and the protective operations that will shield their employer from espionage.

Personnel destined for duties in white positions will receive training in research and analysis and the intelligence arts. They will learn how to use the computer to assist in the collation and coordination of data. They will gain skills in the manipulation of facts so that one slim clue added to another or to several others generates additional data. They will be taught how to detect gaps in the information they need for empirical verification of their assumptions. They will understand when it is necessary to call on their colleagues in black positions.

Personnel destined for duties in black positions will be trained to think like spies, subversives, and terrorists so that they may be prepared to meet the many challenges that counterintelligence must face. They will develop skills in surveillance, electronics, undercover operations, interviewing and interrogation, and general investigative procedures. They will become knowledgeable in the nature of the threats they may anticipate in their particular facility and the types of persons who may be involved. Profiles of possible spies, subversives, and terrorists will be studied so that proactive preventive measures may be undertaken. In short, these personnel will be trained to be alert at all times to the need for protection of the persons and property of the facility—from executive protection to the protection of machinery from sabotage and the protection of trade secrets from spies. Their best defense will lie in knowing the full nature of the offense so they will learn the trade craft of the enemy to the point where they themselves are as knowledgeable as their criminal opponents.

COORDINATING

Controlling the counterintelligence effort will be difficult. The security director who has never been faced with the problem of mounting, supervising, and developing a coordinated counterintelligence effort may have to learn a great deal in a hurry. But if the director chooses the right type of person to head the squad, the director's prior lack of expertise will not be a handicap.

The head of the counterintelligence group must be a leader. The nature of the task is nonroutine and calls for supervision of a superior nature. It is also essential that he or she understand the intelligence function and the need to disseminate accurate, timely, and meaningful information to those with the right to know and need to know. He or she should have a flair for investigation and a talent for controlling personnel who must be allowed to make decisions about their actions. The entire operation deals with sensitive matters and demands both finesse and sensitivity. Ideally the head of the squad should be schooled in the high technology of the trade craft and be aware of the latest scientific developments that may be employed against the facility. Never forgetting, of course, that technology alone is not the entire problem or solution, that the spy has to get some physical access to the sought-after materials or, alternatively, access to a person who has the knowledge required. A very large percentage of really valuable information is obtained by corrupting those who control physical access or those who have access themselves and can deliver the goods.

The counterintelligence effort must also be coordinated with the general management and employees of the facility. The squad and the security department cannot do the entire job themselves. All of the fine perimeter construction, access controls, guard patrols, closed circuit television, and locks and alarms will accomplish a great deal, but ultimately counterintelligence, like security generally, depends on people for its success. The security director and the head of counterintelligence need to get the message across to everyone from the chief executive officer to workers on the factory floor. Security consciousness today has a new dimension. It is a proper concern for all employees; it is a necessary concern for management at all levels.

FACILITY-WIDE PARTICIPATION

Top management and directors of the various functional departments can contribute to the counterintelligence effort. Top management can ensure that the security department and its counterintelligence component are adequately supplied with funds and resources. Top management can issue policy statements that indicate its concern about the threat of industrial espionage and offering advice to all employees to comply with the efforts of the security department in preventing information leaks concerning the company, as well as criminal access to confidential and secret material. Finally, since the corruption of employees is a major tool of the espionage agent, top management can make every possible effort to generate high morale, good motivation, and job satisfaction. It is surely less likely that employees who have pride in their work and the company's products will succumb to subversion, bribery, or ideological ploys. Satisfied employees are not likely to tolerate any attempt to infiltrate or penetrate industrial secrets or confidential information. To the extent that top management can improve industrial relations, the target will be hardened and the job of security will be facilitated.

Top management cannot do the entire job alone. Security, and particularly counterintelligence, needs the support of every level of management and the active participation of the heads of functional departments. Management must learn the lessons of the famous Hawthorne experiments, which demonstrated that improvements in productivity were not related to improved physical conditions but simply to the fact that the workers concerned knew that they were being studied and this gave them an interest in their work that was otherwise lacking. The Hawthorne experiments tell us that management should take a real interest in their employees and what they are doing and let the employees know of this interest. To put it another way, the task of management is greater than a mere technical operation; management must create a climate in which everyone can participate and with which every employee can identify. Such management tools as job enlargement and career development for subordinates will help motivation and morale. Employees want to feel a sense of responsibility and pride in their work, and those who are so motivated will likely resist temptations that are corruptive and destructive.

RECORD KEEPING

Coordinating will be more effective if it is supported by good records management. Records management envisions a top-management-directed program that maintains surveillance over all records to ensure effective control. This can be achieved through the application of systematic and scientific controls to the recorded information that is essential for the organization. Organization-wide controls enable us to provide necessary data for management problem solving and decision-making processes. The many sources of records include correspondence, forms, reports and studies, and instructions and guidelines.

Efficiency will be improved if there is a system of forms control exercised over the various input documents. Effectiveness also depends on distribution control of such records. Standards need to be devised for dissemination. How many copies of records should go to whom? What restrictions (classification) should be placed on access to these records? How shall the information be used?

An important aspect of record keeping is the maintenance of these record files. Here the extensive record-keeping capabilities of electronic data processing and storage should be used, always keeping in mind the vulnerabilities of computer storage and providing for backup in hard copy or tape form. Other aspects of record storage and retrieval that should be considered include the use of microfilm or microfiche.

Electronic systems enable vast amounts of data to be stored in very little space, and they provide instant retrieval. Electronic storage also allows authorized users to have remote access to the records. Security measures assist in controlling access and ensuring that the information is available to those who have the right and need to know.

The control of records requires standards for retention and preservation of records. Some records may be destroyed after a designated time. Other records need to be preserved for long periods of time or indefinitely if they are archival in nature. Appropriate periodic purging of the files increases the effectiveness of system operations.

The objectives of record management are:

1. To provide accurate and complete information when and where needed to appropriate persons.
2. To process, store, and disseminate information effectively.
3. To maintain cost-effective safeguards for data.
4. To provide maximum service to authorized users of the system.

In order to ensure that the records are both effective and secure, good records management is vital in the counterintelligence environment. There must be tight control over records in the security department, particularly over intelligence files and records. However, there must also be a concern about record-keeping practices throughout the facility. Wherever and whenever sensitive information—confidential processes, restricted blueprints, trade secret data, proprietary lists, and other material—is stored, security protections and good records-control practices must be insisted on. Records management is the essential ingredient and the vital prerequisite of a secure counterintelligence information system.

BUDGETING

Planning and organizing for counterintelligence calls for sound budgeting practices. Just as good records management is the handmaid of secure information systems, so the scientific management of the budget process is a necessary adjunct of the thrust to defeat espionage. Budgets are basically plans expressed in dollars. They are management tools and may be used as control devices. Budgets can be used to evaluate in financial terms the progress being made toward the achievement of goals and objectives. Since success in counterintelligence rests to a large extent on overall security measures, budgetary concerns must be broader than immediate financial requirements for specific counterintelligence resources.

Performance-type budgets place an emphasis on what is accomplished by programs with their resource allocations rather than on the specific items that the budget dollars buy. Line-item budgets, on the other hand, are accounting oriented. They provide fiscal control by using an account number for every item purchased. Most advanced public and private agencies currently use a combination program (or performance) budget with a base line-item budget.

General security administration can use the modified program budget combined with a line-item budget. It is less certain whether it would be wise to use the modified program budget for listing intelligence and counterintelligence resource requirements.

Most public agencies that deal with intelligence matters have flexible program budgets that are not generally burdened with specific line-item designations. Following a similar course in developing budgets for industrial intelligence and counterintelligence programs would be wise.

Efforts in the private sector can probably be more discreet than those in the public sector because there is no need to account publicly, and attention from the media is likely to be slight. Nevertheless, private industry must budget for counterintelligence in such a way that resources are available for unexpected operations. The counterintelligence budget therefore should not be burdened with line-item requirements. The program (or performance) budget should evaluate overall costs according to accomplishments rather than by specific expenditures.

The general budget process requires careful preplanning, which should be on a continuous basis utilizing feedback and optimum input from all involved. The budget should be subject to evaluation, inventory, and audit controls. These processes may be augmented by computerization. Performance and impact evaluation are needed. Performance evaluations ensure that the squad is accomplishing in planned time frames the quantity and quality of tasks to meet program anticipation. Impact evaluations ascertain whether program performance is accomplishing its purpose in terms of goals and objectives. Once again, these budget aspects are consistent with general security operations.

Some question may arise as to the viability of these general budget controls in the intelligence and counterintelligence environment. This is probably one of the more important management challenges for the security director who has established a counterintelligence component. Just as the general budget requires preplanning, the counterintelligence budget requires even greater efforts to attempt to anticipate resource needs. Just as the general budget must be subject to controls and itself be a management control tool, the counterintelligence budget must be controlled and itself be a management control tool. The objectives are similar, but the means may differ.

Skillful budgeting and sophisticated control are needed. If we become too specific, we sacrifice flexibility; if we become too variable, we may lose control. The best avenue appears to be the use of program budgeting techniques for the overall industrial counterintelligence budget, combined with tight internal audit and control. Security managers and assistant managers for counterintelligence must know where budget funds are being expended, keep cost-effectiveness in mind, and evaluate operations. Are we carrying out programs as planned? Are these planned programs achieving the objectives intended? If the answers are negative, programs must be reevaluated. Perhaps one of the greatest threats the counterintelligence thrust may face is the charge that those responsible are expending large sums of money with little accountability and with little to show for their efforts.

PERSONNEL DEPARTMENT

The integrity of insiders is so crucial to the success or failure of a company that the security department should maintain constant assessments of all personnel. A cooperative arrangement with the personnel manager for an ongoing exchange of information should be productive in terms of cutting down on employee theft generally and vulnerability to industrial espionage in particular. One of the special problems of dealing with employee misconduct in disclosing information, selling secrets, or otherwise engaging in espionage on behalf of a competitor, a foreign government, or a broker of industrial secrets is that the miscreant may be highly placed in the company. It may very well represent white-collar crime at the highest levels. If this is the case, the security director has to be certain that he or she has developed sufficient evidence to overcome the presumptions and prove that apparently reputable officials are actually traitors to their own business. No matter who may be involved, full and fair discipline, including the possibility of arrest, must be invoked swiftly to be certain that the message is clear to all employees.

In order for the security director to operate knowledgeably and in order for the head of the counterintelligence unit to prevent the incursion of spies, personnel intelligence must be maintained.

These files should be highly confidential and contain both routine personnel information as well as intelligence developed through various sources, including information from official public agency files. One of the prime functions of the commander of the counterintelligence group is to cultivate sources both public and private that may help block spies and agents from suborning facility personnel. In the United States, it is difficult to obtain much direct assistance from government sources unless there is evidence of a clear and present danger to national security in the political and military sense. Therefore security is very much on its own and needs to be resourceful. Nowhere more than in the intelligence area is there a need for innovative approaches and excellent contacts in order to have effective operational intelligence files.

A number of measures relating to personnel and the prevention of industrial espionage should be given serious consideration:

1. A thorough briefing of all old and new employees before they are exposed to trade secrets and other business confidential data so that they are aware of the sensitive nature of the information they possess and realize their obligation not to disclose such information in any unauthorized manner.
2. A requirement for employees to sign nondisclosure agreements.
3. Careful monitoring of positively identified sensitive papers and documents. Cover sheets and hand receipts should be used.
4. Controlled reproduction of such documents so that there is complete accountability for all copies.
5. Maintenance of current clearance lists with identities of persons with the right to know and lists of persons with the need to know.
6. Constant review of the classified status of information for possible upgrading or downgrading to reflect current conditions.
7. Controlled access by media, nonemployees, and others to program-related information, denying any access to trade secrets unless specifically authorized by management and the corporate patent attorney.

Thus the counterintelligence effort will be directly assisted by coordination with the personnel department and other functional areas within the facility. All have a direct bearing on the successful prevention of espionage, although some areas appear to have special impact. Obviously the corporate legal patent activity and the various program managers involved in proprietary confidential operations are of particular importance. The public relations department can be a source of concern or a means of assistance depending on its understanding and cooperation with the goals of preventing industrial espionage, subversion, and terrorism. The public relations department should be able to advise whether the chief executive officer or the company itself is a target for terrorist groups. Press releases must not puff the company to the extent that a confidential matter is inadvertently broadcast. Emphasis should be placed on the establishment of strict security and advanced executive protection so that the public and potential spies and terrorists may seek easier marks.

MARKET RESEARCH

Virtually every competitive business needs to perform market research. Indeed, a great deal of covert industrial espionage is conducted under the euphemism of market research. It is in the best interest of security and the facility itself that it restrain and control its market research activities so that such research is limited to overt collection of information about competitors and their products. The facility is greatly disadvantaged in its attempts to thwart industrial espionage by others when it is known that the company itself is engaged in such illegal practices. To the extent that the security director can monitor the activities of in-house market researchers and maintain intelligence concerning possible illegal acts will the security department be in a better position to deal with industrial espionage from without.

There is a world of information available and numerous sources exist for information gathering on a legitimate basis, including:

1. Reverse engineering (analysis of a competitor's product).
2. Attendance at trade shows.
3. Comparative shopping.
4. Discussions of the competitor and/or its products with other competitors, present and former employees of the competitor, dealers and distributors and others who know the competitor and his products.
5. Publications, legislative hearings, advertisements, and similar materials.

The security director must also be aware that competitors may not exercise restraint. Today there is likely to be a highly competitive market and a desire for personal or company profit (particularly if the market research department head has stock options). Due to executive mobility, there is likely to be a decline in loyalty to any single company; also, the question arises about who owns what is in an employee's head. The high cost and criticality of research make trade secrets increasingly valuable. The vulnerability of computer storage, transmission, and programming to industrial spies all add to the risk of espionage activity.

How is this illegally obtained information extracted by market researchers? Basically, it is accomplished through the competitor's own personnel or hired consultants: the overenthusiastic sales representative, the naive secretary, the careless public relations person, the peripatetic consultant, the disgruntled employee, the mobile executive, the egotistical researcher, and, of course, the corrupted official or employee. The leader of the counterintelligence squad should be aware that market researchers may try to gain information illegally. He or she must be alert not only as to what competitors are doing to the facility but what company personnel are doing that aggravates the potential for successful penetration by competitors.

ORGANIZED CRIME

Another area that deserves the special attention of the security department generally, and of the counterintelligence group in particular, is the operations and methods of organized crime vis-à-vis industrial espionage. It should be noted that we are talking about organized crime in general, as well as that important aspect of organized crime variously called the Mafia, or La Cosa Nostra (LCN).

Dealing first with the most recently exposed operations of organized criminals we note that their depredations in the Silicon Valley of California have been reasonably well documented. Keeping in mind that what has come to public attention in California is probably, if not most assuredly, just the tip of the iceberg, we observe a highly organized criminal conspiracy engaged in selling high technology to domestic and foreign competitors. The so-called Silicon Valley gray market has been hurt by recent FBI sting investigations, but it is far from being put out of business. This thriving underground bazaar services tens of millions of dollars of stolen electronics, some of which are sold to foreign countries and end up in the hands of communist nations. This market is alleged to be undermining national security, as well as generating a growing criminal element engaged in industrial espionage.

The reason this bazaar is called a gray market is that some of the business of selling surplus silicon chips is legal, but greed and avarice have caused the conspiracy to become a true black market. It is organized and serves as a key source of industrial espionage for embargoed countries such as the Soviet Union. It often obtains the services of inside men by offering them narcotics, and it is not at all concerned with the ultimate destination of their stolen technology. Indeed, such spying has become an industry in itself, and suspicion grows that where the KGB cannot obtain secrets directly, they obtain them indirectly through the Japanese.

This is not to say that LCN is not involved in many aspects of industrial espionage. The organized black market that has been exposed in California is only a small sample of what goes on in Route 128, near Boston; in Phoenix, Arizona; in New York's Westchester County; in the Washington, D.C., area; and elsewhere. There are organized criminals, not necessarily affiliated with LCN operating in all these places, as well as in California. And there is LCN involvement in all these locations also. Because of the unusual competence of LCN in dealing with organized criminal activity, very few of their activities have come to public attention. But we can be certain that the huge profits gained through industrial espionage have not been overlooked. Just as organized crime was able to penetrate the brokerage houses of Wall Street and steal millions of negotiable securities before the New York stock market was even aware of the threat, so they are now penetrating industrial firms and stealing trade secrets.

Industry seems to be increasingly aware of LCN involvement and has expanded counterintelligence efforts accordingly. However, there still is no effective coordination of counterintelligence efforts within industry and only minimal support from official agencies. It is the same old story of trying to cope with organized crime in a disorganized fashion. This is what has made LCN so incredibly wealthy, powerful, and an ever-present threat to our business economy. With its uncanny ability to corrupt and its deserved reputation for ruthless enforcement, LCN can outmaneuver the largest industrial facilities.

LCN is a special threat in terms of industrial espionage because it is often interested in actually taking over a business, as well as stealing its secrets. After taking over a firm, it often skims the profits, or, using the technique of planned bankruptcy, scams the business. In other cases it may hold on to the facility and conduct its business in an illegal manner. In still other cases it may maintain the company's operations to provide a legitimate front and phony jobs to satisfy the Internal Revenue Service. In all cases, infiltration by organized crime is serious; the security director and the head of the counterintelligence group should be alert to this potential infiltration. The infiltration may begin with bookmaking and numbers running and advance to loan sharking and narcotics, but once LCN has its foot in the door, it may be too late. The best defense against any organized crime penetration, in addition to good security practices generally, is a top-notch intelligence operation. Local organized crime figures are generally known to the police, and some police organizations have excellent intelligence files. Security directors and counterintelligence commanders should seek the support of the law enforcement authorities in his area, including the FBI in appropriate cases.

TOTAL SYSTEMS APPROACH

Successful defense against industrial espionage depends on an all-hands approach to the problem. It is necessary to consider a special squad within the security department to conduct both overt and covert operations to combat the infiltration and penetration of industrial spies. It is important that the security director be given necessary funds and resources to lead the battle against industrial espionage. In the final accounting, the success or failure of the effort will depend on a system-wide approach. All departments and all employees at all levels must be coordinated in a rational effort to block penetration by industrial spies. The systems approach will provide many more eyes and ears of security-conscious persons than could possibly be mustered in the security department alone. It will provide for feedback and early warning. It will aid in the development of defensive intelligence and present a solid front against the spoilers.

SUMMARY

This chapter has examined the many aspects of planning and organizing to combat industrial espionage. It began with the process of threat assessment and the conduct of a formal survey to evaluate the needs for asset protection. In some cases it may be desirable to employ an outside professional to conduct the inspection. The results of the security survey should provide the basis for rational planning efforts.

Normative planning (What should we do and why?), strategic planning (What can we do and how?), and operational planning (What will we do and when?) are needed in turn. Goal setting is a response to the survey-generated problem statement. Goal setting should be within the context of the overall goals of the facility and within its resources. These broad statements of desirable goals need to be reduced to time-phased and measurable objectives so that specific programs and projects can be set up to accomplish them. Implementation of programs and projects need to be followed up by evaluation. Evaluation may be performance and/or impact related.

In order to achieve goals and objectives, an organization must be set up to conduct programs and projects. Usually the organization is represented by an organization chart with accompanying manuals of regulations and procedures.

In the staffing of the counterintelligence squad, some selectees will be slated for white positions as researchers and analysts, and others will serve in black positions practicing the trade craft of counterintelligence in the field. The counterintelligence group as a whole needs special training.

Coordinating the counterespionage effort is important. This coordination must encompass the entire facility, as well as the security department itself. There should be facility-wide participation in the effort. This should include top management, as well as every level of management and the heads of functional departments.

Counterintelligence has special requirements in the management fields of record keeping and budgeting. These management functions are important to security generally but are essential to mounting a successful intelligence and counterintelligence program.

The personnel department can make a number of contributions to the counterintelligence effort. The security department must maintain personnel intelligence files. The corporate legal and patent activities have a role, as does the public relations department.

The market research department must act in the best interests of security. It should limit its research to overt sources. But competing market researchers may not abide by such ethical standards. The leader of the counterintelligence squad must be aware as to what competitors are doing. He or she must also be alert as to what company personnel are doing that may aggravate the potential for successful penetration by competitors.

Organized crime must receive special attention in reference to industrial espionage. The recent exposure of a highly organized criminal conspiracy in California's Silicon Valley should alert us to the threat of organized crime operations.

A total systems approach to industrial espionage is needed. Ultimately, the success or failure of counterintelligence will depend on having all departments and all employees coordinated in a rational effort to block penetration by industrial spies.

6. Investigative Methods

Now there are five sorts of secret agents to be employed.
—Sun Tzu (500 B.C.)

Field agents support the counterintelligence effort by conducting investigations. They are outside personnel; researchers are inside personnel. This distinction in no way inhibits the investigator from using a desk. Nor does it prevent the researcher from leaving the office to meet with a liaison source. Although both investigators and researchers prepare reports, investigators focus on narrow issues and brief reports, while researchers see more of the big picture and prepare in-depth documents. Researchers stay away from covert activity and do little traveling. Field agents thrive on travel and the clandestine side of their investigations.

Counterintelligence field agents are usually separated administratively from the research section, although both sides communicate actively with each other. Research personnel send requests for information (collection instruments) to field agents and debrief agents after a collection trip or undercover mission. Field agents often make information demands of the researchers. For instance, an undercover agent who locates materials he or she cannot understand will ask research personnel for an explanation or interpretation and further advice on how to deal with the material. In one case, a field agent was working undercover in the corporate research laboratory area. He noted that one scientist regularly took home what appeared to be research notes. Not knowing the importance of that information, the agent managed to photograph some of these notations and submit this material to counterintelligence research. It proved to be theoretical computations predicting the next Super Bowl championship.

There is an age-old maxim in intelligence: field agents enjoy discomfort, danger, low pay, impossible assignments, and infrequent promotion; researchers enjoy comfort, regular hours, good pay, and fast promotion. Despite the half-truths contained in this old maxim, young men and women are normally drawn to the active life as exemplified by investigative duties. These duties, the subject of this chapter, include communications, undercover assignment, informant development, doubling espionage agents, escape routes and safe houses, reconnaissance and surveillance, and background investigation.

COMMUNICATIONS

Electronic countermeasures represent a growing aspect of counter-intelligence work. The revolution in electronic technology has not been ignored by those who plan industrial espionage or foreign technology transfer. (Chapters 7 and 13 deal extensively with electronic countermeasures.)

Field agents must locate, neutralize, or destroy all optical or audio instruments used in the commission of espionage. Locations include homes, offices, vehicles, restaurants, and all social settings. Eavesdropping devices are placed anywhere that sensitive information can be found. Found, in this case, includes overheard.

Counterintelligence goals may include finding and disconnecting the eavesdropping devices. Alternatively, the counterintelligence goals may involve gathering evidence to be presented to law enforcement agencies for criminal prosecution. A third choice is to arrange for false and misleading information to be fed into the eavesdropping devices. Decisions on how to proceed should be made by the senior counterintelligence staff with advice and consent from management and the legal staff.

Eavesdropping devices may be found by physical and/or electronic countermeasures. A physical search combined with an electronic sweep is a regular counterintelligence chore. The presence of eavesdropping devices is often learned from the reports of counterintelligence agents or their informants. The successful compromise and recruitment of an espionage agent represents another good way to locate eavesdropping devices.

No commercial counterintelligence unit should violate state or federal laws protecting the U.S. mail or the privacy of individuals with regard to their communications. Corporate attorneys are useful in determining the laws applicable in this delicate area. Privacy legislation is discussed in Chapters 4 and 7. Foreign laws may bear on this issue if the counterintelligence unit operates overseas.

There is no law against what the police call overheards. People in public places are sometimes careless enough to reveal incriminating facts or details that can be usefully applied to other counterintelligence information. Anything a suspect says could be of benefit later. These communications should be lawfully intercepted whenever possible.

The Fourth Amendment to the U.S. Constitution protects against illegal searches and seizures. The courts have constantly held that this prohibition applies to public officials. Private citizens are governed by the Fourth Amendment when in the company of law enforcement officers. At other times, the applicability is less certain. Communications, for example, fall under the search and seizure umbrella. We believe that corporate counterintelligence personnel must consider the legality of interception of all communications to which suspects are party. The only impediment to such actions should be legal prohibitions such as those concerning wiretapping, bugging, and interference with the U.S. mail.

Communications used to mislead are called disinformation (or propaganda when they are used against the enemy in wartime). We will refer to communications designed to mislead espionage agents as false communications. There is nothing criminal about lying to spies and nothing immoral about it.

False communications can help counterintelligence in several ways. Lies about the location of sensitive data delay espionage. Lies about the transfer of sensitive data reduce the chance of its interception. Lies about the direction of counterintelligence can give the spy a false sense of security.

False communications are very useful in forcing espionage agents to make moves that counterintelligence personnel can monitor. Take the time a suspect was given accidental access to the combination of a cabinet believed to contain secret formulas. Prior to this contrived security slipup, a hidden closed circuit television camera was installed to monitor activity around the data cabinet. The cabinet actually contained materials almost identical to the formulas but different in critical aspects. Two evenings later, the suspect was videotaped while opening the cabinet and photographing the contents. He was allowed to leave the facility under active surveillance. The next morning, the suspect called in sick. He left his house, under surveillance, and drove to a meeting with a foreign national. At this point a federal agency was notified. Joint investigation was successful in terminating this espionage attempt.

UNDERCOVER ASSIGNMENT

An FBI undercover operation in 1982 trapped Japanese businessmen who were trying to steal IBM secrets. FBI Director William Webster, commenting on IBM's cooperation during the investigation, announced, "This is a classic example of the value of an undercover operation to ferret out the theft of high technology."

Undercover personnel who assist counterintelligence are paid employees of business or government who pretend to be someone else. Their purpose is to gather information or evidence used to create intelligence. The evidence also is used for arrest and prosecution of offenders. We believe that undercover agents represent the most significant resource for the investigative side of counterintelligence. The secret agent, famed in literature and media productions, is simply an undercover employee.

Undercover agents above all seek not to be exposed and thus to protect their cover. Exposure causes compromise of the investigation and attendant bad publicity. At worst, the undercover agent may suffer serious or fatal physical damage.

There is a clear distinction between an undercover spy and an undercover counterintelligence agent. The undercover spy represents a hostile government, an unethical competitor, organized crime, or a terrorist group. In other words, the undercover spy is the extension of a corporate enemy. Undercover counterintelligence agents seek undercover spies. Counterintelligence agents seek to plug gaps in corporate security. Their purpose is to locate the industrial espionage agent and then expose, neutralize, or recruit the spy. Since the industrial spy has little or no scruples, the danger to counterintelligence agents is high.

Counterintelligence undercover agents may be used to trace the use of stolen patent rights or trade secrets by a competitor. Agents are assigned to penetrate the competitor's environment in the guise of employee, visitor, or customer. The counterintelligence agent stays long enough to determine if the competitor is in fact illegally using another company's secrets. Evidence gathered will be turned over to corporate officials, courts, and law enforcement agencies as deemed appropriate. This type of counterintelligence operation is normally brief in duration.

Industrial spies will commit illegal acts—such as murder, robbery, extortion, narcotics offenses, wiretapping, and bugging—in their work. In fact, almost everything they do is illegal or unethical. Industrial spies are after high rewards and are not deterred by high risks.

Counterintelligence agents must be careful not to commit illegal acts. The issue of unethical acts performed to aid the counterintelligence mission is not always clear-cut, however. Spy versus counterspy is often dirty as well as dangerous work. Counterintelligence operates in a real world not of its making.

Selection and training are key to the success or failure of espionage agents. But this often-repeated axiom is little honored in the corporate practice of espionage. Impatience to launch an espionage operation may cause disregard of agent safety. Hostile nations often spend years preparing an espionage agent for U.S. assignment. Terrorists, too, are known as methodical, careful planners of each operation they attempt. Only competitors and organized crime practice undercover spying in careless or crude fashion.

Selection and training are also key to the success or failure of undercover counterintelligence agents. Allan Pinkerton is said to have interviewed hundreds before selecting one undercover agent. His exact criteria are unknown, but Pinkerton had fantastic success in undercover operations for bankers, railroads, mineowners, and others. The governing principles in all personnel selection are fitness for the work and the ability to function in a particular environment. Consider a case in southern California in about 1970. A Spanish-speaking American of Mexican heritage was selected to perform an undercover mission at a warehouse that employed many Mexican immigrants. His own background was middle class and his tastes reflected this. The other workers had low economic standing. On his first day, the undercover agent, knowing that other workers brought their own lunches, produced his brown bag. The workers gathered for lunch, and all eyes were on the new employee. As he pulled his steak sandwich out of the bag, the undercover agent realized his error. The other bags contained beans and tortillas. The agent did not report back to work after lunch. He had been burned. (The master actor may fit into every situation. Actual undercover agents understand limitations imposed by racial, cultural, educational, and economic backgrounds.)

Undercover agents need similar attributes. They must have mental quickness since they operate in a fluid situation. Mental quickness is usually the only tool an undercover agent can use to deal with potential danger.

Control of self is equally vital. Undercover agents cannot reveal their true feelings or react in natural fashion to words and events. Instead they must outwardly appear to react according to role while imposing strict internal self-control.

Motivation is a third vital attribute for undercover work. Not all agents operate as James Bond did. Most undercover work requires considerable personal sacrifice. The environment is often unpleasant and, in any case, cannot be fully enjoyed due to the pressures of the assignment.

Counterintelligence agent selection may offer a solution to undercover requirements. Instead of choosing a member of the regular counterintelligence staff for undercover work, it may be better to select a person with the right background and train him or her in counterintelligence methods. Many people feel, wrongly, that undercover activity is dirty or polluted in some fashion. Care must be taken to sound-out a potential candidate on the subject of counterintelligence before mentioning the opportunity.

The person in regular contact with undercover agents is sometimes called the control. This control agent is the link between the undercover agent and management. All instructions and reports filter through control, who also is responsible for meeting agent resource requirements.

The control agent or agent handler must be able to establish a base of mutual trust and respect with the undercover agent. Control agents should have genuine concern for an agent's welfare, not just concern for the goals of the counterintelligence operation. Realism and competency are qualities of a good control agent.

Undercover agents may be free of legal requirements for state registration that could jeopardize their identity. For example, California's Administrative Code (Title 16, Article 3, Section 678) requires employers to keep records of all employees at their principal place of business and make such records available for state inspection. Later legislation exempted undercover agents from this requirement for thirty days. Longer assignment requires exemption approval from the director of California's Department of Professional and Vocational Standards. Undercover records are not considered public records in California. Each state has its own codes in regard to private security. They must be consulted before planning the counterintelligence undercover operation.

There are several important elements in undercover training: detailed knowledge of the environment; detailed knowledge concerning suspect(s); trade craft; and a full understanding of the scenario, or plan of operation.

Spies, the targets of counterintelligence agents, may operate in one or more environments, reflecting the location of desired data or the location of individuals spied on. Data are usually at a work location, although many executives take sensitive data home. Sensitive data may be carried by executives on business trips or be shipped in the form of convention exhibits. Also data are transmitted over telephone lines and by microwave links. The undercover spy seeking data is usually to be found at or near the business or industrial plant.

Individuals who possess or have access to sensitive data can usually be found in one of four environments: the work place; home; a religious, fraternal, or social organization; or a travel setting.

Undercover spies can coexist with the sought individual at one or more of these environments. They may pose as coworkers. They can move into the same neighborhood or apartment building. They may join the targeted individual's church, fraternal society, or hobby or social club, posing as a fellow enthusiasist. Travelers often band together in remote places. Undercover spies can pretend to be on vacation or in town on business that is noncompetitive to the target. The undercover spy may adopt any guise, be found in any place. Veteran counterintelligence personnel often become suspicious of almost everyone. This suspision is based solidly on the knowledge that almost anyone is subject to a spy's compromise efforts based on ancient formulas.

Counterintelligence agents must fit into the same type of environment(s) selected for the espionage operation. Training should supply sufficient detail of the hunt environment. These details allow the counterintelligence agent to concentrate on the mission rather than the process.

Environmental training includes briefings by people familiar with the area. Since the undercover counterintelligence agent must preserve anonymity, the briefing should be to a third party. It can be secretly monitored by the agent or taped.

Maps, photos, and site plans familiarize the agent with the layout of the environment, making it easier to follow suspected spies. The agent has a better chance of survival if he or she must withdraw from the environment under dangerous circumstances. The counterintelligence agent may need to pretend unfamiliarity with the environment as the scenario dictates.

Knowledge about suspects should be as comprehensive as possible. During the training phase, complete background files on suspects must be provided to the counterintelligence agent. The names of the suspect's associates, as well as their backgrounds, are of particular importance. Any one of them could be assisting the spy either as an informant or as the supervisor (control).

Habits, likes and dislikes, and prejudices of suspects are worth knowing. It is much easier to move in close to the subject if the counterintelligence agent shares the suspect's ideas and expresses dislike of the same things.

The suspects' travel patterns need to be understood for surveillance purposes. How do they get to work? What shopping areas are frequented and what routes are usually taken to and from such areas? After-work and weekend travel patterns are important. Most people follow a particular route. Knowing these travel patterns allows the counter-intelligence agent to predict the suspect's destination early in the surveillance. That makes it possible to arrive at a destination before the suspect does. This knowledge eliminates the need for a close (tight) surveillance that itself is dangerous because it is often noticed.

Tradecraft encompasses all the skills an agent needs. Undercover counterintelligence personnel need good skills in particular tradecraft areas. Memorization skills are necessary since the agent will not have the opportunity to take notes openly. Surveillance skills will allow the counterintelligence agent to follow suspects without being noticed. Cryptographic (codes and cyphers) skills are needed to transmit and understand code messages. Other tradecraft skills may be useful depending on the pretext role adopted by the counterintelligence agent.

Tradecraft training is practical in nature. Each skill deemed important for the scenario must receive close attention. Practice is the key to successful employment of tradecraft.

The scenario includes many factors. Good scenario development includes a simulation of the projected investigation. During the simulation, the perspective of headquarters becomes reconciled with the limitations of the field.

A scenario is a complete plan of how the undercover agent will function throughout the duration of the assignment. Each stage of the plan receives careful attention from the training staff, headquarters, and the individual undergoing training. Questions must be asked to take into account possible future events and action alternatives.

During training, the issues of ethics and lawful activity must be defined. Is it permissible to intercept a suspect's mail? It is a felony to interfere with the postal service. What about deliveries of United Parcel Service (UPS), messenger services, or personally delivered communications? Does the same rule apply? Those questions need precise answers. Counterintelligence agents need training in prudence lest their zeal involve the employer in criminal and civil liability.

They need training on withdrawal techniques. Even more important is training on how to recognize signs that their cover is being stripped away. This is a good time to reinforce a cardinal rule of tradecraft: always have a fallback cover story. In fact, it is better to have two or three extra cover stories in case those probing the agent's identity are thorough. Suspicious espionage agents or their informants routinely look into the purported background of new faces in the environment.

Possible fallback cover stories for the counterintelligence agent include hiding from a vindictive ex-spouse, financial embarassment due to gambling or loan shark debts, setting up a criminal activity such as embezzlement or burglary, and secretly representing a competitor for the purpose of industrial espionage.

The cover story of being a fugitive from criminal charges or being an escaped prisoner is virtually useless. Not only can such a claim be easily verified, it raises questions as to what type of individual would adopt such a story in the first place.

During the scripting of the investigation, it is wise to have the counterintelligence trainee accompany others in a site reconnaissance. This may require a disguise for the trainee. The use of a surveillance van is recommended as another technique to keep the trainee from view during the reconnaissance.

Communication techniques are important and must be specified and tested during the scenario development phase of the training period. One of the most common communication errors in undercover operations is to require the agent to report personally to a location that makes people think of security. Even more dangerous is direct communications with a security executive in a public location. All undercover communication must be done through the use of a third party, called a cut-out in intelligence jargon. The cut-out must also be insulated from direct personal contact with counterintelligence personnel.

Field agents often believe they are undersupported by those operating safely at headquarters. This belief is extremely dangerous to the success of the scenario because an unhappy agent is unlikely to operate efficiently. Points of contention that have plagued past undercover operations often concern resources allocated, especially money. Equipment is another possible bone of contention. Not least of the support questions is headquarters' response time. When a counterintelligence agent needs answers, time is usually of the essence. Headquarters' delay, especially if alibied with holiday or after-hours complaints, is seldom accepted calmly by the field agent.

Many disagreements can be eliminated by clear understanding of resources available to the agent on request. Limits must be set as to money available. Response time to agent requests must be guaranteed, with suitable allowance for the unexpected and the time of day and day of the week.

An evaluation procedure should be included in the scenario. Management will have expectations of counterintelligence success. These expectations include a time limitation. Expectations need to be clear. If the counterintelligence staff finds management has asked for too much or asked for it too soon, those expectations can be lowered. Harm to the reputation of the counterintelligence team, and especially the undercover agent playing the main role, will be avoided.

The counterintelligence director or manager will have expectations different from overall management goals. These include how the undercover effort will augment the credibility of the counterintelligence team. The undercover agent must assess the expectations correctly, lest he or she disappoint the boss and injure their professional relationship.

The counterintelligence agent will have personal professional expectations. Anticipated dangers are of particular interest to those with families. The concern of loved ones may overwhelm the agent, interfering with his or her judgment. A bonus or extra vacation may be more useful than letters of praise for a successful effort. Both agent and management should see eye-to-eye on the rewards for success.

PLACING AGENTS

Each investigative environment offers its own initial challenges that must be met soon after the agent has reached the scene. Many people will be watching the new arrival, some of them worried about discovery.

Neighborhood settings are not likely to show suspicion when the counterintelligence agent moves in. Children, however, can be a problem as they tend to be curious and gossipy. Most neighborhoods also have an adult snooper who keeps an eye on all neighbors' habits, comings and goings, and so forth. Such a person should have been located before the agent takes his or her place on the scene, and the agent must act in a manner least likely to cause the gossip's suspisions. Another neighborhood worry is the person who makes a habit of dropping in uninvited.

Apartment buildings are easier for incoming agents since anonymity is usually the role among tenants. More curious than fellow tenants may be the manager and his or her family. A good manager quickly learns each tenant's behavior and habits.

The agent should move into the new neighborhood in an open, normal style. Neighbors should be spoken to in a friendly manner, especially if they are espionage suspects. Shopping should be done in nearby stores, preferably recommended by other residents who will be flattered that their advice has been taken. A borrowing expedition for milk, sugar, tea, salt, or other normal commodities is a good way for the agent to become acquainted with neighbors.

If the espionage suspects are married, have children, or are living with someone else, the counterintelligence agent should have a partner who can remain at home during working hours to gather information from the suspect's family.

Work place environments do not require special attention to procedure since the company will have some established method of integrating new employees. The counterintelligence agent, however, must not appear eager or overly concerned with individual morality.

Other employees are sure to check the new employee's attitudes by telling stories or jokes that may be designed to provoke the listener. Since the suspects' prejudices should be known, the agent must be careful not to offend those individuals by careless remarks or laughing at the wrong jokes.

The first days in the work environment should pass casually for the counterintelligence agent. It is a time for eyes and ears to be open, but not too obviously, and for the mouth to remain shut most of the time.

The agent cannot afford to begin investigation rapidly, no matter how thorough training may have appeared. No scenario practice can equal the real environment. Also some of the training will be out of date by the time the agent is placed at the scene.

Clubs and organizations are often easy to enter but may exclude some people by certain requirements. The agent should seek membership nomination from an officer of the group but not from the suspect. Since clubs and organizations are constantly short on funds, they often welcome dues-paying applicants, especially those who promise to be active. Newcomers are usually welcomed at a public meeting. They are expected to get to know as many other members as possible. These settings are excellent to make contact with suspects and to keep track of them. If they are particularly active members, the task is even easier.

Informality is usually the rule in any organization after the formal ceremonies, if any, are accomplished. This informal period is a good time to discuss hobbies that happen to be identical to those of the suspect(s). Whatever the hobby, the counterespionage agent should have useful knowledge to offer. Top-flight hobby equipment, not too new, should be available to the agent because it is sure to attract the interest of the suspect.

Travel, for business or pleasure, represents a critical espionage aspect. The counterintelligence agent may have the assignment of accompanying an executive or a scientist. In order to be effective, the agent needs equal status. The initial difficulty involves establishing a relationship with the suspect or protected person. That relationship is necessary for the agent to be in the right company without seeming to be pushy or nosy.

Another difficult aspect of the travel or recreational environment is surveillance. The agent often finds it necessary to follow suspects in unfamiliar areas and under circumstances that do not permit a reconnaissance. Foreign locations offer additional language complications. Depending on the location, help from headquarters may be all but impossible for the counterintelligence agent.

Becoming part of a new environment is a challenge to anyone. Experienced counterintelligence agents often refer to the following methods for acceptance by the group: achieve proximity to the suspect, share the suspect's grievances, denounce the suspect's enemies, flatter the suspect, and demonstrate the agent's human nature by exposing a petty vice. The agent must also be careful not to appear too smart, too quick, too efficient, too nosy, or too evident.

Agents cannot perform well until they have established trust. Story telling often helps. When one person in a group tells a story or joke, others naturally respond, and a group bond is established. Recognizing and speaking to odd characters in certain environments is another way for the undercover agent to appear less than totally upright—an important measure of acceptance in the suspect's eyes.

Excess friendliness must be avoided. The suspects should feel drawn to the counterintelligence agent, not the other way around. Flashing money or displaying valuable jewelry is to be avoided. Obvious note taking is certainly bound to cause suspicion. Frequent absences will be difficult to explain. Too many messages or telephone calls will call unwanted attention.

If suspicion seems insurmountable, experienced agents use the transference method; they cast suspicion on another person, producing evidence previously prepared.

The use of leading statements assists the agent in locating espionage suspects and other criminals. Examples of such leading statements are: I'll never be able to afford this . . ., Only the wealthy can have such . . ., I'll work twenty years and never have . . .

IDENTIFYING ENEMY AGENTS

Many counterintelligence efforts fail to unmask an espionage agent because there was none operating at the time of the undercover investigation. This does not mean failure of counterintelligence. The extreme financial danger posed by the industrial espionage agent requires repeated, ongoing undercover efforts to prevent major leaks.

The counterintelligence agent must scan the environment for signs of the industrial spy and informants. These signs have to do with the appearance, activities, financial dealings and general behavior that often accompanies espionage agents.

Spies and their informants are not clearly recognizable. There is no one classification that spies fall into. Industrial spies tend not to be flamboyant; they often make an effort to appear ordinary, especially in regard to clothing, hair style, and mannerisms. Informants, on the other hand, often long-term members of the environment, are likely to be flamboyant since their financial status has been improved by payments for espionage.

Spies are secretive. Their activities are often shrouded in mystery, with late hours and strange comings and goings. They move in shadows to avoid recognition. Spies often are loners. But their informants may act in opposite fashion, acting as bait to ensnare others for their information.

All spies have hidden financial dealings. The money paid by their employer comes to them in a roundabout way. Evidence of this extra money may appear in the form of equipment, especially optical or audio equipment.

Informants also have unexplained sources of income. Having less training than espionage agents, informants are likely to flash money around or suddenly pay long-standing debts. Expensive vehicles and fancy vacations are common.

Both the spy and informants eventually ask too many questions and visit areas they have little reason to be in. They seek the company of others who have access to secrets. Both prey on weak people, hoping to use them as espionage tools. Both tend to be suspicious and jumpy around newcomers and are prone to test newcomers.

INFORMANT DEVELOPMENT

Both sides use informants. Industrial spies need informants to get secrets. Counterintelligence relies on informants to spot espionage behavior in the environment. Neither side has a problem with finding informants, but the quality of the information furnished is often poor.

Informants may be witting or unwitting. If witting, they may be motivated by greed, sex, revenge, loyalty, excitement, or avocation. Counterintelligence, however, cannot offer the inducement of sex for legal and ethical reasons. The other motivations can be used by counterintelligence to recruit informants; each prospective informant has a weakness. Although every person is a prospective informant, care should be taken in informant selection.

Mistakes in selection can ruin an investigation. Bad informants may boast of their activities to others, implicating the counterintelligence agent. They may be too active in amateur investigation, exciting the suspicion of espionage agents. Making up information is another informant failing; so is an overactive imagination.

Take the case of the informant who reported not espionage but a narcotics distribution network. He had observed cars at mysterious times stopped along back roads while an occupant exited to paint white directional marks on the road. The informant, a volunteer, had scouted out the environment and reported that similar signs had been painted on other roads. All signs led to a lonely farmhouse occupied by newcomers. The informant became convinced that the painted road marks would serve to guide dope dealers to the premises of a major narcotics distributor. He had taken the further step of painting out some marks, only to discover later that the directional marks reappeared. One week later the informant admitted an error in his assumption. The marks had been for bicycle riders on a cross-country event.

Counterintelligence must use informants despite their many limitations. Each informant represents additional eyes and ears. Conditions may not permit the counterintelligence agent to get close enough to a particular suspect. Cultural and ethic concerns often make an informant necessary to the investigation.

Counterintelligence headquarters must investigate the background of prospective informants. The agent can use a plausible pretext to recruit informants, careful not to tell them about the counterintelligence operation. There should not be any overtones of law enforcement or security if these can be avoided. Informants should never be considered toally reliable and should never be given more than the absolute minimum of information.

Undercover operations and informant development have received little attention by researchers. Little of substance has been written. The best sources of information are those investigators who have survived multiple operations.

Legal restraints to the use of undercover agents exist in regard to an employee's union activities. Since espionage suspects may be union members, great care must be taken in record keeping not to include the reporting of union activity. The National Labor Relations Act makes it an unfair labor practice for an employer to interfere with employees' right to organize for collective bargaining purposes. Union meetings and strikes are covered by this prohibition.

William Webster has written that "the area of undercover operations raises some unique management problems, but like good lawyers, we don't turn down operations because there is a problem. We try to find an appropriate solution so that the project, if worthy, can function effectively and within the rule of law."[1] Webster was commenting on the FBI's expanded use of undercover agents in the areas of foreign counterintelligence, organized crime, white-collar crime, and property crimes. His message is applicable, however, to business counterintelligence.

---

[1] "Director's Message," *FBI Law Enforcement Bulletin* (September 1980).

DOUBLING ESPIONAGE AGENTS

Counterintelligence, commercially operated or as an instrument of national policy, benefits from the recruitment of double agents. These individuals are often in direct contact with the opposing espionage control. Counterintelligence can gain information about the espionage effort from the double agent. A further benefit involves giving the double agent false information to pass back to the control source. Double agents are extremely valuable, but they are in a dangerous position and require careful monitoring.

Spies who change allegiance once may change it again to suit their needs. If the espionage control discovers that one of his or her spies has gone over to counterintelligence, that spy may be in danger. Alternatively, espionage control may decide to allow the spy to operate while removing any access to important data.

Successful creation of a double agent often requires the compromise of an espionage practitioner. Corporate ethics do not allow the use of sex as the compromise tool. This is a favorite of certain espionage practitioners. The USSR often uses sex to blackmail people with access to sensitive data.

Greed may or may not be effective in bringing the espionage agent over to the counterintelligence camp. It is dangerous to rely on money as bait unless the agent is sure that the spy has a desire for material possessions and that the offer will not be topped by someone else interested in that individual's loyalty.

The threat of a long prison term will have effect on the competitive spy, but terrorists and organized crime espionage agents are unlikely to be frightened by this possibility. An agent of a hostile government is not easily frightened by imprisonment either.

More effective than sex, greed, or the threat of prison is professional compromise. This doubling tactic involves providing apparent evidence that the spy has already been compromised and is serving counterintelligence. Surreptitious photography and voice recordings must be used to record the event. Careful stage management is necessary to create the effect that the spy is cooperating with counterintelligence. Ideally, the spy should not realize the setup until presented with evidence of the compromise.

Doubling of espionage agents is a confusing activity for all concerned. There is always a risk the spy will not change allegiance, preferring to risk the threat of exposure. The spy may pretend to change sides in order to acquire sensitive counterintelligence data.

The administration of the polygraph or psychological stress evaluator by a competent operator is, perhaps, the best way to be secure about a double agent's state of mind, loyalty, and intentions.

ESCAPE ROUTES AND SAFE HOUSES

The use of undercover agents involves an obligation to extract them from danger. The same is true of informants and of double agents. Therefore escape routes for these field agents must be planned, with other field agents used to cover the escape. They must be alert to possible inerception for the purposes of kidnapping or assassination. These covering agents may have to use force in their role as a protective detail. Suitable armament and bullet-resistant vests are recommended.

Safe houses are rendezvous points used for regular meetings and as way stations during escape. These locations must be free of eavesdropping devices. Adequate food and other supplies should be on hand. Safe houses can be single or multi-dwelling units or even motor homes. Mobile safe houses have definite advantages in that vehicles and locations can be changed easily, and fewer personnel are needed to guard the mobile safe house. Several individuals must guard all sides and approaches to the regular safe house.

The complete escape plan will include alternative routes out of the danger area, emergency codes to alert the escape team, rendezvous points, and the safe houses themselves. These details will be supplied to the counterintelligence agent during training. Informants and double agents should not be given more than an emergency contact number and code; they are not to be trusted with escape details in advance.

RECONNAISSANCE AND SURVEILLANCE

Reconnaissance is a preliminary activity to surveillance. (Chapter 14 discusses surveillance also.) Preliminary visits to a site, area, or route are designed to make later surveillance of an area or a person easier. A reconnaissance usually includes driving over routes the suspect is expected to follow. All locations frequented by the suspect are visited. The time of day or night for a reconnaissance should approximate the time the suspect frequents the area.

Photographs of people, buildings, or open areas are a useful by-product of reconnaissance. Agents chosen for surveillance duties can study them if they have been unable to accompany the reconnaissance team. Reconnaissance personnel will use the photographs to refresh their own memories before conducting a surveillance. Annotated maps tracing routes and highlighting landmarks make surveillance easier.

Reconnaissance reports should indicate road conditions, detours and construction, and traffic signals. Driving times from point to point should be noted. In addition, these reports must note ideal places for stationary surveillance and those places to avoid. Police and security patrol patterns represent additional reconnaissance information. The surveillance team will be able to anticipate such patrols if they know these schedules.

Vehicles are frequently used for a reconnaissance. It is even better to walk the area or route, if practical. Certainly it is wise to walk the area where the surveillance vehicles are likely to be parked. Much can be seen while on foot or riding a bicycle that will be easily missed from a car or truck. Motorcycles represent a reconnaissance alternative, but their noise is likely to attract attention.

The reconnaissance team must be careful not to draw attention to itself. If reconnaissance is detected, the suspect will become suspicious and more careful. The chance of detection will be reduced if reconnaissance takes place when suspects are elsewhere. Other prudent safeguards include care that vehicles and personnel fit smoothly into the environment and do not stay in one location for long.

Surveillance is much more difficult than reconnaissance. It lasts longer and takes place when suspects are present. There are times when it is necessary, as when undercover investigation has been ruled out. Situations favoring surveillance include: after-hours espionage at a business location; a tip of impending espionage; when the espionage suspect is an upper-management employee; or if the union contract makes it difficult to insert a counterintelligence agent in the work environment.

We have spent thousands of hours in moving and stationary surveillance. With authority, we note that there are many difficult moments. There is cold, heat, boredom, hunger, thirst, and the need for a toilet. Endless hours where nothing occurs may be the biggest drawback.

Other difficulties relate to losing track of a suspect in or out of his vehicle. If the surveillance team loses concentration or turns away for a second, the suspect may have vanished. Many vehicles look alike. So do people. It is easy to follow the wrong vehicle or person. Frequently suspects drive fast, making it very difficult to keep up without being stopped by the police.

Traffic jams, lights that turn at the wrong time, accidents, missed turns, staying too close or too far back are perils of surveillance. Any surveillance agent knows the feeling of helplessness where things go wrong. For example, one of the authors once got his car stuck in a field during a surveillance and had to walk miles to a volunteer fire department for help.

Headquarters cannot see what surveillance personnel are doing. They call on the radio at the wrong time and then are offended when the surveillance agent or team does not answer immediately. Flashlights are known to give out and tape recorders fail at critical times. The local police get a call from the local busybody, and there is an unwanted visitor in blue, frequently with a flashing strobe light.

Sometimes the suspect seems highly suspicious, sometimes oblivious to activity going on, but a surveillance agent can never be sure if he or she has been recognized unless the suspect taps him or her on the shoulder.

"I lost him" is the most intolerable sentence in surveillance, but it happens to the best surveillance agents. It is always better to lose the suspect than to be recognized. Employed surveillance agents do not lose their suspects often or regularly, however.

A surveillance can last minutes, days, weeks, or months. There is a story that an FBI team has been watching the door to a Manhattan apartment building since the 1950s. It seems that a communist espionage agent entered the building in 1951 and has not come out yet. The story illustrates one of the problems of stationary surveillance. Is there a back door? Have we covered all the exits?

The suspects' car frequently seems more powerful than our own. Their route often leads to strange and unfamiliar places. Our car or our radio fails, never theirs. The suspect eats, drinks, and makes love while the surveillance agents crouch in a car or stripped apartment, cursing and sipping cold coffee. Family and friends begin to lose interest in surveillance agents. Their hours are too irregular and long. They come home to sleep and then leave, often in the middle of the night after an urgent telephone call.

Surveillance can be indeed frustrating and affect negatively the private lives of surveillance agents. Why, then, do they persist? We believe that the thrill of the hunt leads them on. Surveillance is not an end in itself; it is designed to trap and record the espionage agent and followers in an act of treachery—recorded, possibly filmed, for all time. The deer or duck hunter in a blind or a tree stand understands the feeling that surveillance agents have, although those other hunters are much more likely to enjoy regular success.

The basics of surveillance are patience, a concern for detail, the ability to think ahead, a good memory, proper preparation, and, above all, optimism.

Surveillance begins at a predetermined time and may continue indefinitely or finish when a suspect has gone to bed. Sometimes the suspect will take a plane or other form of public transportation. Agents must have credit cards or cash to handle these emergencies. Most times the surveillance team will be reasonably sure of the suspect's plans and route and be able to plan ahead.

The overwhelming difference between surveillances conducted by federal agents and others, such as corporate counterintelligence, is in relation to resources. Federal agents can field all the vehicles and personnel they feel are needed. The corporate counterintelligence team will be fortunate to have more than minimum resources.

Minimum resources are two vehicles if the suspect is driving. Walking teams should include no fewer than three. The purpose of multiple vehicles and agents is such that they can change places to reduce the likelihood of becoming noticed. Surveillance in a stationary vehicle or apartment requires at least two people per shift.

No matter how the surveillance is to be conducted, team members need radios to keep in contact with each other and with headquarters. Tape recorders are a useful supplement to pen and paper for note taking. If there is only one person in a moving-vehicle surveillance, that person must have a tape recorder since he or she cannot easily write and drive simultaneously. Binoculars and cameras are necessary. One camera is enough for the team in many situations, but each surveillance agent needs binoculars.

Careful records of a suspect's movements or area activity must be kept. The records, a minute-by-minute account of all relevant activity, will be useful for reports and court testimony. The exact times of departure and arrival, the suspect's description, and that of any associates belong in the surveillance log. Routes taken must be broken down by streets, turns, and changes of direction. Since surveillance may be preliminary to a raid or other counterintelligence action, headquarters must be kept advised of all significant developments as they occur.

Concentration is one key to successful surveillance. Too often surveillance team members pay close attention to members of the opposite sex. At other times, boredom causes them to take turns telling stories calculated to interest and impress. Each agent should have a certain location determined by the surveillance team leader. The agents should be assigned specific tasks, also.

BACKGROUND INVESTIGATION

Field agents must check the personnel files of all employees with access or potential access to corporate secrets. The personnel director will be able to assist in the evaluation of this material.

During the study of employee backgrounds, a decision must be made on the frequency for background updates. Even if an employee seems to have an untarnished background, events might alter his or her morals or loyalties, to the detriment of the employer. A good counterintelligence division will maintain a file that signals, by color coding or similar device, those employees due for updated background checks.

Updates assume that a satisfactory clearing of the employee took place in the past, but most corporations fall down on investigating the background of those hired for sensitive, responsible positions. Counterintelligence will likely have to develop essential, original background investigations.

Good background investigations include checking on employees' present and former neighborhoods; former employments; credit history; criminal history; litigation history; references on file; and educational history. In addition, a thorough background investigation will include reconnaissance of the subject's home and haunts. Finally, counterintelligence performs a limited surveillance of the employee to establish his or her habits.

Neighborhood investigations include the present residence and several former neighborhoods if possible. At least three present or former neighbors should be interviewed about the employee's strengths and weaknesses. Information about family and their activities should be developed. Any negative information developed must be verified by subsequent investigation or ignored as malicious rumor.

Apartment house managers and landlords usually are good interview subjects. They have regular contact with tenants, maintain records, and often have long memories regarding problem tenants.

Because of the Fair Credit Trade Act and other privacy legislation, former employers may be reluctant to furnish official information about past employees. This official information is unlikely to be of much use to counterintelligence, anyway. The best interview subjects in this category are those who directly supervised the employee and those who worked in close proximity. Coworkers are best approached off the job. Where time does not allow the interview after hours, the promotion pretext rarely fails. The background investigator claims to work for the employee's present company and says that the employee is being considered for a promotion with a large salary increase. The interview then becomes a prepromotion investigation. Cooperation is usually extensive when this pretext is used. Even if the employee learns about the visit to the former employer, he or she will be flattered rather than frightened by the news.

Generally background interviews develop either positive or negative information. Since no one is angel or devil the interviewer must press the informant to humanize his or her remarks about the subject by giving both the good and the bad. He or she might say, "No one is all perfect. If my report does not disclose any human failings, it will be discarded. Even mass murderers have some good in them. Tell me anything at all that makes this character seem warm-blooded!" Interviews that fail to unearth both positive and some negative information should be discarded as totally prejudiced or inadequate.

Employment patterns are useful in predicting behavior, especially during times of stress, personal as well as occupational. The employment phase of the background investigation should include several past employments if possible.

Credit history is the term applied to a person's financial dealings— applications for credit, debt payment records, credit cards, bankruptcy, liens, civil actions to which the individual has been a party, major purchases, and the like. Credit bureaus can retain negative information for a limited number of years; however, they have contacts nationwide and can provide credit information no matter where an individual has resided within the United States or Canada.

Many corporations have access to credit bureaus because they themselves extend credit. If this is not the case, banks that maintain corporate accounts can provide credit history information since they contract with credit bureaus to gather facts on loan applicants.

Credit information may not provide the total information on an individual's financial dealings. Many spies, for example, pay cash for major purchases. They frequently maintain accounts under fictitious names that will not appear on their credit history. It is useful to reconcile the apparent credit position of an employee with the material possessions owned. The determination of material status is best made through reconnaissance, surveillance, and neighborhood investigation. For example, if the credit history indicates moderate purchases but the employee is seen with expensive vehicles, boats, or jewelry, questions should be raised.

Criminal history information is unlikely to uncover an industrial spy, but it is useful in determining those who in the past have been attracted to easy-money schemes and have been caught in the process Sometimes credit records contain criminal history information, making further search necessary. Local conviction records can often be obtained by application to the court clerk.

Neighborhood investigations and other interviews may also turn up leads on past criminal activity, but these sources need corroboration.

The best source of criminal history information is the law enforcement agency in whose jurisdiction the act occurred.

Conviction information is a matter of public record. It is not protected by privacy legislation until a certain number of years have passed or if the court has sealed the records. Some jurisdictions do allow the expungement of criminal conviction records in certain cases. These exceptions should not stop the pursuit of conviction information.

An investigator might have to visit every county courthouse where a trial might have occurred, in addition to checking with appropriate federal district courts. Pennsylvania's Criminal History Information Act allows anyone who pays a fee access to state police conviction records. Although there are gaps in this information—for instance, county clerks do not always forward final trial disposition—the act does amount to considerable time saving for background investigators.

Litigation (civil action) is also a matter of public record provided the record depository is known. Courthouse employees can prove invaluable in locating the proper index files and records. Some clerks keep records far into the past. These records may have been slated for destruction but instead were stored. Properly approached, court clerks have been known to produce startling facts such as Communist party membership rolls dating back to the time when party members expressed this preference during voter registration.

Guilt by association is not an acceptable reason to doubt anyone's honesty if used as a sole criterion. Yet it is a good idea to explore gently into the family background and activities of the immediate family members of the individual being investigated.

Federal tax liens, as well as state and local legal matters, are registered in the local courthouse. Land records and the transfer of real estate can reveal purchases inexplicable by known income. Care must be taken to investigate the possibility that purchases were made in the name of relatives, nominees, or using an alias. Since property tax bills are normally mailed to the real owner, tax assessors can determine the extent of an individual's property holdings.

Counterintelligence background investigations should be done under a suitable pretext. An agent cannot tell the interview subject that he or she is checking out that person's espionage links. The agent cannot claim to be investigating how likely the subject might be to succumb to blackmail or greed. Revealing the purpose is wrong on two counts. First, if the subject is indeed involved in espionage, he or she will be alerted to the investigation. Second, the people being asked to provide information are likely to be offended or frightened. Either reaction is likely to ruin the investigation.

Background investigations have lost much favor in recent years, partly because of their expense. Americans are increasingly mobile.

An individual under investigation probably has held several previous jobs in different geographical locations. A good background investigation under such conditions involves travel time and expense most corporations are unwilling to allocate.

Other reasons for the decline in background investigations are the Privacy Act, the Federal Freedom of Information Act, the Fair Credit Reporting Act, and various state privacy legislation. They serve to inhibit the free exchange of information in both the law enforcement community and the business sector. These laws all but preclude exchange of data between law enforcement and the private sector. Confusing statutes are partially to blame. Sensationalized press accounts charging invasion of privacy have served to make corporations unsure of what information they may keep on employees and how much of that information can be released to outsiders. Law enforcement agencies, aware that they are liable to civil and criminal penalties for the loose handling of information, have opted at times to close their files to other law enforcement agencies.

The situation today is much better than during the mid- and late 1970s. Cooperation is beginning to be reestablished warily. Counterintelligence needs to take full advantage of any relaxation of controls in regard to information exchange.

The question of expense requires much attention. Counterintelligence relies on the background investigation as both a preventive measure and an active investigation tool. Without the ability to delve into employees' and suspects' backgrounds, counterintelligence is ineffective.

Cost-effectiveness is the only way to convince management of the need for background investigations. Espionage potential is easily calculated based on the value a company puts on its own secrets. It follows naturally that those closest to these secrets represent the greatest espionage hazard, through witting or unwitting action. Certain employees must be considered critical to ongoing profitability. An investment equivalent to that person's salary for one week is a reasonable minimum to spend on initial backgrounding. The same minimum should apply to routine upgrading of sensitive employees.

Upgrading of clearance should be done whenever promotion is contemplated, and it should accompany assignment to a sensitive project. Upgrading should occur automatically when the personnel or security department receives complaints on an employee with access to sensitive proprietary data. Routine upgrading of clearance is recommended no later than two years after the initial and subsequent upgraded background investigations.

The upgraded clearance investigation will usually be briefer than the initial backgrounding unless there is reason for active suspicion. It should center around present activities and those in the recent past.

SUMMARY

Counterintelligence investigation is a field activity but has research aspects. There are seven categories of investigation.

Communications includes electronic countermeasures. Illegal eavesdropping devices must be located and neutralized. Physical searches and the electronic sweep are common countermeasure methods. Informants and double agents can provide information on the extent and location of transmitting or recording devices. Counterintelligence agents must be mindful of legal prohibitions on the interception of communications, even those of spies. Communications can be used to mislead the spy.

Undercover assignments may represent the most significant counterintelligence resource. Counterintelligence agents on undercover assignment are hunting espionage agents, a potentially dangerous situation. Industrial spies do not hesitate to commit illegal acts. Selection and training are key to successful undercover work. Mental quickness, self-control, and motivation are important attributes. The control agent must be selected with care. Undercover training should include environment knowledge, suspect knowledge, tradecraft, and a full understanding of the plan of action (scenario). All undercover agents need several cover stories.

There are many ways to identify espionage agents and their dupes. The counterintelligence agent must avoid displaying these attributes while searching the environment for less discreet spies. Informants may be needed by counterintelligence agents. They must be approved by headquarters. Informants should be carefully monitored and given little counterintelligence data.

Double agents have much value when properly handled. They are in a very dangerous position since they have betrayed their masters. Creation of a double agent usually requires the compromise of an espionage agent. Counterintelligence must be careful in choosing methods used in compromise attempts. The method must be legal and appropriate to the motivation of the spy.

Operation of *escape routes* and *safe houses* is an important part of counterintelligence investigation duties. Undercover agents, informants, and double agents may require an escape route in time of danger. Safe houses serve as halfway houses and as secure meeting locations. Mobile safe houses are a promising modern development.

Reconnaissance and *surveillance* are investigative responsiblities. Reconnaissance is a preliminary activity designed to make surveillance easier and less prone to failure. The more detail provided by a reconnaissance, the better the surveillance will be.

Surveillance is more difficult, but it may be necessary for a variety of reasons. For example, undercover investigation may not be possible due to circumstances. There are many negative aspects to surveillance. Boredom may be the biggest drawback to the agent. Long and irregular hours interfere with personal lives. But the thrill of the hunt motivates agents assigned to surveillance. Corporate counterintelligence will probably have available only minimum surveillance resources.

Background investigation is fundamental to counterintelligence. Field investigations explore every aspect of a suspect or critical employee's background. The expense must be judged against the hazard of overlooking an espionage agent. Background investigations should be updated regularly and as needed. It is important to speak with people well acquainted with the subject of the investigation.

7. Scientific and Technical Aids

Steam is no stronger now than it was a hundred years ago, but it is put to better use. —Ralph Waldo Emerson

There is a tendency for many people to think of scientific and technical aids as being related to the physical sciences only. They overlook the fact that there are equally important types of scientific aids generated by the social and behavioral sciences. This chapter discusses both the physical and behavioral sciences and their technologies as they relate to industrial espionage.

AIDS FOR DATA COLLECTION

Library of Relevant Literature

In order to maximize the amount of reliable information available to assist in the mission, it is essential to use the expertise of librarians and the discipline of library science. Much information is available to those who take advantage of resources found in books, newspapers, periodicals, pamphlets, and other documents. Closely associated with literature as a source of information are art and artifacts. They may convey messages that should not be overlooked in our search for data. Documents may be reduced to microfiche and made readily retrievable by computerized programs. Information may be stored in oral tape recordings, videotapes, motion pictures, and recordings of the musical arts and drama.

Scientific Analyses

Information and data may be extracted from real evidence through the application of the forensic sciences, including chemical and spectrographic techniques and clinical pathology. Information may be developed through the application of devices such as the polygraph, psychological stress evaluation (PSE), and pencil and paper testing instruments of various types. It may also be elicited through the use of chemicals such as scopolomine. Interviewing and interrogation techniques are standard methods to generate information. Document examination is a useful tool. Skillful listening, questioning, and confidence development usually elicit valuable and relevant data. Information may also be gained through the use of graphology and hypnosis. Intelligence techniques refine raw data and process them into a more useful form through the steps of evaluation of the information's reliability and validity, collation, (putting the data in order and in retrieval form), analysis, and dissemination.

Computer Programs and Linkages

Few people today remain unaware of the power and capabilities of computer systems to store, process, disseminate, and provide remote access to information. Perhaps less recognized is the wealth of information available through sophisticated programming of available data. Programs not only retrieve data but can generate additional information by the synthesis of already stored information. Programs are becoming more complex and more responsive to the information and intelligence needs of the counterintelligence community.

At the same time, there has been an explosion of data banks of all kinds, some or all of which can be linked together to provide a wealth of data. There are large computer systems in both the public and private arena. The FBI's National Crime Information Center has millions of information items readily accessible to authorized users. Equifax of Atlanta and TRW of California have computerized credit information on virtually every adult in the nation. An interface with these kinds of systems could produce an inexhaustible source of data for counterintelligence efforts.

In examining the potentials of computer applications to defeat industrial espionage, we should not overlook the many security programs that can:

1. Control access to computers and lock out unauthorized access, both in-house and remote.

2. Cybernetic systems that monitor everything from a nuclear reactor to the opening and closing of a fence gate.
3. Computer memory systems that can detect variances on the closed circuit television monitors and signal attention or that can detect any change in the environment of their location, thereby signaling that something has been moved. The latter may be as thin as wafers and, concealed under an art object, for example, they will memorize the underside of the protected object and if it is lifted an alarm is triggered.

Finally, the supervisor of the industrial counterintelligence unit should seek computer capabilities for his or her own intelligence files and try to interface his or her computer system with other intelligence files, both public and private. There is probably no more productive potential for a counterintelligence information system than to share data with other relevant systems. Too often there is a reluctance to share data for fear of compromise, but failing to join a group that shares intelligence is, in effect, compromising the viability of the system by limiting its potential. Some very effective orgnized crime intelligence networks have been developed. If it can work with organized crime, it is surely likely to work in the industrial espionage environment.

AIDS FOR RESEARCH

Behavioral Sciences

The assistance of sociology and psychology is available for industrial counterintelligence research. Any security director and/or supervisor of the counterintelligence group is bound to feel the need for research. Some research may be highly theoretical and may have primarily long-range application, but much can be directly applied to strategic and tactical intelligence here and now.

Profiles can be prepared of the types of employees who are most likely to be suborned by industrial spies and foreign agents. This knowledge should provide an early warning system and permit a focus of scarce resources on preventive techniques that will be applied discretely rather than on a shotgun basis. Such insights might also be helpful to the entire personnel operation to help prevent the hiring, promotion, and sensitive assignment of potential spies.

Studies of employee morale and motivation should help the facility provide greater employee contentment and job satisfaction and generate employee pride in the company and its products, thus lessening the likelihood of penetration by spies and agents. It is a fact of life in the fields of industrial espionage, subversion, and terrorism that a hardened target is least likely to be hit. There are always easy marks around that make the espionage less onerous and more predictable in terms of successful penetration.

Psychological, sociological, and socio-psychological insights can combine with the economic disciplines to provide clues as to the likelihood of certain documents, processes, know-how, and secret information being more or less critical to the industrial spy.

It is of longer-range advantage to obtain analyses of trends in a particular industry. Research can help anticipate future problems likely to be faced in creating and maintaining an effective, proactive, and preventive counterespionage defense. Research can tell what techniques have been successful and what have not.

Operations Research

At least two kinds of operations research can aid in counterintelligence endeavors. The first is relatively unsophisticated; it is reverse engineering, or the purchase of a competitor's product and breaking it down into its component parts to see how it was put together. This process may develop evidence that the competitor has managed to purloin some classified information and point to the need for even more dedicated counterintelligence efforts. Another facet of reverse engineering is the application of espionage tactics against our own facility in order to seek out weak spots in its defenses. If research indicates that competitors are likely to mount an offensive against us because of the attractiveness of our products or because we have scored a technological breakthrough, we must stage a scenario similar to that which our research has predicted from our competitors. Like war games, these espionage maneuvers should expose vulnerabilities and provide knowledge useful for tightening up defense against industrial spies.

The second type of operations research is the actual application of such engineering principles as linear programming, simulation, gaming techniques, and queueing technology. Perhaps the simplest of these to explain is simulation. Although most of these types of operations research techniques require the coordination or cooperation of the company's engineering department or the hiring of a consultant to assist with the program, simulations are not too technical to be formulated by the security director or the supervisor of the counterintelligence unit. Also commercial programs are available. Essentially, the simulation technique involves modeling. The security director or counterintelligence supervisor sets up his or her concept of an ideal defense design for countering industrial espionage against the company. It is possible to use the model as a vehicle to test what could happen under a number of scenarios with a host of variables. The computer program, in effect, creates the actual defense situation and passes through it the various possible attempts at penetration. The statistical likelihood of successful penetration under a variety of circumstances enables the user to refine the design for maximum cost-effective counterintelligence. Thus, not even a pilot program needs to be mounted. The model can be tested, adjusted, evaluated, and fine-tuned by computer simulation before it is installed.

Evaluation Techniques

Because planning is a continuous process, it is essential that there be techniques to evaluate the results of prior planning with a view to adjusting, correcting, or discarding previous plans. Evaluation shows whether more planning is necessary. Prior planning may be suboptimal, poor, or satisfactory. We need to know in order to waste no time in getting involved in rethinking prior planning and making major adjustments or minor changes, as indicated. If prior planning is doing the job, no further effort is needed. But whatever the case, evaluation is needed on a continuous basis, for even if planning were viable last month, it may no longer be viable today. There are many possible interventions of national or local conditions or new technologies may result in the obsolescence of plans that were working well only a short while ago.

Evaluations relate to performance or to impact. Performance evaluations tell whether programs and projects are being pursued according to plan. Usually performance is measured quantitatively, but more sophisticated performance evaluations will also be concerned with qualitative evaluation. Thus, in the counterintelligence field, one might evaluate performance in terms of the number of individuals who were arrested attempting to breach the facility perimeter, or the number of persons who were challenged with unauthorized entry into restricted areas, or cited for careless custody of confidential and/or secret documents, processes, or procedures. These performance evaluations will show whether personnel are performing according to plan. They do not, however, tell whether goals and objectives are being met. To enable a determination of progress toward achieving goals and objectives, impact evaluation is needed.

Suppose we have set up as a goal or objective reducing the number of successful penetrations during the past twelve months by spies and agents by 50 percent during the current twelve months. We can measure the number of known penetration and can determine whether programs and projects are on target at any time or point in the twelve-month period. If we are not having the necessary preventive or protective impact on the rate of successful espionage efforts, we need to reevaluate programs and projects or perhaps set up a more realistic goal or objective. In any case, evaluation, whether performance or impact, will assist in getting the job done as efficiently and effectively as possible because we will be aware of and be knowledgeable about the success or failure of all or part of a planned effort.

Computer Research

Computers are critical for research in counterintelligence. One other form of computer research not yet discussed is at least of equal importance with the others; it is the heuristic (teaching) programs that can help in the wise use of security resources. Perhaps one of the most important elements of an effective counterintelligence program is to make certain that the facility's computers and their programs themselves are secure. There is widespread piracy of computer programs and an unknown amount of information theft achieved by computer penetrations. Research by computers into ways to make computers more secure is needed.

Aside from tightening up the computer systems themselves, these sophisticated programs may provide guidance as to how best to assign personnel, as to what equipment will be the most practical and effective, and also provide projections of immediate and long-range threats of espionage and the best configuration of security tactics and strategies to cope with such threats. The research capabilities of computers are limited only by human imagination.

AIDS FOR IDENTIFICATION

Fingerprinting

The most universal technical aid for identification is the art and science of fingerprinting. If a known suspect's prints are left at the scene of a criminal act of industrial espionage, it is possible that the suspect's identity and presence at the scene can be verified. Note that we said a known suspect who left fingerprints at the scene. The fact that the perpetrator left fingerprints at the crime scene will not ordinarily lead to the identification of that perpetrator unless he or she is a known suspect. If we have the prints plus the name of the suspect, we can use the major state and FBI fingerprint files, which may help us to identify the presence of the suspect at the crime scene. Unfortunately, most people believe that where a burglar or spy has left a print or prints at the scene, that person can be readily identified and the previously unknown perpetrator revealed, but this is not so.

All large fingerprint files are ordered according to formulas derived from sets of ten-finger prints. Thus, the 20 million sets of fingerprints in the criminal fingerprint files of the FBI are classified and filed using the Henry system, which provides formulas basically derived from analysis of full sets of the ten fingers of the persons printed. If there is an unknown perpetrator, in the most unlikely event that he or she left a clear set of ten fingerprints, those prints could be searched against the main files in what is known as a technical search, based on the formula derived from the crime scene prints. But only rarely does a criminal leave behind a full set of prints. Only once in history has a perpetrator in New York State been careless enough to leave behind such incriminating evidence. In the usual situation where, after careful search, the investigator discovers prints left by the perpetrator these discovered prints are likely to be fragmentary and at most of one or two fingers only. As a practical matter, such prints, referred to as latent prints, cannot be searched against the main fingerprint files of state and federal identification bureaus.

In order to compensate to some extent for this situation, the FBI and state identification bureaus generally maintain special files containing a limited number of persons whose prints are broken down finger by finger and filed so that a search is possible where only one, two, or three individual fingerprints may be found at the crime scene. Large states, however, have only about 20,000 individuals in their single-fingerprint (latent) files. If an industrial spy is arrested, his or her prints can be entered into this special file, and, if he or she leaves crime scene prints in that same state in future penetrations he or she can be identified as being present at the scene of the crime. In states and regions where industrial espionage is particularly virulent, security organizations may be wise to request local authorities to enter the prints of spies in their latent files. Some of these single fingerprint files are now automated and very efficient.

Since many persons involved in espionage may be employees of the target company, it would be desirable to be able to fingerprint employees. If the security director is able to maintain a file of single prints of all employees in sensitive positions, it might help to clear the innocent and narrow down the number of employee suspects for a more manageable investigation.

Criminal History Files

Closely allied to the art and science of fingerprinting are CORI (criminal offender record information) files or criminal history files, as they are sometimes called. These are files compiled of all persons arrested and fingerprinted over a period of many years. Access to these sensitive files is usually by the submission of a new set of arrest fingerprints, which generates a response to the submitting authorities of the fingerprinted person's prior criminal history. Generally the police submit copies of the arrestee's fingerprints to both the FBI and the state bureaus of identification and receive criminal history records from both.

In recent years there has been a thrust to computerize fingerprint and criminal history files for more rapid response to the agencies served, for greater economy of system maintenance, and to open up vast sources of data for criminological research. Some states, most notably New York, now have fully automated fingerprint identification systems. Attempts by the FBI to extend its National Crime Information Center (NCIC) to include computerized criminal history records have been partially stymied by persons concerned with the privacy implications of a nationwide, computerized criminal-history system. This same concern for privacy has limited the access of private security, and its counterinteligence component, to criminal history records. Greater access to both arrest and conviction records would assist the counterintelligence capabilities of industry, particularly where there is no restriction on fingerprinting employees.

Since private security is very much on its own in combating industrial espionage, except in those cases where a government agency may be involved, it seems that there should not be undue restrictions placed on private security. Where it is doing a job that is vital to our nation's economic health and survival, private security should be supported by public aids for identification.

Modus Operandi Files

Another frequently used aid for identification is the maintenance of modus operandi files, records ordered by the nature of the criminal offender's patterns of conduct while commiting crime. Thus, if the counterintelligence commander can analyze the techniques previously used by known spies, he or she may be able to match their modus operandi with the way in which otherwise unidentified spies committed acts of espionage currently under investigation. The technique is based on the theory that criminals, including agents and spies, develop patterns of operations that are identifiable as being uniquely their own. In this manner we can actually identify the perpetrator(s) in some cases or at least develop potential leads. In other situations, cases under investigation can be grouped by methods of operation and have confidence that a particular person (or persons) unknown is responsible for that group of cases. The great advantage of this is that each case may provide some clue as to the identity of the perpetrator(s), and with it all added together identification may result. In the event of such an arrest, many cases may be cleared.

A host of other sources and files serve as aids for identification and should be used by the counterintelligence unit whenever appropriate. These files may be categorized as technical information files in the investigative sense and as scientific techniques and files that are largely based on the physical sciences.

Technical information sources and files include the following:

1. Intelligence files maintained by federal, state, and local official agencies.
2. Intelligence files maintained by industrial firms to combat espionage.
3. National Auto Theft Bureau, Jericho, NY.
4. World Association of Detectives, San Mateo, CA.
5. Society of Former Special Agents of the Federal Bureau of Investigation, New York, NY.
6. Security Equipment Industry Association, Santa Monica, CA.
7. National Security Industrial Association, Washington, D.C.
8. National Crime Prevention Association, Washington, D.C.
9. Jewelers Security Alliance of the U.S., New York, NY.
10. National Burglar and Fire Alarm Association, Washington, D.C.
11. International Association of Credit Card Investigators, Navato, CA.
12. Computer Security Institute, Hudson, MA.
13. Dun and Bradstreet, New York, NY.
14. Equifax (formerly Retail Credit Co.) Atlanta, GA.
15. T.R.W., Redondo Beach, CA.
16. International Criminal Police Organization (Interpol), Paris, France.

17. The Credit Index offered by Hooper-Holmes Bureau, Morristown, NJ.
18. Insurance Crime Prevention Bureau, Boston, MA.

This list provides only an indication of the wealth of cooperating agencies that security directors and heads of counterintelligence squads can turn to for assistance. Most of those listed are nongovernmental sources and files. Proper liaison with federal, state, and local law enforcement officials should provide access to many confidential information sources in the public sphere. For example, state motor vehicle bureau files contain valuable data for investigative purposes, including photographs of licensees in many cases. In addition to other sources at the local level, there are extensive records of births, deaths, marriages, property titles, trade names, and, in the local school system, student records, which may be very revealing in terms of grades, psychological and medical tests, and assessments by teachers, counselors, and administrators.

The most insightful confidential information sources are those at the national level. In these days of monstrous computer systems, sometimes interfaced with one another, there can be rapid retrieval of vast amounts of information about virtually any person in the country. It is almost impossible to be a citizen or legal alien and not appear many times over in various federal files. Some indication of the scope of federal files may be gleaned from the fact that the Department of Justice has more than 160 million fingerprints on file, not counting the FBI's 20 million or so criminal files. Immigration files, Internal Revenue files, Veterans Administration files, Social Security files, and so on document the days of our lives.

Scientific techniques and files include the following:

1. Single-fingerprint (latent) files.
2. Laundry and dry-cleaning mark files.
3. Typewriter samples.
4. Handwriting exemplars for graphological analysis.
5. Fraudulent-check files.
6. Personal-appearance files.
7. Voiceprints.
8. Ballistic test records and firearms identification.
9. Paint-sample files.
10. Physiological testing for alcohol ingestion.
11. Drug and poison files.
12. Soil samples.

13. Physiological fluid identifiers.
14. Lectins and blood groupings.
15. Fiber identification of textile and nontextile origin.
16. Tire tread, shoeprint, and other track identification.
17. Casts and replicas.
18. Forensic photography, composite drawings, and Identi-kit (a mechanical aid for constructing a visual representation of facial features of perpetrators in cooperation with victims or witnesses).
19. Human and animal hair.
20. Cosmetic identifiers and dyes.
21. Glass fractures and identity analysis.
22. Metalographic examinations.
23. Examination of plastics.
24. Investigation of tool marks.
25. Arson investigation.
26. Investigation and identification of explosives.
27. Document examination, indented writing, and restoration of burned documents.
28. Use of lasers, x-rays, ultraviolet, and infrared lighting systems.

This is not an exhaustive list of available scientific techniques and files that are available to security directors and supervisors of counterintelligence squads. They should become familiar with some or all of these and other scientific capabilities in order to ensure that full advantage is taken of the many aids for identification.

AIDS FOR SURVEILLANCE

A number of kinds of surveillance are involved in the field of industrial espionage and counterintelligence. Some types of surveillance are more suitable for espionage; others are appropriately used for counterespionage. We discuss scientific aids for surveillance from the standpoint of both the spy and the counterintelligence officer. There are four distinct types of surveillance that we will comment on: data surveillance, psychological surveillance, physical surveillance, and electronic surveillance.

Data Surveillance

It has been said that there are no more frontiers. A century or so ago, if a person fouled up in the old home town, all he had to do was to pack up and head west. If he were running away from something real bad he would change his name. This flight to the frontier was memorialized in the song, "What Was Your Name in the States?" But today there are no frontiers to run away to. With the advent of computer technology and the storage of vast amounts of data about all of us in readily retrievable form, it is very difficult to try to escape from one's past. In fact, some civil libertarians have said that we are all in a data prison.

In terms of counterintelligence, data surveillance can be a boon to efforts to fight corruption of employees. More information is available faster than ever before. Significant background checks can be made on employees without leaving one's desk. This is not to say that we should fail to follow-up leads and fail to do neighborhood checks as vital ingredients of the employment process. It is to say, however, that we can have a great deal of confidence in the various data systems that serve investigative needs. They are more complete, more accurate, and more revealing than previously, and the retrieval of a full dossier of relevant data is a matter of minutes or hours rather than weeks or months. We have but to make use of these scientific aids to benefit from them. We may be sure that the espionage agent will also try to use them, for the more he knows about our employees the more adroit and discreet can be his approaches to turning one or more of our employees into a spy. Unfortunately, the potentials of data surveillance cut both ways. It certainly behooves the security director and the head of the counterintelligence unit to be as wise as the enemy and try to anticipate through data analysis those employees who, for one reason or another, may succumb to the wiles of an espionage agent.

PSYCHOLOGICAL SURVEILLANCE

Almost from the day we entered first grade, we have been tested and retested and tested again. We have been exposed to IQ tests, Minnesota Multiphasic Psychological Inventory tests, Rorschach tests, and a score of other tests designed to discover intelligence, stability, emotional stress, introversion or extroversion, oral or anal fixations, sexual preferences, and so on. The vast majority of these tests are not protected from disclosure by a doctor/patient relationship. Now that these test results can be entered by well-meaning people into computer data banks, all of us are trapped by psychological surveillance. Since these records are difficult to purge from the computer data bank, psychological profiles captured years ago are still available.

If we can obtain any derogatory information first, we may be able to rid ourselves of potential spies. If the espionage agents happen to act on the data first, then they may have been able to find a chink in our armor, with devastating consequences.

Most of these psychological tests were probably given by government agencies of one kind or another and as such may be accessible through the Freedom of Information Act. There is good reason to fear that industrial espionage agents may obtain access to this information and then use it. Many people are intimidated by psychological surveillance and the computerization of the test results without their having any knowledge of what the files contain. One can imagine how such people would react if confronted with derogatory data from those files by an espionage agent seeking to turn the person into a spy.

Physical Surveillance

Physical surveillance can be as unsophisticated in terms of scientific applications as the mere following and unobtrusive observation of a subject. Such mere following may become a great deal more complex if the subject suspects the surveillance. If the subject is on foot he or she may double back, wait in a doorway, or wait around a corner to frustrate the tail. If the subject is using public transportation he or she may wait until the train is just about to pull out before boarding, leaving the pursuer flat-footed at the station.

Deftly switching from train, to bus, to motor car, and back again, the experienced and well-trained operative can often shake the close surveillance. Loose physical surveillances are likely to be more difficult to detect, but an experienced and knowledgeable operative will take no chances and assume a "tail." He or she will use evasive tactics as a matter of course. If the surveillance turns into an automobile tail, a number of evasive driving tactics may be employed to confound the pursuer. Driving into a dead-end street may upset the surveillance, and the use of an entire repertoire of evasive maneuvers may lose the pursuer entirely. On the other hand, there are electronic devices that can be attached to the person(s) or vehicle(s) of the pursued so that the surveillance person(s) can readily follow the subject even though he or she may be temporarily out of sight.

Physical surveillance may be aided by various devices that increase the range of vision and record what is observed. Binoculars, spyglasses, sniperscopes and snooperscopes that enable users to see in the dark, and optical systems that need only low light levels for closed circuit television and other pictures are excellent aids for physical surveillance. Optical systems that can read license plates or other identifiers and process the information through a computer can enable immediate feedback as to the registered owner of the vehicle, boat, or other identified object. Self-activating cameras may be employed for a variety of physical surveillance purposes, such as monitoring a secret process, a dead drop, a suspected safe house, or other meeting place. Remotely activated cameras are also commonly used for surveillance in banks and other locations that may be subject to robbery or other emergency. Physical surveillance, unless supported by electronic surveillance, is usually dependent on the sense of sight, but the senses of smell, taste, and touch may also be involved in some cases. For instance, odors emanating from premises may indicate marijuana smoking inside. The taste of certain other drugs may aid a surveillance, and the feel of the hood of an auto may provide information about its recent use.

Physical surveillance under covert conditions, such as the observation of employees, may provide a great deal of information about those employees. We may discover who is stealing from the facility; we may discover liaisons we had not expected; we may find that some employees are meeting surreptitiously with outsiders and are apparently passing merchandise or valuable confidential matters to them for a price.

Physical surveillance of restricted and sensitive areas is essential to frustrate industrial spies. Physical surveillance of compliance with security regulations, coupled with all of the varieties of physical surveillance involved in prevention and protection of the facility, and its very valuable confidential and secret components, are critical to the counterintelligence system.

Electronic Surveillance

Electronic surveillance is the highly technical employment of scientific advances. It is sophisticated and controversial at the same time. If it were not so effective, of course, there would not be so much debate about its use. Perhaps the most effective means of surveillance is wiretapping and bugging, yet there is nothing that arouses public concern so much. One aspect of this concern is that it is directed toward the legitimate use of these powerful tools, whereas the media and the public seem to be unaware that for every legal electronic surveillance, there are probably hundreds of illegal bugs and taps installed by criminals and spies, both foreign and domestic. Restrictions on private security in its efforts to obtain court-supervised eavesdropping orders places counterintelligence in a disadvantaged position.

The telephone is perhaps the most likely candidate for wiretap; the tapping of computer communication lines and general cables is of considerable significance as well. Telephone wiretapping can be as simple as using a telephone handset at the junction box and connecting the pairs and cables, or it can be more sophisticated and complex, such as using induction pickup or coil methods for obtaining the data on the line, or, indeed, tapping off the telephone instrument itself.

A telephone can be tapped and bugged at the same time. The so-called harmonica bug may be installed in the victim's telephone. The spy from a remote telephone, even thousands of miles away, dials the victim's number and sounds a note that prevents the victim's phone from ringing and at the same time activates the bug so that the eavesdropper can hear any discussion in the vicinity of the phone. The microphone bug will remain active as long as the spy keeps the line open by having the receiver out of the cradle. The bug will be powered indefinitely by the current in the telephone system.

Miniature transmitters and the entire scope of microelectronics has provided aid to the bugging operations of espionage agents. Equipment for eavesdropping can be made so small as to be concealed in virtually any orifice of the human body. Combined microphones and transmitters can be fitted into a cigarette lighter, a ballpoint pen, a wristwatch, a tie clip, or even into a capsule of food. If the victim swallows the capsule along with his food, everything that person says for hours afterward can be overheard by a remote listener. Minimicrophones and transmitters may be supplemented by miniature recorders. Since the recorder is not a transmitting device, it is not readily detectable electronically. Counterintelligence agents would have to do an embarrassingly thorough search of the suspect's body and his or her belongings to expose the instrument. Woe to the officer who picked the wrong person, particularly if the suspect was a woman!

Microphones possess unique capabilities. They can be independently installed, and, if miniaturized, may be readily concealed almost anywhere. If they are installed by a competent technician they may be extremely difficult to locate. Equipment already on the premises such as telephones, radios, televisions, or intercoms may be converted into microphones. Some microphones can sense sound vibrations against a wall. This is the type known as a pointed sensor, or spike; it is inserted into a drilled hole that stops short of the surface of the wall of an adjoining room or office. Another type operates on the principle of a stethoscope and has flexible tubing that can bend around corners. A directional microphone (parabolic mike) can be aimed at a subject, or subjects, from a considerable distance and pick up sound that may be unintelligible to the naked ear because of intervening noises such as traffic or other conversations. Filtering devices can be used to eradicate the noise and bring the desired conversation forward loudly and clearly. One can readily imagine the utility of the parabolic mike when combined with a telescopic camera. One begins to wonder if there is anyplace left where one can discuss confidential matters without the possibility of being overheard.

The detection of electronic listening devices is exceedingly difficult and involves both physical and electronic inspection of the area. Metal detectors may be used to sweep for microphones or wiring; however, some devices use materials that would not be picked up by the sweep. Theoretically there are devices that can check telephone lines for possible taps. One of the authors recalls having been involved with a legal tap on the home telephone of an electronics expert whose customers were members of organized crime. While on the wire, we overheard a conversation with a bookmaker. When the bookmaker hesitated to mention names and places, the electronics expert told him not to worry because he had invented a gold box, which he had installed to warn him if there was a tap on his line. He convinced the bookie to order two of the gold boxes at five thousand dollars each, and the conversation continued. As a result of our legal tap that "didn't exist, according to the 'gold box,'" the electronics expert and several bookies and numbers bankers were arrested and convicted. There could be such devices that could be relied on to detect any tap no matter how skillfully it may have been installed, but the counterintelligence officer should be somewhat skeptical.

When an electronic sweep is conducted, the sweep ordinarily will not locate devices that are not operating or are operating outside the radio frequency spectrum. Thus, devices that are not operating at the time and other devices may not be picked up by the sweep. Unfortunately, many business people do not want their offices to go through the upset of being debugged during the work week. A weekend search may fail because the espionage agent has most likely remotely turned off his radio-transmitting devices. One answer to this problem is the recently available non-linear junction box detector. This device does not require that the bug be in an operating mode. The junction box may be detected, regardless.

Many of these electronic surveillance aids, while they may be important scientific advances, seem to be tilted in favor of espionage rather than counterintelligence, which means that we have to revert to the use of electronic aids for security generally, as well as for specific types of counterintelligence. The remainder of this chapter therefore is devoted to modern advances in electronic surveillance that are applicable to the entire spectrum of security prevention and protection.

It is not the intent of this chapter to go into detail concerning electronic surveillance of electronic security.[1] (Chapter 13 will serve that purpose.)

Some important advances have been made in the area of security alarms, primarily in connection with the sensors. Among the many in use are the following:

1. Photoelectric installations using invisible beams of light that signal an interruption of the continuous beam.
2. Sonic alarms activated by noise.
3. Motion detection alarm systems dependent on the disturbance of radio frequency waves or ultrasonic waves.
4. Vibration detectors that are highly sensitive to movement and may be attached directly to the protected object.
5. Pressure alarms that detect pressure on a carpet, mat, or other object that provides concealment for the device.
6. Capacitance alarms that create an electromagnetic field around the protected object.
7. Laser beams that can be bent around corners and curves.[2]

In regard to electronic surveillance by closed circuit television systems, new digital intrusion detector analyzers have been developed. These systems are designed to replace guards monitoring television cameras. Instead of making a visual image, the camera records and memorizes 65,000 bits of information about the area being guarded. Whenever these bits are disturbed, an alarm is sounded automatically.

Electronic-access devices control keyless entry by reading identification cards or by recognizing hand configurations or fingerprints.

Audio security systems scan premises, including remote locations, automatically discriminating and locking in any local or remote alarm sounds.

One final word about electronic eavesdropping: the Omnibus Crime Control Act of 1968 makes it a felony:

(a) To willfully intercept, try to intercept, or procure another to intercept any wire or oral communication or (b) to use or try to use or procure another to use or try to use any electronic, mechanical, or other device to intercept any oral communication when such device transmits a signal by radio or interferes with radio transmission or when it is affixed to or transmits a

---

[1] Electronic security material is adapted from Robert R.J. Gallati, *Introduction to Private Security* (Englewood Cliffs, N.J.: Prentice-Hall, 1983), chap. 21.
[2] See, also, *Security & Loss Control*, Bottom and Kostanoski, Macmillan, 1983, chapter 7.

signal through connections used in wire communications, or when the user
knows that the device or any part has been transported in the mails or in
interstate commerce, or when the use takes place within or develops information relative to the operations of a business whose operations affect
interstate commerce.[3]

It is also a felony according to the act to engage in the:

manufacture, assembly, possession, sale, and transmission through mails
or in interstate commerce of any electronic, mechanical, or other device
whose design renders it primarily useful for the purpose of surreptitious
interception of oral or wire communications, with knowledge or reason to
know of such primary purpose and of the past or future interstate or mail
transmission, are prohibited, as is advertising any such device in such a way
as to promote it for such purpose. The penalty in these cases is also five
years and $10,000.[4]

There is also a special right to civil damages accorded to victims
by this act. The civil right is in addition to the other civil remedies
available to victims of industrial espionage. We should not, however,
be lulled into a false sense of security because of the provisions of this
act. Espionage agents know they are violating many laws, yet this does
not deter them. It is not likely that any spy will fail to use whatever
electronic surveillance methods and devices he or she deems necessary.

SUMMARY

We have conducted an overview in this chapter of four categories of
scientific and technical aids: aids for data collection, aids for research,
aids for identification, and aids for surveillance.

Among the aids for data collection are libraries, scientific analyses,
and computer programs and linkages. Among the aids for research are
the behavioral sciences and the assistance these sciences can provide.
We can profile employees who may be suborned. We can study
employee morale and motivation to ensure pride and loyalty among
employees. The behavioral sciences coupled with the economic
disciplines can provide clues as to the likelihood of particular facets of

---

[3] 18 U.S.C. 2510 et seq., as interpreted by Timothy J. Walsh and Richard J.
Healy, *Protecting Your Business against Espionage* (New York: Amacom, Division
of American Management Associations, 1973), pp. 78, 79. Excerpted by permission
of the publisher. All rights reserved.

[4] Ibid.

a facility being targeted by industrial spies. Research and rational analyses can help us anticipate future problems in a particular industry.

Operations research was dealt with at some length. We distinguished between reverse engineering and the actual application of such engineering principles as linear programming, simulations, gaming techniques, and queueing technology. We also discussed evaluation research techniques. We described both performance evaluations and impact evaluations and their differential employments in the industrial espionage environment. Computer research was dealt with both from the standpoint of the computer system as potential victim and the computer as an ally in counterintelligence efforts.

Various aids for identification include fingerprinting, latent prints, criminal history files, modus operandi files, technical information sources, and scientific techniques and files.

Aids for surveillance are data surveillance, psychological surveillance, physical surveillance, and electronic surveillance.

Data surveillance has been aided by computer technology, enabling security directors to obtain more information about employees. Industrial spies also use these data to target individuals who may be likely to succumb.

Psychological surveillance is the end product of the various tests Americans are subjected to as they progress through life. Some of these are very revealing and can be used by the forces of counterintelligence to provide insights about potential spies among employees. If the spy masters can obtain access to these data, they can employ them by threatening subjects with blackmail or by selecting dupes.

Physical surveillance was dealt with in terms of basic observation of persons, places, and things and tracking the activities of targeted persons. These activities can be assisted by various technical surveillance devices such as binoculars, spyglasses, sniperscopes (and snooperscopes), and an entire array of optical systems.

Electronic surveillance is highly important to counterespionage. The provisions of the Omnibus Crime Control Act of 1968, however, call for harsh penalties for illegal eavesdropping and the manufacture, assembly, possession, sale, advertising, and transmission of eavesdropping devices. The law has not been very effective. Espionage agents are not intimidated.

8. Research Activity

In fair weather prepare for foul. —Thomas Fuller

The word *espionage* often brings to mind a Hollywood image of romantic, sinister, and frequently violent activity in dark and exotic locations. Spy pursued by counterspy suggests direct and life-threatening confrontations between deadly field agents armed with exotic technology. But behind this myth lies the reality and importance of research activity. Active investigation is meaningless without the direction provided by thorough research. Refinement of the investigation and the analysis of investigative results requires additional research effort. Preparation of the final report is a research effort, as is evaluation of the entire mission.

Corporations that have made a policy decision to combat industrial espionage normally have the necessary resources to carry out counterintelligence research activities. Those corporate departments that perform research as a matter of normal business can assist the counterintelligence team. Of course, it is best that few people know the purpose of this research since untrustworthy employees may be found in any department.

The uncovering of espionage is a counterintelligence function. Successful espionage requires access to people, places, and/or things. Counterintelligence personnel seek to deny that access by security measures. They also seek to identify espionage agents through active investigation. Necessary planning and guidance for the counterintelligence mission depend on research to limit wasted counterintelligence activity and to speed success. Research locates the ways and means as well as helps to determine counterintelligence priorities.

A survey of corporate weaknesses aggravating the industrial espionage threat is the first research step. This survey should provide information on at least the following categories:

1. Previous industrial espionage losses.
2. Industry-wide espionage experience.
3. Trademarks, patents, and trade secrets essential to corporate survival and profitability.
4. Sensitive information now loosely disseminated.
5. Morale problems and the percentage of unhappy or dissatisfied employees.
6. Poor physical or procedural controls or the ignoring of same.

Previous losses provide case studies to analyze for past vulnerabilities (which may remain uncorrected) to industrial espionage. Loss histories also direct attention to those agencies or corporations that directed any previous espionage attacks because these adversaries may be considered possible future users of industrial espionage techniques. Thus, they represent a class of espionage users.

The best sources for espionage loss-history information are senior management employees. Espionage losses may not have been reported to the police, perhaps because of a lack of real evidence, but senior personnel often have reasonable suspicions that such a loss occurred. Overseas managers should be contacted since espionage effects may have become apparent only in the overseas marketplace. Establishing the dollar amount of loss is of less importance than learning the espionage techniques used, as well as who is suspected of ordering the espionage.

Industry-wide espionage losses may be harder to track down because many corporations do not reveal their espionage problems publicly. Liaison is helpful in learning about such espionage activity. Industry journals often speculate on possible espionage targets or print brief accounts of attempts and successes. This information helps complete the threat appreciation begun with a single corporation's loss history. Espionage attacks against competitors are likely to be similar to future attacks on any and all corporations in the industry.

Trademarks, patents, trade secrets, and other sensitive proprietary information need to be cataloged much as householders are advised to take an inventory of valuable possessions. This list should include some measure of valuation or ranking in relation to corporate survival and profitability.

Most corporate executives lack an appreciation of the amount of sensitive information under their control. Therefore, to complete this research project, it will be necessary to contact the head of each corporate department, with special attention to production, research and development, data processing, and planning. Research efforts should include detailed consideration of all categories of information held with a view to locating vulnerabilities previously overlooked. (Information in this context means prototypes and design models as well as data.)

Sensitive information may be given away in the form of officially sanctioned information sharing—through newsletters, announcements (written and verbal), promotional materials, and the like. Corporations routinely honor outside requests for data under the guise of educational research. Too often visitors are improperly escorted or allowed free access. Vital data may be discarded regularly in the trash. Such give-aways are not deliberate assistance to espionage agents, but they cause as much damage to corporate assets as does true espionage.

Articles published in trade or scientific journals, authored by employees, may reveal far too much information. Scientists often scoff at requests for secrecy. They need help in understanding espionage threats.

Existing morale has a direct effect on how employees carry out their responsibilities or react to opportunities to commit dishonest acts, such as the theft of company secrets or assisting an espionage agent. Dissatisfaction and low morale affect efficiency and loyalty negatively. Thus, it is important to establish the corporate morale level, especially in sensitive operations like data processing and R&D. The higher the morale, the easier it is to involve employees in counter-intelligence efforts. The lower the morale, the higher the internal espionage threat and the external threat.

To gauge morale, it may be necessary to use an undercover agent (see Chapter 6). Another applicable research activity is to analyze the rise and fall of overall losses (shrinkage). Declining losses usually indicate reasonable employee morale. Rising losses almost always indicate overall employee dissatisfaction. Peer pressure is the best method to reduce all losses. These include successful industrial espionage. Attitude surveys represent a method to gauge employee morale. They should be designed by psychologists.

Employee carelessness is a constant problem. It may be the result of poor physical, procedural, or document security. Lax enforcement of security standards is another cause. Often carelessness stems from a simple lack of security awareness on the part of employees who are loyal but do not realize the jeopardy caused by careless handling of company secrets. These people do not realize that their own jobs and reputations can be lost through their careless acts. This lack of aware-ness is partly the fault of the security department or management policy or both. Management must openly support counterintelligence and the security department. That department must formulate an attractive educational program that will cause employees to be alert to the dangers of espionage. Employees who persist in careless acts, such as failing to lock document cabinets or talking indiscreetly at social events and conventions, must be fired. An analysis of security hardware, personnel, and procedures should be completed with an eye to their effectiveness in relation to the industrual espionage threat. (See Chapter 12.) Management policy in the form of written rules should be measured against the same threat. Supervisors can pinpoint any careless employee in their charge. Security inspections will also help to locate the careless individual. Carelessness, of course, may be either accidental (error) or deliberate (crime or unethical practice).

Some possible findings from preliminary research activity follow. These examples illustrate how research activities serve to prepare for those investigative methods discussed in Chapter 6:

1. Industrial espionage loss history of XYZ Corporation: Negative local records. Suspicion that an advanced production process was copied by another corporation although it may have developed the process independently. Suspicion is based on the fact that a former key production employee left XYZ for the other corporation shortly before it adopted the same production process.

2. Industry-wide industrial espionage experience: Competitor sued former employee who left to start his own business. Suit was unsuccessful. It could not be proved that the secrets had been safeguarded by the company in any way. Trade journals expressed concern that the Freedom of Information Act could damage domestic corporations through disclosure of proprietary information. A competitor was damaged through overseas trademark piracy.

3. XYZ Corporation's crucial proprietary information: Board minutes. Expansion plans. Sales projections. Promotional campaigns. R&D projects. Proprietary data are mostly computerized. Merger negotiations. Less than strict controls on any of this data at this time.

4. Loosely disseminated information at XYZ Corporation: No evidence that compromise is likely from corporate newsletters or publications of staff. No program in respect to visitor questions. Researchers allowed to use corporate library after hours and without supervision. Visitors loosely supervised.

5. Morale problems at XYZ Corporation: Poor morale at the blue-collar level partially due to frequent layoffs and concessions demanded by management with respect to union

contracts. Average morale among supervisors unsure of layoffs to come, affecting them. Excellent management morale.

6. Carelessness at XYZ Corporation: Good physical access controls (locks, lights, alarms). Employees generally ignore security and safety rules. So does management.

FORMATS FOR COLLECTION INSTRUMENTS

Instructions must be issued to those prepared to carry out the counter-intelligence mission. These instructions become a format for efforts to gather information. This is part of the direction phase of counter-intelligence. Formats are modified as information is collected and analyzed (see Figure 8-1).

Based on research activities, the security department designs counterintelligence questionnaires, usually called *collection instruments*. They may be general instructions or include considerable detail. Information bearing on counterintelligence can be collected by personnel in various corporate divisions, but all information must be reported to a central facility, ideally the corporate security staff. Since the volume of data may be considerable, it is wise to make use of the data-processing department. Special computer programs can be written to ease the burden of sorting information and establishing linkages.

Four sample collection instruments follow. The requirements of each reflect the results of research activity previously conducted.

Specific Counterintelligence Collection Format 1

Subject: Visitors

According to the new security policy, all visitors must sign in and sign out, indicating their company and purpose of visit. Guards must annotate the log to indicate who provided the escort and where the visitor was conducted.

Investigators will contact the listed escorts and locate all individuals who spoke with randomly selected visitors. These employees will be queried as to the questions asked by the visitor and subjects discussed. Company materials and data to which the visitor had access will be determined. Investigators will pay particular note to unusual requests or unnecessarily detailed questions. This information will be compiled on a weekly basis and furnished to the director of security.

Specific Counterintelligence Collection Format 2

Subject: Board Minutes

Board minutes are supplied to all board members. The chief executive officer's secretary is authorized to distribute copies to other executives at their request.

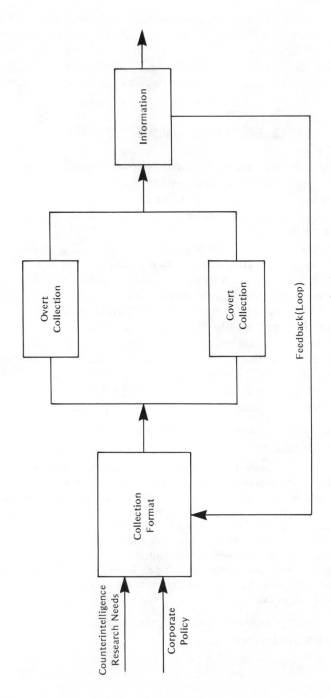

Figure 8-1. Format for gathering information

The CEO's secretary will keep a log of all requests for board minutes. This log will be furnished to the security department on a weekly basis.

The security department will determine if these minutes are further copied after distribution and where the additional copies are kept and under what conditions.

General Counterintelligence Collection Format 1

Subject: Employee Morale

Guard personnel will take specific notes (including names and details) concerning employee morale problems encountered during daily tours of duty. This information will be transferred to the Remarks section of their daily report.

General Counterintelligence Collection Format 2

Subject: Conventions

Employees attending conventions will report all contacts with competitors outside of normal business intercourse. This information will be furnished to their supervisor who will forward same with comments to the security department no later than seven days after the close of the convention.

Collection formats must be fully discussed with affected employees. There must be no feeling that XYZ Corporation is trying to restrict personal freedom or free associations. If the collection instrument is disseminated only in written form, it may be misunderstood. In some cases it is better to keep such instructions verbal to prevent media distortion.

LIAISON

Public Agency

Liaison has been defined as "a linking up or connecting of the parts of a whole, intended to bring about proper coordination of activities."[1] This linking up is invaluable in meeting all security responsibilities. Liaison frequently hinges on goodwill or mutual respect. Individuals are sometimes ordered to cooperate with outsiders, but such orders rarely accomplish their purpose. Rather, a tight individual relationship cutting across organizational lines represents the best type of liaison because it often produces information generally unknown to supervisory personnel who cannot be bothered with details.

---

[1] *Webster's New Twentieth Century Dictionary Unabridged*, 2d ed. (New York: Simon and Schuster, 1979), p. 1042.

The local police represent one type of law enforcement agency that can be of assistance to corporate counterintelligence. The U.S. DoD, through the Defense Investigative Service (DIS), will assist in any matters that might involve compromise of defense information in violation of Title 18 of the U.S. Code. The FBI is vitally concerned with preventing foreign technology transfer and cooperates with business on this subject. The postal service has inspectors concerned with misuse of the mail. Mailing counterfeit or pirated items is a federal offense.

Part of the responsibilities of the U.S. Department of Commerce and the U.S. Department of State is to assist American business. Both departments supply printed information and employ officers who assist in answering corporate inquiries. The State Department assigns a variety of attachés and security officers to foreign embassies. These people can provide detailed information on local conditions and local business interests, including suspicion of piracy as well as other industrial espionage concerns.

Different federal agencies may prove valuable in liaison depending on the product or industry threatened with espionage. These agencies include the Nuclear Regulatory Agency, Securities & Exchange Commission, Department of Transportation, Secret Service, Department of the Interior, Department of Energy, Consumer Product Safety Commission, and the U.S. Congress. Members of Congress on certain committees are concerned with espionage and respond to business concerns nationwide.

True liaison means one-on-one contact, not simply letter writing or blind telephone calls. Corporations must expend significant effort in learning which employees in each relevant agency can be of help in counterintelligence efforts. Referral is the best way to develop liaison links. A way to start is with one federal employee, law enforcement or non-law enforcement, interested in curbing industrial espionage. That federal employee can make introductions to useful people with the same interests in other agencies. Each of those individuals has liaison sources who may be willing to share information.

Continued liaison depends on regular mutual sharing and assistance. Cooperation will not be achieved unless there is frankness on both sides. Trust is fundamental in liaison. Should the corporate representatives refuse to explain why information is required, the public employee may be unwilling to cooperate. In one situation, a telephone company supervisor in Tennessee called a sheriff's detective who happened to be her neighbor. "Please give me information on Mr. X, a former employee of the sheriff's department." The detective asked the reason for the request. "I can't tell you, the telephone company has its secrets, you know." This telephone supervisor was advised to call the company's own security representative.

This story highlights another important liaison rule: do not ignore existing contacts between your company and the public agency in question. The detective mentioned the telephone security representative. He was on a first-name basis with that representative and met with him monthly. This liaison provided a clear conduit for information between the sheriff's department and the telephone company. Think of the chaos created if every supervisor decided to establish his or her own liaison link with each public agency!

To avoid the problem of confusion and annoyance, it is normal to go through channels. A second method calls for appointing a liaison officer in the company whose job is to transmit requests and information and receive the same from public agencies. The liaison officer becomes the key contact between outside agencies and the corporation. Such an individual needs to be intelligent, friendly, and personable.

Liaison should not be confused with public relations, nor should the public relations staff be assigned the sensitive liaison demanded by the threat of industrial espionage. Often the director of the security staff or the number two person has the liaison responsibility. This is not a good practice since the regular meetings required to keep liaison active cut too deeply into the time of such executives. Instead a junior security staff member can be trained as a liaison officer.

The employee assigned to the liaison assignment must keep a central record of contacts, including addresses and telephone numbers, made at each agency. These files should indicate how often liaison contact is made and the type of information exchanged. Files must be updated regularly because of transfer and retirements among the liaison links. The liaison officer must make sure he or she is introduced to the incoming public employee by the retiring or transferred liaison source. These introductions help continuity. Failure to ensure a smooth transfer may inhibit liaison at that agency for some time.

Going through channels can be effective in learning who has the information required, but this method has problems. Contact may be refused or bureaucratic meddling stirred up. A far better method is informal referral from one liaison contact to the next.

Commercial Sector

Unlike the public agency that has a duty to the citizenry and by extension to business, private corporations hug their information jealously. One of the continuing problems in combating terrorism is the sharing of information among corporations. Each corporation guards its own contingency plans for fear it may be imitated or compromised. Each guards such things as information on terrorist intentions because it may create a competitive advantage. Consider the situation in Tehran, Iran, just before the shah was deposed. There was considerable uncertainty in the foreign business community. The U.S. State Department was unclear on its signals. Several corporations pulled out their assets, in time, despite U.S. government assurances of a stable situation. Many corporations were taken by surprise and lost everything in the takeover by the Ayatolla's forces. Why did some corporations get the correct information? Why did they not share it? We will probably never know. Obviously there was a lack of useful liaison.

We believe that the threat of industrial espionage and foreign technology transfer may be even greater than that of terrorism. Thus the corporate sector's refusal to cooperate among its own is short-sighted. Security directors, knowing that peer exchanges are essential to loss control, are forced to conduct clandestine liaison at times with a certain amount of mistrust.

Previous research activity dealing with industry-wide espionage losses may turn up some useful liaison sources. Security meetings, such as those sponsored by the American Society of Industrial Security, the International Security Conferences, Canadian Professional Protection Seminars, and meetings of specialist groups such as the Academy of Security Educators & Trainers (ASET), provide a good environment in which to develop liaison links on industrial espionage.

Informal luncheon meetings between security directors with similar problems are useful in liaison. The settings provide for periodic exchanges of information. More important, the meetings create human relationships, always the best basis for successful liaison. Sometimes events take place between meetings and are too urgent to save until the next time; therefore some method of transferring tactical (hot) counterintelligence should be devised. The method can be as simple as using home telephone numbers, but emergencies may dictate other communications methods, which should be planned in advance and tested at least once. The type of information that needs immediate transmittal includes knowledge that an espionage penetration is under-way. Another critical topic is information that an employee is offering secrets to a competitor.

The matter of security ethics is not clear. Security professionals must prevent unethical acts by their employers, but they must do this work carefully. Liaison can be used to pass along information that a particular corporation is planning to mount an industrial espionage attack on a competitor. If it prevents the espionage act, it will save the guilty corporation much later trouble and expense.

BRIEFING AND DEBRIEFING

Briefings may be prepared in advance to give instructions or warnings to corporate employees regarding industrial espionage. They are also used to explain collection formats to investigators or others assigned to gather information or to maintain certain records. The second use concerns us in this discussion.

Consider the four collection formats given as examples earlier in this chapter. Specific Counterintelligence Collection Format 1 deals with visitors. The object of this format is to gather information on visitors and what happens during their visits. The purpose of such information is to gauge if a visitor is seeking sensitive information or exhibiting suspicious activity not in line with stated purpose of the visit. A number of employees may be involved with visitors, starting with the guard-receptionist. Other employees may be scientific, technical, or managerial. If they fully understand the purpose of the format, they are likely to cooperate. In fact, they may be able to suggest improvements over time. Each of these employees must be briefed. There must be consideration of their background and place in the corporate structure. Lack of briefing often leads to the ignoring of any rule, including counterintelligence collection requirements.

General Counterintelligence Collection Format 1 of the XYZ Corporation refers to the problem of employee morale in reference to industrial espionage vulnerability. The issue is a delicate one. All employees gripe, and their complaints do not automatically mean they will engage in industrial espionage. In this case, briefing the line security officers becomes critical. We do not want every expletive reported. We do not need to know that Mr. B did not want to work on a single day in June. On the other hand, it would not do to ignore the fact that supervisors regularly ignore their responsibilities. That would serve to worsen employee morale. We need to know if deviant acts, theft, pilferage, or safety violations occur without comment by senior employees. This would mean a lack of peer pressure, damaging to overall morale.

Debriefing is entirely different; it calls for information from others. Debriefing is suggested for all employees who leave any corporation for any reason. We believe that such employees will speak frankly on departure and give information of use to security and other departments. Debriefing is also beneficial to research analysts assigned to speak with investigators after a mission. Information developed from these investigators may have been unincluded previously in reports. It may be information of importance not recognized by the investigator until asked the right questions by the debriefer.

Terminating employees may receive verbal and written debriefings, which should take place on or about the last day of their employment. Verbal debriefing should take place first. It will serve to put the employee in the correct frame of mind. The written report will be enriched by the thought processes that accompanied the verbal debriefing session. During the verbal segment, the employee must have explained or reexplained to him or her the methods of industrial espionage agents. It is not necessary for the debriefing agent to dwell on the potential damage to the corporation of industrial espionage since the employee will be leaving the corporation. Most individuals love to play detective and will identify anyone they think may be suspicious. Any such information furnished must be evaluated in the light of the source's reputation and prejudices.

With the employee's permission, the debriefing session should be recorded. Verbal debriefing is not an interrogation; it is an interview. The debriefer should be an experienced interviewer. Specific questions should relate to current appreciation of the espionage threat.

The written phase of debriefing is more difficult for most young Americans. The ability to compose is becoming a vanishing skill. Nevertheless, we must address the problem. There are two alternatives. The first involves asking the employee to write out those methods that would diminish the industrial espionage threat and point out current weaknesses. The second alternative is to design a series of written questions that require short answers. Industrial espionage debriefing usually represents a neglected area. Exit debriefing should cover a variety of concerns. Industrial espionage questions will represent only a small percentage of the exercise, but a vital part.

OPEN SOURCES

Counterintelligence depends on up-to-date information that will be analyzed and used in decision making. Because its only concern is the threat of espionage, the information needed is rather specialized.

Collection of information can be done overtly or covertly (sometimes called clandestinely). Overt collection uses open sources. It is perfectly legal and above board. As a matter of record, covert collection is not necessarily illegal or immoral. The problem with utilizing overt sources is simply one of location. Where are they to be found?

Researchers, generally, have a great fear of overlooking an overt source that could be useful.

One of the problems with overt sources is the information glut. The number of news media offerings, journals, books, speeches, proceedings, and so forth is immense. Therefore the problem with overt sources is one of quality. Researchers must be able to locate the most critical facts in a limited time. They must review numerous journals and newspapers each month. The following fields could prove useful: marketing, business, management, automotive, electronics, chemistry, telecommunications, oil and gas, labor, economics, public relations, drug and cosmetic, restaurant, air conditioning, heating and refrigeration, telephony, cybernetics, engineering, and banking. From 1975 through 1980, the *Business Periodical Review Index* noted articles dealing with industrial espionage in journals representing each of the fields listed above. A host of general purpose news magazines, such as *U.S. News & World Report* have carried industrial espionage articles. *Playboy* has published serious articles addressing the threat. We must not forget the security journals now published in England, Canada, South America, Europe, and the United States.

Clipping services can be hired to read the publications and extract the industrial espionage articles. A search of the various periodical indexes found in every public library saves considerable time and provides precise article reference for easy retrieval. Liaison may aid in locating important periodical articles.

There is a shortage of books discussing the industrial espionage problem, although a considerable literature deals with national intelligence in one context or other. Because counterintelligence is an intelligence function, overt sources include all books that treat intelligence seriously. The Association of Former Intelligence Officers publishes a newsletter that includes reviews of books on intelligence.[1] The "Foreign Intelligence Literary Scene", a bimonthly newsletter/book review is a useful source on intelligence materials.[2] University libraries frequently carry a wide selection of intelligence books used by students of government and criminal justice, and Reserve Officer Training Corps cadets. Local libraries can borrow books through interlibrary loan. Copies of periodical articles can be secured in the same way.

Industrial espionage writings of interest are published throughout the world. These cannot be overlooked or ignored simply because the

---

[1] AFIO, 6723 Whittier Avenue, Suite 303A, McLean, VA 22101.
[2] Thomas F. Troy, ed. 6101 Rudyard Ave., Bethesda, MD 20814.

language is foreign. Perhaps employees in overseas subsidiaries can be directed to search foreign language publications for industrial espionage material and translate the material into English. The alternative is to use an overseas agency that functions much as an American clipping service. It may be necessary to hire a translater.

Television, especially the U.S. Public Broadcasting Service, the British Broadcasting Corporation, and other state-owned broadcasting networks, is another type of open source. Television special presentations may focus on the subject of industrial espionage and foreign technology transfer, which may be useful as background information to create awareness among corporate employees. The problem is not in securing a copy of the tape; it can be purchased. Rather, the problem is learning that the tape exists. Radio, too, may be the medium for a special show or interview on industrial espionage.

University researchers have made contributions to various security subjects, including intelligence. Many of these reports are not published. They may or may not be the basis for a speech or paper presentation at a professional society meeting. Locating this material will be made much easier by developing some acquaintances in the academic area. Scholars usually keep abreast of research conducted by colleagues by means of telephone contacts, association newsletters, scientific journals, and attendance at professional meetings. Faculty members with an interest in industrial espionage could represent any one of many disciplines. Business, government, security, and criminal justice are likely places to start.

Much scholastic research goes into the preparation of doctoral dissertations. They are available in microform or printed form from University Microfilms, Ann Arbor, Michigan. Dissertation abstracts are regularly published in volumes available at college libraries.

Trial transcripts are overt sources of special value. Testimony presented may highlight espionage methods used and the deficiencies that allowed the espionage to succeed. Corporate attorneys should be able to locate the citations of industrial espionage criminal trials and tort actions. Current court actions might be worth observing during crucial testimony periods.

Overt sources include individuals who have personal knowledge of espionage as a victim, witness, or participant. Much as in employee debriefing, these individuals, if they are willing to cooperate, can provide useful information. Other people who represent overt sources include liaison links from the public and private sector.

In short, anything or any person who can be approached openly to learn about industrial espionage represents an overt source for research personnel.

COVERT SOURCES

This is an area to be approached with caution. The line between legal and ethical covert sources, and those that are illegal and unethical, is often slim. Each counterintelligence unit must measure the desire to protect its employer against the dangers of excessive zeal. Mistakes in choosing covert sources or methods can result in both criminal and civil penalties to all parties involved, including the corporation.

Undercover agents are an acceptable method of securing information on criminal acts by employees or outsiders. Espionage is a criminal act in the United States. Counterintelligence would be foolish to ignore this covert investigative source.

The double agent is another covert source that can be employed by corporate counterintelligence. When an espionage agent or his or her dupe is discovered by counterintelligence, that agent may be recruited as an informer. This activity is always highly covert and presents personal danger to the agent so turned.

A number of covert devices can aid counterintelligence research. Any type of silent alarm, for example, especially if coupled with hidden cameras or closed circuit television, provides excellent covert information. Devices are available that silently record the after-hours use of company equipment often involved in espionage, such as telephones and computer terminals.

In general, covert collection is accomplished by investigators rather than research personnel due to the risks. But it is not unusual for a research analyst to brief or debrief an undercover agent or double agent or to suggest the use of covert collection devices.

LINKAGES

Industrial espionage agents fall into patterns of association and conspiratorial activities. This is a result of many things, including shared training, mutual experience, similar interests, and available technology. Agents and their masters link up with each other and others for practical considerations. Research activity seeks to establish these linkages to uncover the extent of industrial espionage and locate all of the players. Research activity seeks to establish linkages as an aid to planning future investigation. As information is gathered, the understandings of these linkages are improved.

Industrial espionage is used by many groups, each for its own reasons. Despite possible future cooperation between groups, it is necessary to establish the identity of each group and its membership at the outset. The main groups to consider are competitors, hostile governments, terrorists, and organized crime.

Each suspect group should be broken down by prominent participants and by incident (suspected or actual espionage operation). Biographical information on the prominent participants should be compiled. Link analysis is used to connect individuals or groups. Circles represent people or organizations; lines show their relationships to each other.

In Figure 8-2, we can see that the key people are represented by the numerals 1 and 2; they have the greatest number of regular intergroup contacts. The information that allowed the construction of this figure will come from the development background files. These individuals may be part of other groups. For instance, individual 2 may be a suspected foreign agent, 3 may have organized crime connections, 7 may be a former employee now working for a competitor, and the other numerals could represent our own research employees. This initial diagramming will aid the establishment of direction criteria for the investigative effort.

Incidents can be linked in similar fashion. The goal is to link individuals to incidents, especially those espionage incidents that involve some of the same people. The link diagram may reveal who is

Figure 8-2. Organizational linkage (individuals suspected as espionage associates)

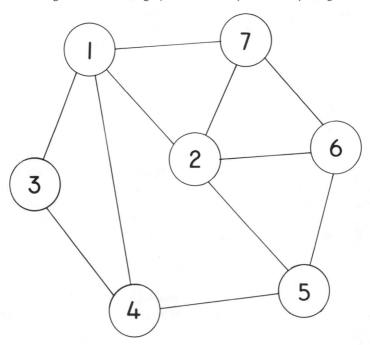

likely to participate in a joint industrial espionage venture and the types of penetration likely to be attempted.

Research has revealed links between terrorism and organized crime. Corporations have been subject to organized crime assaults as well as terrorist attacks. Government agencies have hired criminals and terrorists for specific operations. Corporations have used the services of highly suspect experts with extensive criminal backgrounds. These past associations show that the users of industrial espionage may cooperate in any number of complex arrangements. Counterintelligence cannot be termed successful until the linkages among potential enemies have been explored.

Behavior patterns, operational patterns, time patterns, and choice of targets are another research challenge. These patterns, common in industrial espionage as in other crimes, represent more than the weakness of human nature. Language fluency may limit some espionage agents. Others may favor the use of electronic eavesdropping based on skills. Certain terrorist groups strike only where a certain type of target is available. The list of patterns may include time of day typically chosen for espionage penetration. Tools used, age groupings of cooperating espionage agents, type of vehicles preferred, and choice of disguises or false identities involve patterns that may be established through research.

One method used to examine patterns is extraction of detail from case studies, incident reports, eyewitness accounts, and other data. This detail can be graphically displayed as a means of showing patterns of behavior favored by espionage agents and/or their masters.

Figure 8-3 illustrates that the suspects under scrutiny favor certain time periods for their activity based on case histories of past espionage. Therefore counterintelligence investigation efforts should focus on the peak times developed through the analysis.

Figure 8-4 indicates the false identities preferred by espionage agents over the years. If other information suggests concentration on one type of espionage, appropriate instructions can be given to employees responsible for access control. If the false identity is commonly employed in social or conference situations, sensitive employees should receive special preconference briefings regarding the research performed to locate these patterns. Concentration of counterintelligence resources is aided by what the preliminary patterns reveal.

SIMULATIONS

A simulation is a type of game. The more the simulation reflects actual conditions or events, the better it serves as a research or training

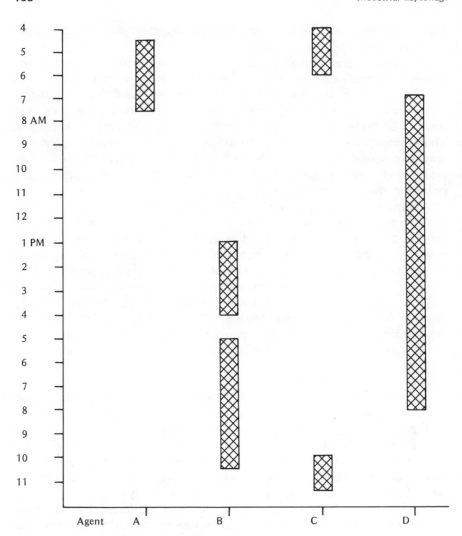

Figure 8-3. Time-of-day espionage pattern

tool. Preparation for an industrial espionage simulation must be detailed. All facts gathered through a search of sources, liaison, debriefings, and linkage and pattern analysis are combined in a simulation to create a realistic industrial espionage scenario.

The simulation exercise may be carried out in several ways. One is role playing; employees are assigned to parts, much as in a play. Characters in one type of scenario might include managers, security personnel, receptionists, executive secretaries, and espionage agents

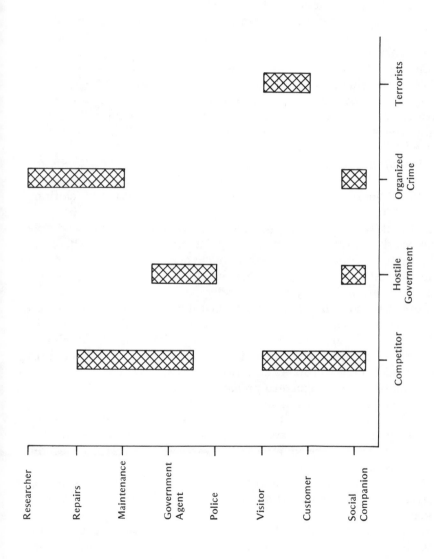

Figure 8-4. False identity espionage pattern

and their dupes. This simulation would address penetration during working hours at corporate headquarters. Another simulation would include the employee-victim, several representatives of a competitor, a bartender, a waitress, and a prostitute. Such an exercise would address the espionage hazards of convention situations.

Closed-circuit television cameras and video recorders make excellent tools for a simulation exercise. The tapes can be played back and reviewed.

Simulation exercises need not be limited to lower-level personnel. A boardroom simulation can be helpful to counterintelligence by creating managerial awareness. A scenario for these players would involve reaction to a particular industrial espionage threat. Another scenario for executives might involve costing an apparent industrial espionage loss of proprietary data.

Simulations, unlike plays, do not provide a complete script for the players. Certain information must be introduced, but players' reactions should be spontaneous in character. Props and clothing should be supplied.

Conflicts are important to the success of any scenario. People seldom work together smoothly during a crisis situation. There are usually opposing points of view strongly advocated. A majority opinion is fine, but at least one of the players should be primed to disturb any simple solution by playing devil's advocate or spoiler.

Both written and verbal communications are part of the action in a successful scenario. Verbal communications will be limited to the players. Written communications can be used by both players and scenario master. The scenario master should be prepared to introduce additional factors if the action seems to bog down.

Simulations are designed to prepare employees for actual espionage attempts. Their participation in the simulation provides them experience in dealing with such attempts. These exercises, widely used by the military, the research community, terrorism trainers, and assessment centers, have proved effective. Research activity provides the basis for simulation design.

Because scenarios require extensive preparation and time for all participants, the camera person, and the scenario master, they cannot take place frequently.

Experience suggests that participants discuss the scenario with others, thereby widening the circle of influence. Key personnel should participate in at least one industrial espionage seminar as a victim. If they participate twice, they should play an espionage agent the second time.

Following each simulation, all participants should attend what is in effect a debriefing session. The principal actors will be asked to explain their thought processes and emotional levels during the exercise. Others will want to ask questions out of curiosity or for the purpose of clarification. The scenario master should lead the discussion so that main points receive discussion. The videotape can be used to settle disagreements among the participants. It should be reviewed later by management personnel.

DATA BASE

Establishment

There is a shocking lack of information available about industrial espionage and foreign technology transfer, and much of the information that is available is not current. There is no central clearinghouse on counterintelligence measures. Therefore each corporation must assemble its own data base on industrial espionage that will allow for intelligent counterintelligence resource allocation and provide a rationale for action.

A data base is more than a drawer full of newspaper clippings or an overstuffed file cabinet. The true data base will have all information integrated, cross-indexed, and otherwise collated for reference purposes. The procedures for the data base must be established at the beginning of a counterintelligence effort. Delays here will result in confusion later.

A long-standing problem with information collection is what do you do with the data. Collection of data is far easier than its processing.

Each organization has resource limitations. Concerns for security affect the establishment of a data base and impose limitations of another kind. The analytical abilities of counterintelligence personnel further influence data base design. Management policy must always be considered, of course. Time is another crucial factor.

Trusted employees from other departments, suitably cleared, may be available to assist. Their research experience and data-processing experience represent an invaluable counterintelligence resource. It is best to recruit managers for this type of cooperation rather than use line employees.

In order to understand the function of a counterintelligence data base, we refer again to the EEI (essential elements of intelligence) concept for handling data: direction, collection, interpretation, evaluation, collation, analysis, and reporting (dissemination).

Direction, specifying what information to seek, precedes any other activity. It means deciding whether to watch the back door or the front door on a surveillance. It means establishing a line of questioning for interview purposes. It means giving the proper key words to a clipping service. Through direction, counterintelligence personnel focus their attention to satisfy management goals. Counterintelligence personnel perform collection in a wide variety of ways: surveillance, interviews, photography, and document searches, among others.

Collection and evaluation are the only investigative phases of counterespionage. All other EEIs focus on research. The data base is the basic resource for research, much as the college library serves as a resource for students preparing for examination or writing papers.

Interpretation is necessary when information collected is in a foreign language, encrypted, or in jargon. Mistakes in interpretation can be dangerous, if sometimes amusing. Some years ago, a researcher in an intelligence library, scanning the card catalog, noticed a card under the heading "Pullman Cars." The report listed had the title "200,000 Sleepers in . . ." When pulled, the report was found to deal with railway cross-ties, what the British call sleepers. This was an obvious error. That error concerned interpretation.

Evaluation means a method of rating both the source of information and the information itself. Because there are sure to be conflicts in information gathered, it is necessary to develop qualitative criteria for all reports filed in the data base.

As an example, consider the following reports that arrived within hours of each other. The first report alleged an espionage penetration would take place at midnight tomorrow at the Houston, Texas, facility. The second report claimed with equal urgency that the penetration would take place the same time and date at the Paris, France, subsidiary. Among the obvious problems of that example is the fact that no one—not even the counterintelligence staff—can be at the same place at the same time.

Normally all information collected receives two evaluations by the investigator preparing a report. These evaluations are alphabetic and numeric. The letter A usually stands for the most reliable source; the number 1 stands for confirmed information. Following is an evaluation scheme for corporate counterintelligence:

A: Reliable source	1: Confirmed information
B: Usually reliable source	2: Probably true
C: Sometimes reliable source	3: Possibly true
D: Questionable source	4: Questionable information
E: Source of unknown reliability	5: No way to confirm information
F: Unreliable source	6: False information

Even reliable sources may sometimes furnish false information, and sources labeled unreliable in the past may furnish an important truth. For those reasons, both types of evaluation need to be applied to all information gathered. This system is subjective rather than objective. Chaos will result if each investigator has a different definition or interpretation of the ratings. Research activity must establish the definitions. Definitions must be passed on in detailed briefing sessions where questions may be freely answered.

Research personnel must reevaluate material during the analysis stage. Counterintelligence experts trust their acquired knowledge about the credibility of the source of the information and also trust analytical abilities to judge the worth of the information itself. Unfortunately for any systematic approach to evaluation, the letters and numbers are too often assigned intuitively rather than by scientific criteria, probably because previous evaluations often are unreliable in judging new data.

Collation is an effort to assemble complementary information. Keeping in mind the old axiom that the whole is more than the sum of the parts, collation becomes an attempt to link up all of the counterintelligence information that bears on a particular espionage problem. These related data include the product of source exploitation and liaison. If, as in the railway sleeper example, a mistake has been made in interpretation, the research activity is likely to overlook important information. Failures in the collection effort mean that relevant information will be unavailable.

Analysis is the most important part of the research process. Faced with a bag of jigsaw puzzle pieces, usually with one or more key pieces absent, the analyst must conclude what the puzzle would show if all pieces were available and properly identified. Analysis involves a lot of inspired guesswork, as well as scientific study. It is little wonder then that counterintelligence research personnel make mistakes!

Reporting, or dissemination, of counterintelligence research activity is the final EEI. Finished counterintelligence may be disseminated in verbal or written form. The danger is that the information will arrive too late or go to the wrong individuals. Either error will render the research activity useless. Reporting may involve the greatest danger in any counterintelligence research effort. A report containing gross error tears down the credibility of the counterintelligence operation. A report that reaches espionage agents does great harm since those agents will know the conclusions drawn by corporate counterintelligence.

Clearly the production of counterintelligence is weighted toward research activity, something far more complex than investigation. Both are needed. Therefore counterintelligence can be described as a combined research-investigation activity.

The establishment of the data base must include strict guidelines in written form for all EEI activity. Supervision is necessary to ensure that guidelines are followed routinely. Individuals can be checked out in the instructions through the use of practice problems.

The storage of information is both a security and a research problem. All information should be housed so as to minimize fire and intrusion threats. The data must be readily accessible to the counter-intelligence team. If data are computerized, the access will be controlled by software. The danger of computer storage is that information cannot be seen. If data have been incorrectly entered in the computer, they may never be found again.

The cataloging effort is vital to easy retrieval of information. Those who prepare catalog cards or encode information for computer storage must understand the needs of counterintelligence. They must be familiar with espionage methods as well as terminology. For this reason counterintelligence personnel are recommended for the catalog-ing of information.

Computers

Computers will never replace human analysis or human intuition; they can assist in the storage and retrieval of information, however. They must be used for counterintelligence research activity.

Computers also present some problems. They will not do the work of the counterintelligence team. They can break down at awkward times. And they have been described as a huge safe with no doors. For this reason, sensitive data must be kept separate from other data storage. Counterintelligence programs must be run only at special times by cleared personnel. Counterintelligence data should never go into the general corporate data base.

JUDGING THE RESEARCH EFFORT

Evaluation is a final procedure common to all research activity—scholarly, technical, or scientific. Too often, research in the criminal justice and other social science fields has been unchallenged through proper evaluation. Only by evaluation can we judge successes and failures.

Evaluation procedures should be set up prior to the actual research or investigation. Four steps require implementation: goal setting, monitoring, arbitration of efforts, and final outcome.

Goal setting involves management policy. This policy determines the counterintelligence thrust. Upper management may desire only a general appreciation of the espionage danger. Alternatively, it may be policy to identify those organizations and individuals likely to attempt industrial espionage. A further management choice leads to uncovering the intentions of those identified as threats. Finally, management may wish counterintelligence to secure evidence that will result in the apprehension and prosecution of espionage agents, their masters, and backers. Goals must be clearly set forth prior to investigative activity, and time allowances must be given.

Monitoring of the research or investigation requires criteria. What is expected in the way of progress daily, weekly, monthly, annually? Those who act as monitors must understand the nature of research. Unless all parties clearly understand the criteria, there are sure to be accusations of inefficiency or unfair requirements. Neither research nor investigation is to be judged as a production-line activity.

Arbitration of efforts should be done by both management and the counterintelligence staff. Each will view the achievements differently according to their perspectives. Each must appreciate the other's evaluation. Arbitration, then, is a joint management-counterintelligence effort. Total agreement may be lacking, but each side is sure to gain a higher appreciation of the other's position.

Final outcome is different from arbitration of efforts. The counterintelligence effort may be judged as poor, but espionage may have been prevented through a combination of fortunate circumstances. Efforts may have been superior, yet an espionage penetration can take place through unfortunate circumstances. The final outcome may be the reason for rejoicing or not. Who judges final outcome? The corporate balance sheet will show losses due to successful espionage. Success seldom has a similar flag to recognize.

SELECTION OF RESEARCH PERSONNEL

Counterintelligence researchers must be able to understand the various data collected. A good analytical mind is necessary since analysis is the crucial research step.

The research staff is basically a group of independent scholars, each working on his or her own projects and sometimes helping others. Researchers must enjoy unsupervised activity and be highly self-motivated to meet deadlines that frequently are moved up due to counterintelligence emergencies. They must be able to organize their work in order to locate data quickly. Researchers must be able to get along well with people they meet through liaison. Investigators must be pampered and appreciated during infrequent contacts with research personnel.

Researchers must be realists. Collection requirements may require field agents to expose their cover stories and, perhaps, their special sources, and the physical well-being of all concerned. An unrealistic collection instrument will draw scorn from field agents, who will be less likely to produce well for the researcher. Field agents are highly suspicious of headquarters personnel. Researchers must be careful not to judge investigators' results too harshly; they must be patient in the face of difficulties experienced by field agents.

Finally, anyone entering counterintelligence research needs a small ego or one easily satisfied. Few will see the results of their work. There will be little praise. The main benefit is pride in a job well done.

SUMMARY

Research activity does not receive much publicity, but it is vital to the counterintelligence mission. Beginning before initial direction of investigation and extending to evaluation of the final report and results of counterintelligence, the contributions of researchers are necessary. There are six categories in the initial research step, a survey of corporate weaknesses to industrial espionage.

Formats for collection instruments are designed by research personnel in the direction phase of counterintelligence. They are based on the initial survey. These formats may be general or specific.

Liaison is another research task. Both public and private sector sources must be developed. These include various federal, state, and local agencies, as well as commerical-sector business and industry. Liaison is a two-way sharing of information to reduce the espionage risk.

Briefings and debriefings are often conducted or planned by research personnel. Briefings involve explaining research needs and ensuring that these are understood by investigators and others. Debriefings are interviews designed to extract valuable information that has gone unreported.

Open sources represent one resource for research personnel. The exploitation of open sources is neither illegal nor unethical. Covert sources represent another resource for research. Some covert sources are lawful; others are not.

Special techniques such as link analysis can benefit preliminary research. This type of charting provides graphic illustration of how people or espionage events are connected. Background files supply the information used to make these charts. Time of day of previous espionage attacks and false identity patterns may be charted too.

Simulations are popular methods for both training and research purposes. These exercises represent an action or discussion play that involves various corporate personnel in role-playing situations. Counterintelligence researchers must design the espionage simulations so that they reflect reality as closely as possible. Simulations can be used to prepare individuals for espionage situations they may encounter.

Industrial espionage information must be brought together for research into a data bank. It will be used for many purposes, including providing a rationale for counterintelligence actions. Corporate information-processing facilities, under security guidelines, can be of great assistance in establishing the data base and designing programs to make use of the stored data. The essential elements of intelligence (EEIs) outline the process for using a data base. They are direction, collection, interpretation, evaluation, collation, analysis, and report writing and dissemination.

Evaluation takes place during and following each counterintelligence project. All research must have an evaluation component. Procedures for evaluation should be installed prior to counterintelligence investigation. These include goal setting, monitoring, arbitration of effort, and final outcome.

Research personnel must have a number of qualities. These include intelligence, analytical ability, love of research, self-motivation, ability to relate to others, and no desire for public recognition. Realism may be the most important quality for counterintelligence research personnel.

III. REFINING COUNTER-INTELLIGENCE DATA

9. Preliminary Analysis

Every fact that is learned becomes a key to other facts—E.L. Youmans

All collected information needs analysis in order to achieve refinement leading toward the production of pure intelligence. Intelligence data helps corporate decision makers avoid some of the undesirable functions of ignorance; the major drawback of ignorance being error. Counterintelligence errors lead to the compromise of trade secrets and proprietary information, the possible loss of business control, and loss of human lives.

Preliminary analysis has many parallels in ordinary life. Indeed, it would be foolish to urge theoretical solutions when commonsense answers exist. No fancy model equals the object or process of preliminary analysis. It can be considered similar to refining gold, up to the point that metal reaches the jewelers, who later produce works of art from natural purity. Finished intelligence is a work of art.

We hear many words in our daily activities. Some of these words we understand immediately as they are meant to be understood. At other times we are not sure of the meaning and ask for clarification. Foreign phrases and technical terms are typical of utterances requiring interpretation. Hours after we have heard a comment, we may suddenly understand what was meant. Similarly, counterintelligence analysts must study all facts and discover their true meaning, just as if they had been encoded or encyphered. In fact, they may have been if the espionage agents are professional.

Another element of daily thought is the selective discarding of the irrelevant. An employer gives various instructions to a group of employees. We remember our own assignment but do not struggle to retain instructions given to others. Similarly, we turn around after hearing "Hey, you!" On noticing the call is for someone else, we forget about it. There are far more data available than anyone or any group can assimilate.

As rational beings, we try to evaluate carefully all information presented. If we did not, confusion would be constant since much information serves to contradict other data. For instance, on an average evening of television there may be four competing beer commercials and three competing feminine hygiene announcements and each network insists that its evening programs are superior to competitors' offerings. The source of all data must be evaluated as well as the information itself.

Cataloging is a library process that has a great effect on the retrievability of information. Mistakes in cataloging can bury valuable information forever. A cataloger examines incoming material deemed important and breaks it down by subject and topic headings. Unless the analyst is familiar with the headings chosen, it is unlikely that files will be of real assistance. In our daily lives we suffer from the mistakes of improper cataloging or the failure to be in tune with the catalog system in use.

Collation is the term for integrating relevant data that bear on a problem. There are many examples of collation in other pursuits. For example, we collate equipment and clothing for a camping trip. If collation has been unsuccessful, we have forgotten something. A handyman knows that a project is much easier if the necessary tools and materials are gathered before commencing the project. Students preparing papers, and businessmen preparing reports, need to gather all relevant facts, in one place, before putting pen to paper.

Every cook and every handyman has realized at some point in the project at hand that a tool, material, or ingredient was lacking. A similar void noticed during the analysis phase of counterintelligence is called a data gap. When a data gap has been encountered, the analysis must stop until the missing data have been secured. The identification of data gaps during preliminary analysis is common.

Selective updating is the correcting of out-of-date facts. Daily weather reports are excellent examples of the selective update process. Counterintelligence researchers must also recognize when information has become out of date. Updating is a re-collection effort designed to verify the correctness of available information or to provide newer and better data.

INTERPRETATION OF DATA

Data interpretation is the first step in any preliminary analysis. Counterintelligence personnel cannot proceed rationally if data interpretation is delayed or ignored. Imagine the chaos resulting from an offensive player's misinterpretation of the football quarterback's play call. Most of us have seen incredible mixups from interpretative errors during Monday, Thursday, or Sunday professional football games.

Interpretation is the key to understanding the actions of an espionage suspect. Much time can be saved by prompt interpretation of a suspect's activities. For example, the counterintelligence surveillance team follows one suspect to a lonely, after-dark meeting. A gentleman who speaks English with a foreign accent meets the suspect. On the surface that looks suspicious and warrants further resource allocation to monitor this suspect's future activities. But wait. Interpretation has shown us that the gentleman with a foreign accent is the pastor of the subject's church. They met under a sign announcing the construction of a church-sponsored retirement home. The suspect has volunteered to donate his time and skills in the land-clearing phase of construction. The lonely meeting was merely a discussion about which trees to save and which to cut down. The apparently sinister has become, through the process of interpretation, an innocent act. Such situations are likely to arise regarding partially overheard conversations too. The first step in preliminary analysis must always be interpretation.

Meaning is the most important benefit of the interpretative process. Language, for example, requires interpretation even if the words are spoken in the listener's native tongue. No one has a complete vocabulary. Any listener to commentator William F. Buckley finds an occasional need for a good dictionary. Slang represents a challenge to interpretation. Each generation has its own catchwords. Each region of the country employs slang expressions not heard or understood elsewhere. Every occupational group develops its own jargon. Computer specialists delight in mystifying outsiders. First- and sometimes later-generation Americans (the Cajuns in Louisiana are a prime example) mix foreign words and phrases with English in their conversations. Ethnic minorities have their own slang. In addition to defining words, it is necessary to interpret the shades of meaning implied. The speaker may have been earnest, sarcastic, cynical, joking, or simply telling a story to create an effect. Tone of voice and body language are helpful signs in interpreting the spoken word. The written word offers less in the way of interpretative opportunity. Some people have a tendency to exaggerate, which must be taken into account. Others are prone to understatement.

Situational meaning is a matter for interpretation. The time of a meeting or other contact by a suspect is suggestive. Other parties to these contacts affect interpretation. Physical environments must be considered as well. Espionage agents do not meet their controllers exclusively in lonely places. In fact, crowded environments often are better for passing purloined data from one agent to another. A suspect who normally favors crowds looks out of place in deserted spots. The normally reclusive individual raises suspicion when he or she suddenly visits a heavily peopled area.

Actions as well as words require interpretation. Erratic actions such as apparently aimless driving or unusual patterns of activity must be interpreted. The suspect may break routine because of some personal problem. If this is so, the actions must be interpreted differently than in the case of erratic activity designed to flush out or avoid surveillance efforts by counterintelligence personnel.

Proper interpretation is assisted by completion in data collection. Photographs, diagrams, the comments of witnesses or bystanders, and many other details assist researchers attempting to interpret data collected on an espionage suspect. Resource allocation greatly influences the ability to interpret materials collected by investigative personnel. For example, analysis of a suspect's background should uncover linguistic abilities that could require a specialist's skills for interpretation. These specialists should be located at the onset of the field investigation due to the need for timely interpretation. Cult groups, fraternal associations, clubs, social organizations, and sports clubs may be involved in the suspect's activities. A knowledgeable individual who can interpret the actions and language typical to the environment must be located early to assist the counterintelligence interpretation effort.

Statisticians and computer programmers are able to process large amounts of data and draw interpretive influences. These specialists should be considered vital components of the analysis team. They need to be included early so that preparations for statistical analysis and computer processing of data will not be delayed.

Psychologists and psychiatrists can aid in interpreting a suspect's words and actions. Handwriting analysts can report the suspect's present stress patterns and, if given handwriting samples prepared at different times, will uncover changes affecting the individual's character.

The voice of a suspect, if opportunity exists to record it legally and note the circumstances of the conversation, can be processed by the operator of a psychological stress evaluator (PSE) to reveal patterns of stress that include efforts at deception.

These examples represent only a fraction of the resources that exist to make interpretation easier. Depending on in-house specialists available, the number of outsiders hired to assist analysis may be minimal or high in number.

The use of outsiders brings us to the next issue in interpretation of data: secrecy. Researchers, often involved in liaison with others, including opposites in other companies and interpretative specialists, must safeguard their raw data, especially when processing information from counterintelligence undercover personnel and their informants. Raw data frequently contain identifiers that could jeopardize the lives of individuals cooperating in the counterintelligence field effort. As the analysis process reaches later stages, it will be harder to pinpoint the source of information due to rewriting of the data as they are integrated with other materials. Researchers should never divulge information to those not previously cleared by the counterintelligence security office. This prohibition is often difficult to follow when time-liness, our next topic, is discussed. Improper haste jeopardizes the lives of field personnel as well as the mission.

Good timing or timeliness is vital to successful interpretation during the preliminary analysis of counterintelligence. Delays in inter-pretation allow mistakes, such as continuing to follow the wrong suspect or persisting in an investigation when counterintelligence resources could be spent elsewhere. Similarly, delay may allow a true suspect to commit an espionage act that could have been prevented by timely interpretation.

Conflicts in interpretation are frequent. Witness the common arguments that begin with: "You said that! No, I didn't!" Therefore the analysis phase must take potential disagreements into consideration before the influx of data begins. The best way to solve disagreements is to put final trust in one person whom we will call the research analyst. Only the research analyst will possess or have access to all information that bears on the interpretation of collected data on espionage suspects.

Some recommend a system of interpretation, perhaps passing collected data through several people for their comments or using the computer to identify significant details that refer to information already stored in the data base, using a special software program.

Early mistakes in analysis, like early mistakes in any other activity, wrench the research process out of perspective and interfere with the counterintelligence mission. All interpretation effort requires the best care that resources can afford.

PURGING IRRELEVANT INFORMATION

One of the greatest problems in our informational age is the surplus of information. Each of us is subject to a constant media barrage through television and junk mail offerings. That barrage of commercial data is augmented by memoranda and announcements at lunch, as well as conversations with associates directly, by letter, teletype, and telephone. Most of us receive professional journals as the result of membership benefits. Additional, general purpose and specific purpose periodicals find their way into our offices, our homes, our airplane seat pockets, and our hotel and convention center rooms. Thousands of new and potentially useful books are published annually in many different countries and languages. There are newsletters, special-interest media programs, newspapers, and news programs.

Counterintelligence field agents can gather volumes of information, much of which on close inspection proves to be irrelevant. There will be pages of daily reports, weekly summaries, special reports, and monthly and annual reports from field agents. Supplements to the reports include tape recordings, photographs, drawings, and maps. Debriefing sessions and liaison meetings produce still more data that must be stored, guarded, and subjected to analysis with the hope that more grain than chaff exists.

Anyone who has served as an intelligence analyst knows that the easiest way to measure data flow is by the yard, meter, pound, or kilogram. It never stops as long as the counterintelligence unit is operating. The multiplier effect is astonishing. The average agent can collect enough information to keep several analysts busy, considering the analysts' liaison and open source acquisitions that must be processed, also. Dangers of overabundance of data include confusion, space problems, difficulty in locating specific information, and unnecessary resource allocation for processing, filing, and guarding information, much of which will prove unnecessary in the end.

Just as dams allow some water to flow while keeping the bulk of it blocked, research personnel need to establish strong criteria for managing information, beginning with the direction phase. This will not be enough to purge irrelevant data as time goes on. Additional effort is necessary to control the extent of information presented. Field personnel must be constantly reminded to exercise restraint and to practice good judgment in their collection activities. Agents who persist in padding reports with data that do not bear on the counterintelligence mission should be dismissed. Also, excessive irrelevant data may be a sign that the field agent is faking activities.

Danger signals from too much information are easy to recognize. Analysts' in-boxes never empty; desk and cabinet space needs increase although no new research personnel are employed. The computer department mentions that your data base storage capacity is being eroded at an abnormal rate (as researchers literally dump information into the data base to get if off their desks). Overtime increases. Research reports may be delayed, despite a full personnel complement. The good counterintelligence administrator takes note of trends in this area in order to purge irrelevant data from the research department.

Confusion results from the inability to make decisions. Analysts may be afraid to discard irrelevant data that they think could be needed later for some unspecified purpose. A keyword system is helpful in this respect. Each analyst should take a turn at a brief review of incoming materials searching for keywords. If such a word is located, the report is directed to a particular analyst's desk. Documents that fail to show keywords are placed aside. Administrators should note the source of the irrelevant materials and keep a log of the discards for future action should the number become excessive.

Desk analysts must keep a similar log since the presence of key words is not a guarantee of quality information. The field agent may sprinkle key words in otherwise worthless material. The counter-intelligence administrator should regularly confer with analysts and check their score cards for problem agents.

Contradictory information is another irrelevant-data problem. Unfortunately, the analysis process must proceed to the next stage, evaluation, before contradictions can be dealt with by the analyst. Contradictions are not necessarily undesirable or without benefit, however. Take the case of the persistent disagreements on the reported activities of a top executive who often took sensitive information home in his large briefcase. The leather briefcase bulged at the seams on his way out at night but appeared almost empty the next morning when he entered the facility. One counterintelligence agent reported that the vice-president was evidencing signs of instability and had secretly booked a quick weekend trip to Belgium. A second source disagreed. This agent reported that the vice-president was continuing to act as the faithful but somewhat eccentric employee who took weekend trips as his sole source of vacation.

Further investigation was necessary. In this case, the executive was determined to be a compulsive thief of office supplies rather than secrets. His trip to Belgium was legitimate enough but for the purpose of bizarre sexual activity. He was granted sick leave and institutionalized for a brief period to relieve his tension and end the compulsive thefts.

Irrelevant data also must be purged for legal reasons. Privacy is an important right in a democratic society, and indiscriminate record keeping can damage privacy rights. As soon as collected data are judged useless, this information should be destroyed.

Irrelevant data will always be collected through error or misdirection. These mistakes are compounded if the data are allowed to accumulate. Civil liability is a potent threat to all loss-control efforts, including counterintelligence. The accumulation of irrelevant data on individuals signifies that counterintelligence has become in fact an espionage unit. Wrongful intrusions into an innocent individual's privacy can cost the corporation heavily. The danger of irrelevant data accumulation extends into the labor relations arena. The National Labor Relations Act forbids employers from spying on union activities.

Fire loading is another reason to purge irrelevant data. The accumulation of files makes any structure more vulnerable to fire. Research analysts who surround themselves with paperstuffed file cabinets and overloaded desks are contributing to fire hazard. Irrelevant data accumulation increases the combustion danger to the important information filed side by side with the irrelevant.

The recognition and disposition of unnecessary data should precede the analysis phase. All discarded data must be destroyed in a secure fashion so that it cannot be recovered and used by others. Shredding, pulverizing, or burning currently are the best document-destruction methods. Computer-stored data normally are erased so as to reuse the storage medium.

Inventory of files is a tedious and time-consuming task, but inventories are the only method by which irrelevant data can be purged. Counterintelligence management needs to set schedules for inventories and to supervise the task. Analysts and their supervisors should jointly examine the inventory results in any effort to reduce the volume of stored data.

EVALUATION

More controversy is inherent in the evaluation process than in any other stage of analysis, primarily because of the subjective nature of the evaluation. Few people see the worth of a source or the information itself in quite the same way. Additional complications result from security precautions that strip a report of identifying data that might help to shape a decision on reliability. Conflicting reports are common too. A known lack of consistency makes the evaluation process chance at best.

The analytical process requires evaluation of two factors pertinent to each report presented: the source of the information and the information itself.

The source affects any report's credibility. Most of us hesitate to believe anything from certain sources (such as the communist press), but give unhesitating credence to even bizarre statements by trusted sources. But we cannot expect any one source to be always right or always wrong. That applies to governments, the media, hostile elements, liaison sources, coworkers, friends, loved ones, and, more importantly, counterintelligence field agents. These agents may be fooled despite their intentions to be objective.

The further the analyst is separated from the source of any data, the harder it is to make an evaluative judgment. A field person's judgment, like that of a referee or umpire, must be accepted most of the time even if misgivings are present.

An arbitrary six-point system can be used to evaluate any type of report. The scheme reported in Chapter 8 using alphabetic and numeric ratings indicating reliability of source and whether information is confirmed is useful in this regard.

A source may be an individual, such as one's own agent, an informant, or another person. There are printed sources, which may or may not indicate the author. A friendly public agency may represent itself as the source of espionage information. Many times, however, the true source is obscured as the data pass from hand to hand. At other times the source is direct, such as when a counterintelligence agent sees something and reports it. The source may be simply an anonymous letter or telephone call.

The third-agency rule, common in the international intelligence community, often serves to mask a source. This general rule is designed to protect sources from the danger of exposed identity. One agency cannot pass along information it has been given by a second agency unless the identity of the original source has been deleted. The third-agency rule makes it virtually impossible to assess the reliability of the original source.

Information contained in a report may be so fresh or so novel that there is no way to judge its reliability. Yet such information can be the most critical to preventing an espionage act. For example, an uncorroborated report may claim that there is an espionage agent in the corporate research division. Do we take it seriously, despite a lack of information, or disregard it until further data are available? Another problem affecting information is vagueness. Suppose the previous report had insisted instead that one of approximately 100,000 corporate employees is a spy. That information may be true, but it is hardly useful. Another problem concerns the category of previously confirmed information. If we know the information already, it does little good to receive confirmation. Counterintelligence needs to move at an early stage in order to prevent and interdict espionage. That posture cannot afford delays that result from an overconcern for confirmation before taking action.

Trying to define the terms such as "unquestioned reliability," "previously confirmed," or "known to be false" creates more difficulty. We have polled many groups without finding general agreement on what constitutes reliability in an individual. Should "previously reliable" mean the source was right eight out of ten times on previous occasions or only six out of ten? The best baseball hitters, the most reliable at homeplate, fail to achieve a hit at least six out of ten times. They, and their fans, think four hits out of ten tries at bat (.400) makes for a fantastic batting average. Analysis needs exact definitions on the terms used.

Information itself offers difficulties as to definition. The numerical measurements for "probably true" and "possibly true" depend a great deal on the background knowledge of the evaluator. They also depend on the evaluator's intuitive abilities. Conservative and liberal attitudes naturally affect any individual's thought processes and color the final evaluation of information under consideration.

Other agencies and liaison sources may not accept the restrictions of anyone else's definitions on reliability or truth. Thus, an A-1 or B-2 evaluation (refer to the code system presented in Chapter 8) may not mean quite the same on any two documents the analyst is working on.

Documents presented to the analyst may have been evaluated previously by the collectors of the information. In this circumstance, the analysts need to consider how credible the evaluator or the agency has been in the past. No report should be taken at face value. There will often be conflicting reports with an equal or higher evaluation code. Conflicts in equally rated data are common. The next chapter examines how best to resolve such conflicts.

Former or current detectives may feel that formal evaluation of counterintelligence information is unnecessary and cumbersome. They might argue that they themselves never devised a system to evaluate street rumors or informant tips, instead relying on commonsense and experience. Unfortunately, counterintelligence, as is the case with all intelligence effort, involves too many people and too many diverse sources to make any casual evaluation effective. Espionage is a far more complex threat than burglary or crimes of passion, such as most homicides.

CATALOGING

Cataloging is usually underrated in the counterintelligence process. Yet, the analyst depends heavily on catalog information, much as the catalog shipper relies on the index, usually located in the middle of a thick volume. Thickness is a good way to view the counterintelligence library. It can also be viewed as a jungle only passable with the help of signs and guides. The signs are keywords and catalog cards. The guides are librarians.

The more detail contained in a report, the more effort is required to catalog the information for later use. The concept of later use is important to recognize. Documents are not catalogued for the pleasure of the cataloger. They are not cataloged for any purpose but later retrieval by analysts. It may be months or years before a need develops for certain stored facts. In the meantime, this information must be safeguarded in a security repository. Locating the data is possible only by reference to catalog files. There is little chance to correct catalog errors. Incorrectly cataloged data simply disappear unless stumbled upon accidentally. Keywords can serve to signal what is in the document. Names of suspects, suspicious activities, threatened secrets, background data, and the like represent the types of facts requiring special note on catalog cards or computerized retrieval systems.

Selection of counterintelligence research personnel was discussed in Chapter 8, but no previous mention has been made of the need to select catalogers or how to make such selection. The first step is to calculate the complexity of information likely to require cataloging. The more complex the data, the greater the challenge to those assigned to the catalog section. Their intelligence and education must be equal to the job. Catalogers need a taste for detail and the ability to abstract all categories of facts in the reports they will examine.

Trial runs represent a good way to test a person's cataloging ability. If possible, these results should be compared with similar exercises by experienced personnel, including other catalogers and analysts.

Breakdown of information into various categories needs guidelines from the research analysts who must later retrieve the data. Each analyst should examine standard breakdown choices for completeness. Anyone who has worked with the Library of Congress cataloging system or the Dewey Decimal System used in most libraries will recognize the disadvantages of either system or both. The research analyst cannot complain about the counterintelligence catalog system if he has been deeply involved in its creation.

Incomplete or partial cataloging is extremely dangerous to successful counterintelligence research. It can be argued that the extent of cataloging has a negative effect on the speed of the catalog effort. Pressure of information flow often suggests a short list of catalog subjects to hasten the process. This pressure should be eased by assigning extra personnel to break down incoming data for subject headings. This is especially important in conjunction with computerized storage of data. Shelved data, even improperly cataloged, may be successfully located with some effort. Information stored in computer data banks cannot be crowsed through as if it were on library shelves. This information can be found only by interrogating the data bank using key words. If these terms are incomplete, needed data will not surface for preliminary analysis.

A discussion of cataloging would be incomplete without mention of appreciation due cataloging personnel. Researchers often take their library for granted, expecting the best results as natural and undeserving of comment. Catalogers should be praised for good efforts and encouraged to broaden their general knowledge of espionage and associated subjects.

COLLATION

Collation, a process of bringing information together for the purpose of analysis, is a major step in producing intelligence. The success of collating information rests partially on the filing system adopted by the unit. This filing system will include, at the minimum, 3 × 5 inch catalog cards, an easy-reference shelf system, and a knowledgeable librarian to assist the researchers in gathering information bearing on an espionage problem. At a maximum, the file system could be totally computerized, with all data transcribed into the computer's memory bank.

Collation means more than merely assembling data in one place. The data must be separated into associative segments. Each analyst develops a preferred collation method that is used consciously or unconsciously during every project. A uniform method of association enables researchers to fill in on the projects of other when necessary. Following is one example of systematized collation:

1. Locate all storage sites where relevant data may be located.
2. Visit storage sites and retrieve data.
3. Assemble data by subject headings.
4. Subdivide data by source-evaluation code and data. (Set aside "source unknown" at this point.)
5. Further subdivide by information-evaluation code. (Set aside "cannot be confirmed" at this point.)
6. Pair conflicting reports having equal or similar evaluation codes.
7. Prepare a list of documents indicating those of a higher or lesser priority using special symbols.

The best way to visualize a collation project may be to consider an actual case history dealing with corporate counterintelligence in the 1980s. A research analyst of the XYZ Corporation was asked to prepare a report from available resources on the hiring practices of a major competitor, ABC Corporation. Specific attention was directed toward recruitment of technical personnel. The researcher began to collate available data. He divided this information into reports from open sources, XYZ counterintelligence reports, XYZ employee reports of recruitment efforts directed toward them, current executive recruiter strategy, loss of XYZ technical personnel in the past twenty-four months, and the identity of their new employers. Major research breakthroughs of the ABC Corporation in the past year was another category. These categories were evident as piles of data on the analyst's desk.

Each source pile was scanned for evaluation codes. The best and most recent were advanced to the top of each pile. "Source unknown" documents were set aside to use during analysis if necessary. "Cannot be confirmed" was treated the same way. Conflicts in reports from the same or other sources were noted, together with their date of origin and evaluation codes. Documents viewed as having more rather than lesser importance were given an asterisk on the major list of documents assembled for the project. A yellow file tag was assigned to each document seen to have major importance.

Index systems are part of all cataloging efforts. The collation process cannot be complete unless researchers thoroughly understand the index system in use by the catalog staff. There are bound to be changes in personnel assigned to cataloging and perhaps also changes in the system in use.

Counterintelligence data are unlikely to be cataloged the same way in more than one agency or corporation. The librarian is the key to unlocking the catalog system(s) used at a particular location. Even the best and most agreeable librarian cannot be expected, however, to unearth all file data that might bear on a particular research project.

Imagination is the key to successful retrieval of file data, whether shelved or stored in a computer. All catalog systems use subject headings. Imagination is necessary to select fruitful subject headings. The analyst must pit his or her mind against the mind-set of the person who originally cataloged the data.

Take the case of the young researcher in a library seeking data that concerned unusual meetings attended by XYZ personnel. The analyst came up with the following key words as subject headings:

- *Unusual*: unexplained, strange, chance, weird, unrelated, odd, novel, eccentric.
- *Meetings*: assemblies, gatherings, rendezvous, encounters, conferences, get-togethers.
- (All combinations of the above.)

Roget's Thesaurus and all other dictionaries, especially those featuring synonyms, are helpful in assembling key words. Analysts should keep a list of key words that have proved useful in the past.

Occasionally necessary files are not where they should be. A security problem may exist if they are lost. More likely, there has been an error in filing. Once information has been misplaced in a computer data bank, its recovery is all but hopeless. More conventional library systems offer hope that the information will eventually turn up. Librarians can speed this process considerably.

Good liaison is essential to collation. This includes both public and private sources who cooperate in sharing espionage information. Even willing sources must be primed with proper keywords to provide access to data sought for analysis. If possible, the analyst should have direct contact with the library or file custodian in order to explain what is sought and to answer questions the librarian will have.

The time factor is an important consideration in planning collation of materials for a research project. Ample time must be allowed. There will be multiple facilities to visit. Liaison sources take vacations and sick days. Librarians have frequent calls on their time. Desired files may have been checked out and are temporarily unavailable. Getting clearance to see certain information always takes days, if not weeks.

Each collation source should lead to others. There is no end to information storage sites. No one can locate them all. Frequently, the most up-to-date data belong to someone else. These types of data are not easy to locate without assistance. The biggest worry to all analysts is that vital information has been overlooked through haste or ignorance in collation.

IDENTIFICATION OF DATA GAPS

There will always be unanswered questions and gaps in data analysis. Some gaps result from incomplete investigation; these are dangerous and must be closed prior to final analysis and report writing. Other missing information, such as detail left off a surveillance log through carelessness, will not be obvious to the researcher studying that report. Hence the unnoticed gap is even more dangerous.

Many researchers share a problem in respect to data acquisition: they hesitate to end the collection process since fresh information may make matters clear once and for all. Of course, that rarely happens. Researchers cannot delay analysis while they seek more and more data. There comes a point when a data sufficiency must be recognized so that analysis can proceed. Timetables and deadlines are a great help in making the decision that existing data must be considered acceptable. At other times, the analyst must call on common sense in order to end the data search.

Recognition that a report is incomplete is not quite the same as spotting a data gap. An example will illustrate the difference. A surveillance log that ends at midnight is incomplete if you want to know what happened two hours later. If the surveillance log is supposed to show entries each hour but there is no entry at 11 P.M., there is a data gap. Similarly, a report of a break-in at the research facility has a data gap if there are no forensic entries. The report is incomplete if it fails to indicate the precise statements of witnesses regarding a suspect's appearance.

Analysts often recognize that information is lacking on a particular report by comparing the details with those furnished on other, similar, documents. The puzzle approach is another method of recognizing data gaps. The analyst charts the pertinent information from surveillance logs and discovers that during some critical periods, the suspect was on his or her own, not under surveillance by counterintelligence. A third way to recognize incomplete information is to measure the amount of data collected on suspect A as opposed to suspect B or suspect C. This method can be applied to locations as well as individuals.

Once gaps have been recognized, their importance to the preliminary analysis project must be estimated. No calculation can be accomplished without studying the purpose of the analysis. If a project is designed to determine whether a market researcher is an espionage agent, it may not be important that we know his college alma mater. On the other hand, if we are trying to learn if this market researcher has links with radical activists, such as terrorists, the identification of his college and years of enrollment could be crucial information.

Time and money are other factors that affect the consideration of incomplete data or data gaps. Time, like money, is not infinite. There will always be limits on counterintelligence time and money resources. Getting more information on a certain individual may be impractical given the deadline. Additional information may be too costly to process.

A research analyst unsure of the need to close a data gap should consult the unit supervisor. The analyst is unlikely to know the precise direction of the counterintelligence unit and its overriding priorities, including the allocation of investigative resources as well as time and money limitations. A number of investigative and research projects are often underway at the same time. Surveillance is particularly demanding on investigative personnel. Not only are many people and vehicles tied up during surveillance, the agents will require rest after a long surveillance. Their vehicles need more than average maintenance due to heavy and unusual use.

Each research analyst naturally believes his or her project has the highest priority. Sadly, that cannot be so. The denial of additional collection resources should not frustrate the analyst who knows further information is needed. All analysts are conversant with how to collect data. They can certainly gather overt materials by themselves. Liaison sources can assist in last-minute collection of data too. There is always the option to cultivate investigative personnel. They often feel unappreciated by researchers and will go out of their way to collect important data for friendly analysts.

It is worth remembering that all intelligence, including counterintelligence, is an attempt to see into and through the dark. For this reason there will seldom be a perfect investigation or a perfect analysis. It is a matter of doing what you can with what you have.

SELECTIVE UPDATING

Selective updating is a constant re-collection effort designed to bring counterintelligence holdings up to date. Another purpose of selective updating is the improvement of data resources that are not quite as complete as could be wished. They may have seemed adequate in the past but are not at this time.

Selective updating is a method of analysis since the analysts point out newer data needs. Analysts locate data gaps and incompleteness in file data. They are aware of research projects scheduled for the future and demand selective updating so that they will be prepared to write reports without causing a delay in the schedule. Analysts peruse great amounts of material daily so it is natural for them to notice what is out of date and desire newer information.

A pathetic case of failure of selective updating was witnessed by one of the authors. Many years ago he was called in, together with another young intelligence employee, and briefed on the embarrassment an older analyst had caused the unit. This older analyst, near retirement, had constructed a research report based on information over twenty years old and from a poor source. He had taken no steps to update the data, merely incorporating the information in an intelligence document, noting the ancient reference in a footnote. The report could not be forwarded as is. It had to be rewritten quickly. The author and his coworker were ordered to drop their own projects immediately.

Correcting old facts is a routine endeavor that benefits from a system. The system should alert research personnel that particular documents, or facts, need fresh investigation or be used to ascertain the present status and correctness of the data. A tickler system should be devised for use with the master index of reports. The master index can be coded—for example, with a color tab—that indicates the month a particular file needs to be pulled for updating.

Since the whole report may not require updating, it is necessary to design a subsystem to identify the parts that need special, periodic attention. Again, color codes can be used. Computerized files need specific retrieval programs for this purpose. The analyst must work closely with data-processing personnel if selective updating needs are to be met.

Each research analyst should be assigned to keep watch on data holdings on a particular subject. This responsibility will include ensuring that no elements of those holdings become out of date. Competitors' activities could represent one area of analyst responsibility. Because there will be a limit on how many competitors one analyst can be assigned, two analysts or more may be given specific competitors to monitor in reference to their espionage potential and/or espionage activities. Research personnel of the XYZ Corporation, the same corporation the analyst works for, need to be watched in regard to compromise attempts or weakness. Periodically it is necessary to perform update background investigations on these sensitive personnel. One analyst might monitor the dates of the most recent background investigation in order to call for additional collection in timely fashion. Another type of analyst assignment relates to liaison with public and private agencies devoted to meeting the industrial espionage–foreign technology transfer danger. This analyst would be responsible for updating liaison information by making contacts and visits to obtain updated information on a regular basis. Counterintelligence files must not become static.

One of the authors, re-reading *The Origins of Intelligence*,[1] discovered that this excellent reference work had not been checked out in over three years. No counterintelligence data should rest undisturbed for more than a few months. Active espionage suspects need daily profile and activity updates.

Regular files may be insufficient for many reasons. Anticipated research projects have been given as one cause of specific file updates. Neglect represents another reason for special updating. Often an analyst

---

[1] Francis Divornik, *The Origins of Intelligence* (New Brunswick: Rutgers University Press, 1974).

will notice that a particular subject, individual, or company poses a higher threat to the XYZ Corporation than before, reason enough for an out-of-turn update. Analysts who take over the files of others often feel certain ones have been neglected and order immediate update.

SUMMARY

Interpretation of data is the first step in preliminary analysis. Unnecessary waste of time and resources is aided by prompt interpretation. Meaning is established by correct interpretation of foreign words, technical terms, and slang. Tone of voice and body language require interpretation. Situational meaning needs definition. Actions require interpretation in relation to breaks in routine. Specialists may be needed to aid the interpretation process.

Secrecy is important to the interpretative effort. Analysts must be careful not to divulge information to those not cleared by counterintelligence.

Conflicts in interpretation are to be expected. Potential disagreements can be limited by fixing responsibility for conflict resolution on the analyst. A system of interpretation is useful.

Counterintelligence field agents can gather volumes of information, much of it useless. Research personnel (analysts) need criteria for managing information and must devise ways to reduce the collection of irrelevant data. Supervisors must look for signs of too much information. Irrelevant data must be purged from the files for many reasons, including a concern for privacy rights. The danger of fire is another reason to purge the irrelevant.

Evaluation of information offers the potential for extensive controversy because the evaluation cannot be objective. Many times it may be impossible to learn the source of a report. Conflicting reports are common.

The third-agency rule hides the identity of the original source. Information may be so fresh there is no base to use in judging reliability. Differing agencies and different analysts may use their own evaluation systems. Analysts must use their own judgment when considering the evaluations of others.

Key words, catalog cards, and librarians are the basis of the cataloging step in preliminary analysis. The analyst needs to participate in the catalog process.

Catalog personnel must be equal to the complexity of information expected. Trial runs represent a good way to test a potential cataloger.

Collation is a process of bringing information together for analysis. The filing system chosen by an agency will have a direct effect on the ease of collation. The collation process cannot be complete unless researchers understand the index system(s) used by the catalog staff. Imagination is useful in assembling possible key words that will allow essential data to be retrieved for analysis. Even willing sources must be primed with key words. Collation sources often lead to new sources. Analysts fear overlooking an important source during this process.

Identification of data gaps often signals an incomplete investigation. Missing information may not be obvious to the analyst. There is a tendency to extend the collection process overlong to fill in perceived and suspected data gaps, but there comes a point when data sufficiency must be recognized so that analysis can proceed.

Data gaps can be recognized by comparing reports, using the jigsaw approach, and comparing the amounts of information collected on various topics or subjects. Recognition of a gap must be followed by a judgment on its importance to the project at hand. Time and money constraints have a major effect on whether the gap is bridged.

Selective updating is an ongoing process done to keep counter-intelligence holdings up to date and to improve their completeness. Selective updating often follows the location of data gaps. Analysts should call for updates by anticipating research requirements as far in advance as possible. Correcting old facts is a routine endeavor that benefits from a system.

10. Producing Intelligence

An error is the more dangerous the more truth it contains.—Amiell

Finished intelligence is the final goal of the research process. That is true whether we are speaking of intelligence in the military combat zone, as practiced in the national strategic arena, or the counterintelligence efforts of the corporate world. Intelligence is created through the process of analysis.

Intelligence is an aid to decision making. Thus failures in intelligence can be costly. There is no doubt that early counterintelligence mistakes that are not rectified while producing intelligence lead to management error. There are at least four types of error that the analyst can make:

1. Espionage threat goes unrecognized.
2. Innocent people are labeled suspects.
3. Conclusions are too general for action.
4. Conclusions are erroneous, in part or in whole.

If a particular threat is not recognized, no action will be taken to reduce the threat and thereby prevent espionage. Resources of a loss-control department are always limited so they will be applied according to the best threat analysis available. When analysts fail to recognize the real threats of individuals, corporations, groups, or foreign powers, it is unlikely the threats will be monitored. Management is unlikely to approve surveillances and background investigations at random. Management depends on the reports and recommendations of analysts. Executives do not have time to go over raw information or participate in debriefings that could change their view of the intelligence conclusions.

For legal and ethical reasons, it is wrong for a corporation to assemble file information on any citizen for capricious reasons. There is also a financial reason for avoiding surveillance on the innocent: available resources in corporate counterintelligence are never going to be as adequate as those of a national intelligence agency. Time, money, and personnel restrictions forbid the waste that occurs when the wrong suspects are given the counterintelligence treatment.

Intelligence analysts often make mistakes in their conclusions, a very good reason that action decisions should be made by others. In their enthusiasm, analysts may see shadows in daylight. They can impute espionage activity where none exists. The ultimate users of the intelligence product (reports) must be alert to the possibility of error in respect to the naming of espionage suspects.

Haste, pressure, insufficient facts, and unwillingness to make a judgment are common reasons for a too general intelligence conclusion. Sometimes the jigsaw puzzle has too many pieces missing for any definite conclusion. A wishy-washy report does not assist corporate decision making. It may instead lead to a blind, intuitive conclusion on the part of management. Inconclusive reports should be rejected by the counterintelligence supervisor before they reach management.

Errors in a report may not be obvious. A report can drift from the true direction much as a sailor drifts off course if a slight compass error has been made. A mistaken logical premise or hypothesis will cause conclusions to go awry. Errors in evaluating the reports of field agents often lead to misplaced trust in one agent or source over all others. Intelligence is meant to be purified information. Information in the raw state is seldom completely true. Lies, half-truths, poor conclusions, and a host of other problems obscure the truth of raw information. Analysts, and all counterintelligence personnel who produce intelligence, must constantly address the problem of error. You can put an underwriters label on a defective electrical appliance; it is still defective. You can put "INTELLIGENCE" on the cover of a garbage report, it is still garbage. Erroneous reports can be the most dangerous errors if they lead to complacency.

This chapter considers the final steps of producing reports for management. There are many choices in analytical methods, although all ultimately are either qualitative or quantitative. Various types of intelligence reports can be produced according to the need of the decision maker. Overall, intelligence reports address the long-term (strategic) or short-term (tactical) future. Conflicts in data must be resolved before an intelligence report can be written. There are several ways to solve conflicts in reported information, though none is perfect.

All intelligence reports must have a designation that serves to limit distribution and access of the information contained in it. But too severe access control limits the utility of the report because the right persons may not be allowed to see it, and too loose access control compromises the work that went into the report. The counterintelligence supervisor can assist in determining the classification for reports produced by counterintelligence research personnel.

Analysts must help decide where to send their reports. The distribution phase is as critical as any other step in producing intelligence. There are many possible beneficiaries of intelligence information, inside and outside the corporation responsible for its production. Liaison sources and public agencies must be considered potential recipients. Various corporate departments may benefit also. However, careless distribution to someone with poor security controls is tantamount to giving intelligence away.

Periodic analysis of available data should take place whether or not management has requested advice or a report. At regular intervals, counterintelligence researchers must make preliminary judgments from their data. This preliminary analysis often uncovers espionage dangers otherwise easy to overlook. There are parallels in ordinary activity. A cook regularly tastes a dish during preparation. We know to service our vehicles at regular intervals without being told. Such routine servicing often uncovers serious problems before they cause a breakdown.

Analysis is the most important step in producing intelligence. In some ways, analysis is a lonely job because so many critical decisions must be made. The analyst does not receive much credit for his or her work since report authorship is often anonymous. Nor does the analyst have the thrill of field activity that motivates collectors of data. The reward of being correct is often withheld because the analyst may not learn how the report is used by management decision makers. Analysis is an intellectual exercise and can be enjoyed only as such. Analysts can take heart from the fact that without them "the intelligence unit is nothing but a file unit."[1]

ANALYTICAL METHODS

The basic function of all analytical techniques is to reduce accumulated data, locate significant relationships, and discover the meaning of such

---

[1] *Basic Elements of Intelligence*, rev. ed. (Washington, D.C.: LEAA, U.S. Department of Justice, 1976), p. 27.

relationships to the project at hand. For example, the analyst may be assigned to compile a report on the espionage potential of research employees at a particular facility. Data available and sure to be collected in anticipation of the assignment will be diverse and usually voluminous. They will include the results of background investigations and the personnel files of all people from the research director down to the lab technicians and janitorial employees. If maintenance or other service personnel make regular visits, background information must be available on each one. Summer employees, part-time employees, as well as regular staff members will be represented by background investigation reports and personnel files.

Surveillance reports, with hour-by-hour and minute-by-minute entries, add to the data mass. They may be supplemented with maps, drawings, pictures, and recordings. Personal observations of investigative personnel will be appended to each log of observed activities. Known associates of research employees will have been ascertained. Each of them will be represented by an individual file that contains background data. Surveillance reports may be included too. Imagine these documents multiplied by 100 individuals. It will give you some idea of the summarization duties for the analyst, regardless of analytical methods employed.

The next stage is to examine the collected data, suitably summarized, for possible indications of present or future espionage threats. The research assignment previously given concerned espionage potential. That suggests present and future threats. Ongoing espionage is certainly evidence of espionage potential. Discovery of weak or venal characters among the research and research-allied staff suggests future potential for espionage should these character flaws become predominant in determining individual actions. The analyst must consider the type of associates who interact with the potential espionage threat to determine their true allegiances. Each individual must be measured against the hypothesis that he or she is an espionage threat or tool possibly serving a hostile government, competitor, organized crime, or terrorists or a combination of these masters.

The third analytical stage, whatever analytical methods may be employed to carry it out, is justification of the conclusions that emerge from the earlier summarization and comparison stages. All conclusions must be supported by hard data, not by intuitive feelings. Unsupported conclusions are likely to be rejected, no matter how correct they are, because they could easily be erroneous and therefore harmful to an indivudual's reputation or the success of the counterintelligence unit. The type and extent of supporting data should be coordinated between the analyst assigned to make the report and his or her supervisor.

Good analysis is always systematic and thorough. There is a wide choice of specific techniques appropriate for the analyst: methodological routines in data examination such as association charting (link diagrams and the transaction matrix), flowcharts, time charts, VIA (visual investigative analysis), and PERT (program evaluation review technique) charting.

Association charting employs figures, geometric or tabular, that indicate bonds between individuals considered potential or actual espionage threats. Other uses for association charts include establishing the relationships of suspects' hobbies, sports or cultural activities, former employers' residences, and any other possible thing, place, or activity that might be shared by individuals who are subjects of the counterintelligence process. Figure 10-1 presents an example of association charting using the link method.

Figure 10-1 shows that the strongest bonds, on the basis of frequent association, extend between Joe and Nick, Joe and Sarah, and George and Sarah. Although all links could prove important, it is the strongest bond the analyst seeks to locate initially. Additional linkages may prove valuable later depending on those individuals

Figure 10-1. Link diagram

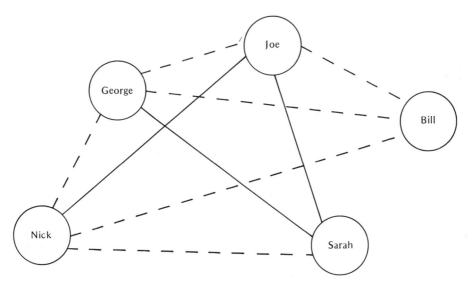

Frequent Association ————
Regular Association — — — —

deemed suspect. Should Joe be the only outsider (a man with an undefined connection to a competitor, for example), all of his contacts with the employees on the chart became meaningful. Figure 10-2 shows the titles of all people whose names appear in Figure 10-1. The link diagram assumes more importance with this added information. Based on the additional data, it is obvious that we need more information about Joe.

The transaction matrix (see Figure 10-3) is used to enumerate how many times individuals interact in a given period of time, six months in our example. Each transaction is counted separately as abstracted from field reports and other file information.

Clearly the transaction matrix goes hand-in-hand with the link diagram and gives the link diagram a solid foundation. If an undercover agent or other counterintelligence staff/member is able to judge the bonds in other ways, rather than simply counting the number of times they meet, that is acceptable too. We may say hello to an otherwise virtual stranger every day on our way to and from work. Each hello is a transaction; however, it is not a relevant or important transaction.

Figure 10-2. Expanded link diagram

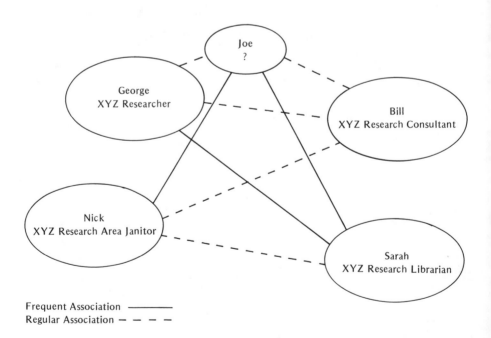

Frequent Association ─────────
Regular Association ─ ─ ─ ─

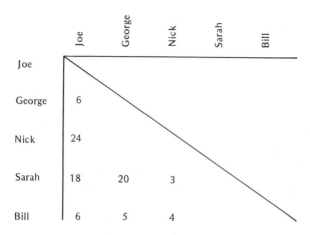

Figure 10-3. Transaction matrix

Flowcharts are diagrams that depict the way things happen. They can be used to show mechanical processes, human interaction, or any other activity. Used in counterintelligence analysis, flowcharts depict how instructions are given or how information is passed from one person to another. For our example, we will continue to use Joe, George, Nick, Sarah, and Bill, presuming them up to no good. Figure 10-4 illustrates how they might interact as an espionage network in respect to instructions and compensation.

Time charts depict when things occur, such as meetings between individuals possibly engaged in industrial espionage. Patterns determined in time charts make it easier to predict future meetings, thus allowing possible interruption or surveillance. Figure 10-5 illustrates one manner of time charting based on previously observed or reported meetings.

Examination of Figure 10-5 reveals that Joe and Sarah, and Joe and Nick meet at fixed times. The others meet at various times. Since agents tend to meet at staggered time intervals to throw off surveillance, it may be wise to rethink our hypothesis if Joe is suspected at this point as the mastermind of the espionage operation. Nick could have an innocent after-work cleaning job at Joe's apartment, or it could be a cover job allowing espionage meetings. Joe and Sarah may be lovers or simply playing the lover's game, using the evening hours as a logical meeting time based on their cover activity. Perhaps we can restore Joe to the head of the espionage operation after all.

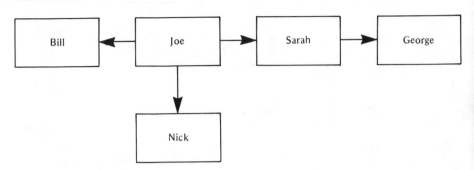

Figure 10-4. Espionage instruction-compensation flowchart

A second method of time charting depicts events. A developing series of events can suggest future activity in time to take counter-intelligence action. At the least, an event time chart presents a picture of what occurred in the proper sequence, knowledge useful in future planning against industrial espionage—foreign technology transfer. Figure 10-6 illustrates how a conspiracy developed that led to the theft of secrets by an agent of a hostile government and his dupes. Because time event charts allow considerable information to be represented on a single page, they are useful for quick presentations to management.

VIA is an offshoot of PERT. Both share the same advantage of breaking down complex activity into individual components. The advantages of separating a series of events into its components include managing a counterintelligence investigation from onset to conclusion, alerting the analyst and hence the decision makers to the preliminary phases of an espionage attempt, scripting scenarios that espionage agents could use against the corporation, and demonstrating to decision makers how espionage attacks are carried out.

PERT was developed as a business management-science tool to be used in planning. Office procedures, assembly-line operations, and distribution systems represent examples of activity often analyzed by PERT for more efficient operation. More recently, law enforcement and private security analysts have begun to use this charting in planning a complex investigative task, including counterintelligence.

The Los Angeles Police Department was the first user of VIA. This technique is a method of incident reconstruction. VIA was used to organize the large amounts of data collected following Robert Kennedy's assassination. Many police departments and intelligence units find VIA helpful in analyzing major crimes and terrorist incidents. It also can be used to reconstruct events leading to espionage. Even better,

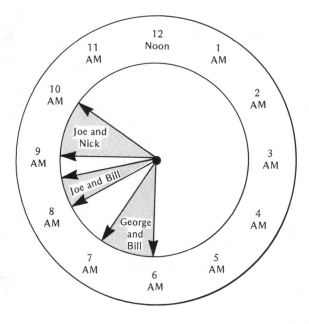

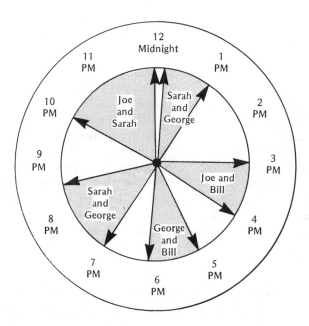

Figure 10-5. Time chart

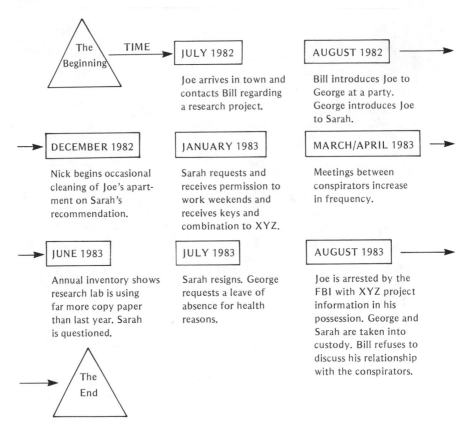

Figure 10-6. Espionage time event chart

counterintelligence analysts can use VIA to make sense of data in hand. This second use of VIA allows prediction of future events or behavior, an activity often required by decision makers.

Both PERT and VIA use the same symbols. Events are represented by circles or triangles. Triangles are used to symbolize the beginning and the end of the incident, as well as to represent particular crisis points. Lines are used to express action. Figure 10-7 is an abbreviated VIA chart of a single incident. An actual VIA chart often extends many yards, depending on how many events are depicted and how finely they are subdivided.

If further detail were required, Bill's exact driving route could be diagrammed with a circle and explanation at each turn he made. Sarah's precise movements while waiting could be represented in the same way. Later surveillance efforts are often aided by providing field agents with the results of VIA analysis because patterns of behavior are easily

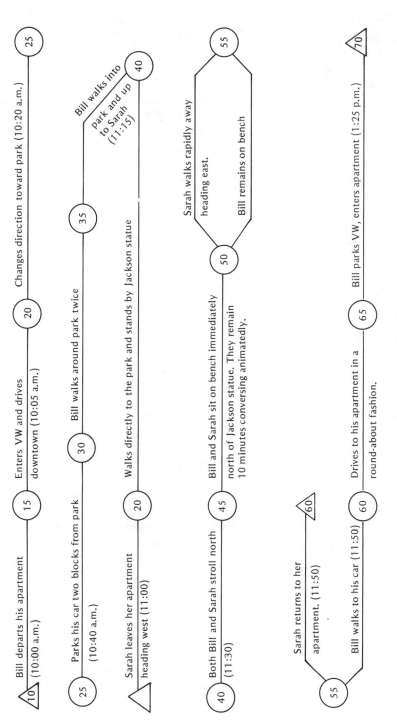

Figure 10-7. VIA Chart

recognized in this way. Even sophisticated espionage agents are likely to fall into patterns of behavior although they may be difficult to recognize at first.

Case studies are an older technique of analysis. All the social sciences, especially political science, delight in using the case study to explain how a process or event took place. A case study is simply a narrative report of something that occurred over minutes, months, or years. Essentially it is a summary highlighting the people involved, causes, and important actions. Major characters receive attention; minor participants usually are nameless. Case studies frequently are used in training classes as a method of stimulating students' interest with a real-life scenario.

Investigators frequently are trained by the case study method. They read files that contain interesting investigations. Analysts study reports of predecessors to understand their own duties. Mature counter-intelligence analysts use the case study method as a research tool, comparing previous cases with ongoing activity in the hope that a parallel will be found that will suggest events to follow. Even better, study of a case history may allow identification of espionage agents who manifest behavior patterns similar to those observed previously and reported in the case history.

Diagrammatic methods can be used to supplement and complete the case study, although that is not an essential to the construction of the study. The briefer a case history, the more likely it is to be understood by the consumers of counterintelligence analysis.

Statistical analysis methods are increasingly common in the field because of advances in computer hardware and software packages. Analysts who wish to use statistics as an aid to research are likely to request the services of a corporate statistician or work closely with the computer programming staff.

We recommend consideration of the Statistical Package for the Social Sciences (SPSS), a system of computer programs designed for use by noncomputer-trained analysts. Many computer systems can use SPSS software despite the different hardware manufacturers involved.

The SPSS allows many types of data analysis. It features both flexibility in data format and a number of statistical routines common to social science analysis. Descriptive statistics, frequency distributions, cross-tabulations, simple correlation, partial correlation, multiple regression, factor analysis, and Guttinan scaling can be provided through use of the SPSS. In addition, the data-management features enable users to modify data files. Statistical procedures such as variable transformations, recoding of variables, sampling, and selecting or weighing are easily accomplished.

The counterintelligence analyst need have no fear of the SPSS. The package was designed for people having little time to master cybernetics but desiring to use computer data handling and analysis capabilities.

The more data collected for counterintelligence, the more attractive computer processing appears. Computer processing used for research purposes is called data analysis; it is an important part of research. A number of procedures must be repeated in routine applications; collectively these procedures represent a program. A program can be applied to immediate and later collections of data. A package, or system of programs, contains related procedures for handling and manipulating data.

Figure 10-8 shows an actual SPSS cross-tabulation run by one of the authors. In this analysis, association membership of suspect employees was broken down by sex. It addresses professional organizations only.

An analyst may prefer to perform statistical analysis himself or herself in the absence of computer resources. Anyone assigned to analysis should be familiar with statistics. Most colleges offer basic courses covering such topics as organizing data, probability distributions, estimation, testing statistical hypothesis, regressions and correlation,

	VAR005		
COUNT ROW PCT COL PCT TCT PCT	MALE 1.00	FEMALE 2.00	RCW TOTAL
VAR014			
0.0	18 48.6 85.7 37.5	19 51.4 70.4 39.6	37 77.1
1.00	3 27.3 14.3 6.3	8 72.7 29.6 16.7	11 22.9
COLUMN TOTAL	21 43.8	27 56.3	48 100.0

CORRECTED CHI SQUARE = 0.82555 WITH 1 DEGREE OF FREEDOM
PHI = 0.13114
CONTENGENCY COEFFICIENT = 0.13003
KENDALL'S TAU B = 0.18111
KENDALL'S TAU C = 0.15104
GAMMA = 0.43284
SOMER'S C = 0.15344

Figure 10-8. Association membership chart (using SPSS) breakdown by sex

conditional probability, and independent events. The analysis of variance and nonparametric tests is also useful.

The value of statistics lies partially in the clearness of this method of presentation. Mathematics, on which statistics is based, remains the clearest manner of expressing concepts. Certain statistical indexes are difficult to discuss any other way. For instance, statistical measures of correlation have no verbal equivalent. Statistics can be used to express information concisely. Statistics provides evidence supporting the analytical report. That evidence is used by the reader to judge the analyst's conclusions, as well as the data available for such conclusions.

TYPES OF REPORTS

Each type of report offers challenges to the analyst trying to prepare an intelligence product. The demand for some reports can be anticipated well in advance; other assignments come suddenly. Sudden demands for reports can be met only by the constant assemblage of good data based on projected research needs. Sometimes the analyst is caught off guard and finds the data on hand to be marginal or insufficient. A report should never go forward without data sufficient to support the conclusions of the analyst. For this reason, the analyst must often scurry around filling last-minute information needs.

Written intelligence reports are the primary responsibility of the research analyst. Intelligence reports may be requested by decision makers or the result of periodic, special-purpose, or maintenance requests of the counterintelligence unit itself. In addition to written reports, the analyst may be asked for an oral response in view of sudden time constraints. The oral response can take the form of answers to questions posed during a meeting. Special briefings may be requested during which the analyst presents an oral report, usually supplemented by charts, tables, diagrams, photographs, and/or slides. If possible, an oral report should be recorded since all reports represent an important resource and should be part of the data base available to all analysts.

Written reports can be formal or informal. In many cases, the analyst will be asked to provide a brief written report quickly. Such a request often fails to explain the reason or need for the report so the analyst must guess its purpose. Short written reports, like oral reports, are usually considered tactical intelligence, sometimes called combat, hot, or operational intelligence. These terms underline the urgency behind the request for a quick report.

Strategic intelligence reports, sometimes called headquarters intelligence reports, are more complete and less hasty productions used to furnish in-depth background information on a problem, facility, organization, or suspect(s). Strategic reports include basic reports, background data, and predictive reports, often called estimates. An estimate tries to take all background information into account while constructing realistic hypotheses of future activity.

A third type of report, a hybrid between the tactical and strategic, is called the periodic report. These are scheduled on a timetable that allows the lapse of a number of weeks or months before a new, periodic report must be written. Periodic reports are necessary in the case of constant problems or areas of concern such as the vulnerability of corporate research to industrial espionage.

All written reports must share a high standard of analysis, evidenced in a clear presentation. It is best if the counterintelligence unit adopts a district report style that serves to reinforce a concern for methodology. Editors are frequently used in national intelligence agencies to smooth reports in respect to style, grammar, spelling, and punctuation. The corporate counterintelligence unit will be unlikely to have the resources of a full-time editorial staff so the supervisor or an analyst with good writing skills can review all draft reports before final typing. Charts and other display materials require editorial guidance to ensure a continuity in the intelligence product. Less important from the standpoint of quality but with a definite effect on perception is the binding, cover stock, paper stock, and printing for the final copies of the intelligence report. The audiovisual staff, often located in personnel or public relations, can assist in choosing materials and colors that tend to produce the desired effect on report readers. Reactions to a document's appearance may be conscious or subconscious, but they are never absent. Evaluation of the performance of the entire counterintelligence unit depends partially on the appearance of its reports.

Decision makers and their planners are the recipients of counterintelligence analysis. They have a right to insist on certain requirements as to content and format. Those reports meant to be used internally should be to the taste of the manager of the counterintelligence unit.

Police intelligence units have been advised to adopt the following format, which can be adopted to corporate needs.[2]

- *Conclusions.* The conclusion section presents the results of the analysis. It should not be confused with a summary of the facts and allegations on which the conclusions were based. The conclusions answer such questions as: What is the signficance of this information? What is the

---

[2] Ibid., p. 132.

meaning for the department? Is there criminal activity involved? What is the relationship between the subject of the report and other types of areas of criminal activity in the jurisdiction? Is there a case or not?

- *Recommendations.* If the intelligence unit believes there is a case, then it should recommend how to approach the problem of evidence gathering and case building. If there is no case yet, what should be done? Should the unit continue to gather information? Should the subject be put on the back burner until other developments occur? Should the assistance of other local or Federal units be requested? Should the case be turned over to a Federal Agency? At the time the intelligence unit's report is finished it knows more about the subject than anyone else in the department; hence its views are important.
- *Summary of Information.* This is a synthesis of the most important elements of information without reporting all the details. The details will be in the intelligence files and available when a decision is reached on the next step.
- *Sources and Reliability of Information.* The analyst should give whatever information he/she has on the validity of the information available when the report was drafted. It is difficult for a chief or other readers to appreciate the value of conclusions unless they have some way of judging the reliability of the information basic to the report.
- *Principal and Alternative Hypothesis.* The reader will also be greatly helped if he/she can see the range of hypotheses the analyst considered before choosing the one presented in the conclusions. It is also important to understand explicitly why the analyst chose a particular hypothesis.
- *Missing Information.* This is an essential base upon which the conclusions and recommendations rest. It tells the reader explicitly what further information will be needed if the hypothesis selected is to be proved. It also points out missing information which must be found if a successful enforcement action is to be launched.

CONFLICTS IN DATA

Conflicts in data pose problems at every stage in the research process. They continue to require resolution during the final stages of intelligence production. Sometimes conflicts must be accepted but noted in the finished report in those sections above titled "Sources and Reliability of Information" and "Missing Information."

Conflicts tend to be in one of two categories: sources or the information furnished by different sources. Analysts cannot fully trust the evaluations of other agencies or their own field agents. Too much subjectivity is involved for blind acceptance. They must refer to past history of the source, as well as the apparent credibility of the information.

Both acquired knowledge and intuition are necessary. Intuition is not a form of witchcraft. Everyone has it to some degree or another. The late John E. Reid, of polygraph fame, once commented that all humans know they have five senses whereas, "Oftentimes certain people are credited with a sixth sense. . . . Actually it was not a sixth sense, *but* a good use of the . . . five senses."[3] However defined, as intuition or subconscious conclusion of the five senses, a good analyst must sometimes make a quantum leap or jump in thought processes to resolve an apparent conflict in data.

Documents with unidentified sources are frequently useful in resolving conflicts in data, especially if the documents came from an outside agency or friendly corporation. The third-agency rule prohibits identifying the source of information if it has passed through two agencies already. The third agency may receive excellent data without being able to appreciate the original source. Information rated highly by an outside agency with a good record should be taken seriously, even if the source is not identified.

Sometimes the analyst must give an either/or conclusion, but this type of conclusion should be kept to a minimum for it implies that the analyst is unable to perform assigned duties properly. Conflicts should be resolved during the analysis process, not passed on to the decision maker who is relying on the report for guidance.

CLASSIFYING REPORTS

The federal government has had a tremendous impact on the safeguarding of classified information. The *Industrial Security Manual* (DoD 5220.22-M) is valuable. No counterintelligence unit should be without a copy of the most recent edition. Revisions appear periodically. They are available from the Government Printing Office.

The information in the *Industrial Security Manual* has been hard won. The private sector has experienced many difficulties over the years in dealing with federal classification requirements. Some insist that the American Society for Industrial Security, International, got its start in response to contractor frustration with government security requirements. While things are happier now with respect to cooperation and understanding between defense contractors and the federal government, problems in classification management still exist, and they will always exist.

---

[3] John E. Reid, "Behavior Symptoms of Polygraph Subjects," *Polygraph* (March 1982):39–40.

Counterintelligence analysts and supervisors share age-old problems in making decisions in regard to how a document should be classified, marked, and protected. Their concerns are on a smaller scale than those of the defense industry in response to government regulation; nevertheless these decisions are vital to the corporation involved in dealing with the threat of industrial espionage.

Classification is a method of determining how sensitive a report is and thereby helping to determine who will have access. The object of classification is to protect data and sources of data. Should either be exposed (compromised), danger is created. That danger, in respect to counterintelligence, ranges from embarrassment to mission failure to loss of life and other corporate assets. The U.S. government views the danger to the nation in definite, if somewhat ambiguous, terms.[4]

"TOP SECRET" is the designation which shall be applied only to information or material the unauthorized disclosure of which could reasonably be expected to cause *exceptionally grave damage* to the national security. Examples of "Exceptionally grave damage" include armed hostilities against the U.S. or its allies; disruption of foreign relations vitally affecting the national security; the compromise of vital national defense plans or complex/cryptologic and communications intelligence systems; the revelation of sensitive intelligence operations; and, the disclosure of scientific or technological developments vital to national security.

"SECRET" is the designation which shall be applied only to information or material the unauthorized disclosure of which could reasonably be expected to cause *serious damage* to the national security. Examples of "serious damage" include disruption of foreign relations significantly affecting the national security; significant impairment of a program or policy directly related to the national security; revelation of significant military plans or intelligence operations; compromise of significant military plans or intelligence operations; and, compromise of significant scientific or technological developments relating to national security.

"CONFIDENTIAL" is the designation which shall be applied to information or material the unauthorized disclosure of which could reasonably be expected to cause *identifiable damage* to the national security. Examples of "identifiable damage" include the compromise of information which indicates strength of ground, air, and naval forces in the U.S. and overseas areas; disclosure of technical information used for training, maintenance, and inspection of classified munitions of war, revelation of performance characteristics, test data, design, and production data on munitions of war.

In addition, the federal government employs a host of special category classifications added on to the general classifications. These

---

[4] U.S. Department of Defense, *Industrial Security Manual for Safeguarding Classified Information* (Washington, D.C.: Government Printing Office, 1981), pp. 3, 7, 8. Emphasis added.

special categories include CRYPTO (cryptographic) and COSMIC (North Atlantic Treaty Organization).

Counterintelligence should make the classification scheme simple and easy to understand. The more categories used, the slower the classification process. Reports cannot go forward without a classification. Therefore a simple system of classification will speed the report to the consumer. Every corporation has the right to protect proprietary information and each has the authority to construct its own classification system. The following example provides a format for corporate classification of proprietary data:

1. Red: Highest protection. Select distribution only. Not to be copied.
2. Yellow: Controlled access. Copied with permission only.
3. Green: Not for public consumption. May be copied for internal use only.

The exact procedures for safeguarding red, yellow, or green documents will be based on physical and procedural security considerations, such as those to be discussed in Chapters 12 and 13. The *Industrial Security Manual* gives precise directions on the safeguarding of information depending on classification. The current literature of security discusses alternatives in protective measures. We recommend the following periodicals for those desiring current information on document classification: *Security Management, Assets Protection, Professional Protection* (Canada), *International Security Review* (England), and the *Journal of Security Administration.*

The most-sensitive rule usually applies to a classification decision. If an analyst includes a red item in a report, the entire report has a red classification, according to the most-sensitive rule. The problem with the rule is obvious: only part of any report or other document may require a high classification. The analyst, abstracting from any classified report, may or may not pull out a classified item. If the item used is indeed red, there is no problem. If the item is, in fact, yellow, green, or not classified, there is no reason to classify the analyst's report as red. Therefore, any information of a partial nature, abstracted from a classified report, must be examined for its true classification. Only very lazy analysts fail to see this done.

The decision process of classification management requires a knowledgeable individual, especially if the information is scientific or technical or unfamiliar to the analyst. Specialists may be needed to decide on the correct level of classification. It may seem an easy solution to classify everything red, but few will have access, and the control problems and associated expense preclude this type of solution.

The matter of classification review is also important. At some point, almost all information becomes public knowledge. Most information becomes outdated and useless at a future date. Storage problems alone make it wise to downgrade and destroy classified documents as soon as possible. At regular intervals, classified materials should be reviewed for this purpose. A register or log of classified documents must be kept. Notification instructions that will cause the retrieval of documents for downgrade review need to be established.

Former government intelligence analysts are able to remember many ludicrous examples of overclassification. Private industry can avoid such errors. Responsible people, given wide latitude, should handle downgrade reviews with the advice and consent of management. Bureaucratic regulations should be minimal in this area. Analysts should be encouraged to identify over- as well as underclassification of documents they examine. Red should be used as a regretful necessity, not as a status symbol for the analyst who prepared the report.

The media have a habit of publishing materials considered proprietary by governments or corporations. Once such information is published, it becomes a matter of public domain. But corporations sometimes continue to regard information that has been publicly released as still under their control, with ludicrous results. Take the case of the utility companies that cooperated with a government-sponsored research project on security vulnerability. A senior researcher was authorized to present the results of this security study to a security organization seminar. Interest was shown by a journal editor in publishing the study as presented. The companies refused at first to allow the researcher to publish his paper, citing the *already released* information as proprietary. It took government pressure before they realized the foolishness of their position.

One of the authors, working as an intelligence analyst, was constantly surprised to see the *New York Times* print information needlessly wrapped in secrecy by overzealous government classification personnel. Corporate counterintelligence units need not fall into the habit of needless classification or overclassification. They can design a policy with guidelines to keep classification in its proper perspective.

Should a corporation share documents it has classified, the receiving corporation must respect the constraints imposed even if they seem unnecessary. To do less is to invite other corporations to treat one's own classification scheme lightly, which could result in needless compromise of one's own sensitive information.

All documents need proper marking to avoid error in handling. The *Industrial Security Manual* is helpful in giving examples of government marking requirements. Documents may not be the only items deemed subject to classification controls. Photographs, charts, tapes, films, slides, and models are other categories of information that may need classification.

Primary responsibility for classifying a document always rests with the supervisor of the counterintelligence unit. Decision makers in management should furnish some guidelines on what they feel should be protected. A team effort is needed to make classification work. Since there is no science of classification, subjective judgment plays a major role in classification.

DISSEMINATION OF REPORTS

Sometimes writers link the process of report writing too closely with the distribution of the reports. They list report writing and dissemination as if it were a single activity. The dissemination of intelligence reports is a distinct step in the production of intelligence. It is the final step, and it is hazardous. Intelligence is a precious commodity, a distillation of raw information, too precious to give away to the general public or enemies of the corporation. Counterintelligence reports do no good if improperly distributed. Care must be taken that the right people receive the intelligence reports and the wrong people are denied access to them.

Need to know is the paramount reason for being on the distribution list of reports from the counterintelligence unit. *Need to know* is a term widely used in the intelligence community but not precisely defined. The concept of need to know must be approached from a commonsense perspective. Here we speak primarily of distribution outside the corporation, although internal distribution, outside the counterintelligence unit, must have similar safeguards. Reports that enable an outside friendly corporation to defend itself better should be distributed to it theoretically. Reports that enable law enforcement agencies to make a case should be passed on. Reports that affect national security should go to the appropriate federal agency.

Knowledge and trust must accompany need-to-know decisions. It is imprudent to place intelligence in the hands of unknown or untrustworthy individuals. The counterintelligence unit needs guidance from outside agencies or organizations that have proved themselves worthy of trust. As in liaison, it is necessary to locate one trustworthy individual who represents an agency or organization and go from there. The personal touch is vital. Even the most prestigious organizations or agencies cannot be accorded blanket trust. A report given away or sold is out of control. Secrecy depends on the abilities and goodwill of the recipient. Care always must be exercised in regard to dissemination.

Common sense is not sufficient. All those who are chosen to receive an intelligence report should have passed a thorough background investigation conducted by corporate counterintelligence field agents.

Established distribution relationships are not uncommon between intelligence units. These call for regular sharing of reports on agreed-on subjects. Such relationships may be based on formal or informal agreements, with the approval of management and subject to regular review. It is prudent to evaluate exchanges in the light of the current situation. Another factor that affects exchange of reports is the legal climate of the times. Of course, the legal climate is a reflection of the cultural, social, political, and economic times.

Rules on report exchange are a good idea. These rules should include penalties for needless exposure of proprietary information. The best penalty, and the most sensible, is dropping the offending agency or organization from the distribution list until it can prove itself more worthy of trust.

Records must be kept of recipients of intelligence reports. These records should be as detailed as possible, indicating the individual as well as the agency. One important principle of management is responsibility. It is impossible to ascertain responsibility unless record keeping is accurate. In normal corporate activity, copies are automatically forwarded year after year to the same addressee. An individual may be dead, retired, or transferred, yet copies continue to be addressed and sent. The distribution of intelligence reports requires special care to ensure that the recipient is not absent.

Disclaimers or nonidentification procedures are sensible when distributing reports outside the corporation of origin. The following disclaimer, although developed for police use by the Illinois Bureau of Investigation, can be adapted to corporate purposes:

> The information furnished is disseminated pursuant to the intelligence division procedures of the Illinois Bureau of Investigation and is the property of that Bureau. Contents may not be disclosed to any person or organization without the express permission of the special agent in charge, Intelligence Division, or the Superintendent, Illinois Bureau of Investigation.

SUMMARY

Producing finished intelligence is the goal of the research process. Intelligence is created through the process of analysis. There are four common analytical errors: an espionage threat goes unnoticed; innocent people are labeled suspects; conclusions are too general for action; and conclusions are erroneous, in part or in whole.

Data must be summarized first. The next stage is examination of data for possible espionage threat indicators.

Good analysis is always systematic and thorough. Methodological routines include link diagrams, the transaction matrix, flowcharts, time charts, VIA, and PERT. Statistical methods, such as the SPSS package, are useful in analysis. Computer processing of data for research purposes is called data analysis.

Finished intelligence can appear in various types of reports, which may be ordered far in advance or be required suddenly. Analysts will produce both written and verbal reports. In most cases reports should be supplemented by charts, tables, diagrams, photographs, and/or slides.

Written reports can be formal or informal. Informal reports are short and usually are considered to be tactical intelligence. Formal reports, allowing the analyst more time and flexibility, are called strategic intelligence. Both background reports and estimates are strategic intelligence. Periodic reports are a hybrid between tactical and strategic intelligence.

All written reports should meet a high standard. All reports require conclusions, recommendations, a summary of information, discussion of sources and reliability of information, principal and alternative hypothesis, and a comment on missing information.

Conflicts in data represent an ongoing problem in intelligence production. If they cannot be resolved, conflicts must be noted in the final report.

All reports require proper classification to prevent unauthorized use. The *Industrial Security Manual* is a helpful document for those who must design a classification system. Corporations can use a simpler system.

The most-sensitive rule is usually applied to a classification decision. Specialized knowledge is often required to determine a classification level. Periodically all documents need review of their classification.

Dissemination of intelligence reports is the final step. Need to know is the paramount reason for access to an intelligence report. There should be written rules on the exchange of intelligence reports with other corporations or agencies.

11. Uses of the Intelligence Product

If Not Now—When?—Hillel

Some of the uses of the finished products of intelligence are self-evident, but others are not so obvious in either structure or content. Intelligence dissemination and use often suffers such pitfalls and maladies as the following:

- Failure to share information.
- Permitting improper access.
- Loss of control of data.
- Underuse of intelligence.
- Lack of imaginative applications.
- Improper disclosure.
- Illegal or unethical practices.
- Insensitivity to public relations.

On the one hand, intelligence needs to be protected zealously; on the other hand, intelligence that is ineffectively used because of excessive restrictions on sharing of data with colleagues or with allies is a waste.

Access must be tightly controlled. Once access is permitted, no disclosure to another may be allowed without the consent of the generator of the intelligence. At no time must the originator lose control of dissemination.

Underuse may be occasioned by the failure of information sharing. It may also be the result of the originator's failure to exploit the potentials of the intelligence produced. Imaginative applications of available intelligence may greatly assist the counterintelligence effort. In the endeavor to maximize the impact of the intelligence product, we must be sensitive to the public relations aspects of counterintelligence.

Generally counterintelligence is more acceptable to the American public than espionage. It is important to define clearly what we are up to and demonstrate the need to employ intelligence to cope with espionage. This is true whether it be purely domestic competitive espionage or foreign power industrial espionage.

Improper disclosure of the counterintelligence operation, or of the information and data gathered, can devastate the entire operation. Such disclosure may result from illegal or unethical practices. Intelligence operations still suffer from the Watergate syndrome. Any disclosure of unconscionable acts involved in industrial counterintelligence will likely destroy the effort, thereby paving the way for spies, spy masters, and control agents to achieve covert technology transference, to the detriment of the United States and U.S. industry. The strength of the industrial economy and the economic viability of the United States are placed in jeopardy by all industrial counterintelligence failures.

The critical role of industrial counterintelligence can be understood by an awareness of its manifold employments. Some of the major uses of the intelligence product are discussed in this chapter. (All that is discussed is within the context of avoiding the pitfalls and maladies previously mentioned.) The following are the subjects of this chapter:

- Threat identification
- Aid in identification of actual possible spies
- Investigation assistance and development of evidence
- Assessment of countermeasures
- Guide to preventive and protective priorities
- Decision making on security measures
- Aid to risk management and legal tactics
- Controlled information sharing and mutual aid
- Combating organized crime and terrorists
- Monitoring gray markets and spy gangs both foreign and domestic

THREAT IDENTIFICATION

The finished intelligence product should assist in a realistic evaluation of the scope and dimensions of the perils we face. Paranoic reactions to industrial espionage can do more harm than good. Thus any assessments must be rational, made on the basis of data and information. The intelligence product can be of great help in identifying threats.

Depending on the particular industry involved in the use of industrial counterintelligence, the threat may be found to be competitive, or it may involve foreign technology transfer to a hostile, or potentially hostile, nation. The reality of the threat must first be determined. Is there in fact a thrust from some person or persons to steal information from our business? Headlines such as these can cause undue alarm:

- Newport, R.I., Seen as Likely Nest for Spies
- American Border Called an Open Sieve
- Silicon Valley Greed Fuels Technology Theft
- Boston's Electronic Highway Infiltrated by Spies
- Massive Increase in Espionage from Soviet Union

The best reference point for an assessment of actual threat is not media hype or public hysteria; it is a sound body of counterintelligence that will objectively show whether there are actual or potential threats in a specific segment of industry. Obviously some industries are more vulnerable than others. Industrial counterintelligence can corroborate the vulnerability; however, such intelligence may demonstrate some anomalies. Certain particular high-technology operations may not be nearly as vulnerable as one would imagine. But special marketing plans, new car models, dress designs, and similar trade secrets may be exceedingly vulnerable and critical in terms of industrial espionage. Consider the secret formulas of specific products like Coca-Cola, Drambuie liqueur, Tribuno vermouth, and so on. Also consider the following. An alert executive of Chrysler Motor Company overheard that the Ford Motor Company's top photographer was in Paris. He contacted a representative of Chrysler in Paris who found out that the photographer was posing a new model Ford car against the Eifel Tower. He also learned that the photographer was next going to Hong Kong. Armed with this intelligence, Chrysler concluded that Ford's advertising would stress the car's popularity as a "world car." To counter this marketing, Chrysler had its new model photographed against American landmarks to show its popularity with Americans. This campaign of the early 1980s was a great success.

Competitive secrets are the basis of corporate economic strength. Loss of trade secrets may seriously affect the victim industry and harm a thriving business, causing losses of jobs, a diminished tax base, and, to the extent the company is in the export business, affect the U.S. foreign trade and balance of payments. The last is particularly true if the stolen secrets are obtained by foreign competitors, as was alleged in the 1982 Hitachi and Mitsubishi silicon chip espionage case. Taking the situation one step further, competitive secret components that are stolen may wind up in the Soviet Union or in a Soviet bloc country. The components may be used for hostile economic or military adventures that jeopardize the strength or even ultimate survival of the United States.

Often counterintelligence reveals a more direct attack on industrial security. It may be that a company is producing products used in military combat or support operations. They may not be directly involved in weaponry but may be used by other industries as components, tools, or processes of military logistics, or they may be strategic materials required for such operations. In some of these cases, the company's business may come under the cognizance of the DoD or some other federal agency, and the industry will obtain a great deal of security support. In other cases, however, we may not be seen by the government as being so immediately critical for national defense that we should enjoy the luxury of government sponsorship of our preventive and protective requirements. In the Soviet Union all the resources of the KGB would be at our disposal. In the United States we are pretty much on our own.

The military-related component of electronics, aerospace, and materials science has generated government support, which has drained research and security talent away from areas with limited military application. Unfortunately the spin-off research and security potential of such supported industries does not filter down to the industrial, commercial, and consumer-oriented segments of the U.S. economy. Research and development, and the security of it, in these areas are left up to industry. As a result of this neglect, America's competitive position has been hurt.

When counterintelligence indicates that threats to security are likely to come from domestic sources, priority should be given accordingly. The security effort should be coordinated with local and state enforcement agencies and resources applied discreetly. On the other hand, if foreign industrial espionage is involved, security efforts should be coordinated with appropriate federal agencies.

Thus counterintelligence can provide information about three types of threats: competitive domestic industrial espionage, competitive espionage with foreign technology transfer implications, and direct foreign espionage by hostile, or potentially hostile nations.

Counterintelligence should also enable a clear identification of the specific sources from which such threats are most likely to come and indicate the specific items or segments of the business that are targeted. Suppose we become aware that competitive companies want to acquire the results of a major research effort we have successfully concluded. We will provide adequate security to prevent leaks of information about the research itself and also about its impact on our new product lines. Or suppose counterintelligence advises that certain confidential or secret processes are being sought by foreign nations. We will apply resources to deal with this type of threat. Foreign nations, whether currently friendly or hostile, are likely to set up sophisticated networks of spies and use advanced technology and infiltration techniques. Our counterintelligence helps to focus security efforts on specific targets and specific espionage rings.

The loss of trade secrets is seldom compensated by court actions for damages. An ounce of security is worth many pounds of after-the-fact legal action. Counterintelligence serves as an early warning system. If adequate security measures are undertaken, the industrial espionage effort may be blocked or at least shunted off to a less-well-secured company.

AID IN IDENTIFYING ACTUAL AND POSSIBLE SPIES

Counterintelligence can also assist in maintaining a ready alert system as to actual spies or those who are prone to become spies.

Often industry does not take adequate protection. Employees may obtain jobs without a background check. Many employers are especially loath to subject a high-level applicant to a rigorous check, not wanting to alienate or embarrass a prospective executive. Yet applicants for employment often lie about their educational background, substance abuse record, and motives for seeking the position. The applicant may be an agent of a competitor or may have heard that the company is a good place to steal from, sell drugs, or engage in other illegal acts. Counterintelligence can help keep subversives and the unqualified from becoming insiders.

Some prescreened employees may succumb to spy masters. Greed, anger, fear of exposure, and concern about relatives are but a few of the many reasons they can be recruited for espionage attempts. Consider the following cases:

- The wife of a West German scientist performing secret research was living in East Germany. The husband, making efforts to have her come to West Germany, was approached by an East German espionage agent and was told that his wife would be allowed to travel to West Germany if he worked for the espionage network. For more than three years he provided the agent with data about the laboratory. He also handed over to the Russians scientific pamphlets of British, German, and American information in highly specialized subjects including laser techniques and plasma physics.

- An anonymous spy said he had been able to steal oil exploration maps worth millions of dollars by bribing a half-dozen armed plant guards. He was thereby enabled to photograph the maps and replace them. To this day the company thinks that the spy's client got to the oil first because it had better researchers.
- Kodak Corporation developed for its own use a number of secret processes. Diachemie, an East German firm, employed a professional industrial spy from Belgium to obtain these secrets. The spy corrupted two of Kodak's employees by offering substantial financial inducements. He obtained the secret information and passed it on to East Germany.

Each case shows a failure to maintain security in depth and to maintain checks and balances. They also illustrate the age-old spy tactics of money corruption, and pressure brought against an individual who seeks to protect his family.

Counterintelligence may be designed to defeat these espionage efforts by being aware of the activities of espionage agents and maintaining surveillance of their activities. Counterespionage may also provide profiles of the types of employees who may become victims of the espionage conspiracy. As previously mentioned, we tend to expend great effort to keep outsiders out of our facilities. We set up highly sophisticated physical security to protect sensitive areas and materials. This is all to the good, but much of this endeavor may be in vain if we employ the wrong people. If we permit high-risk personnel access to secret data and devices, we are in trouble, regardless of the effectiveness of physical security operations and methods. In short, personnel security is at least as critical as physical security. To the extent possible, a potential spy should never be employed. A person who has the potential for being compromised should never be promoted. A person who fits the profile of a potential espionage victim should never have access to sensitive persons, places, or things.

It is the responsibility of the counterintelligence component to screen employees and others who are insiders on their original appointment and on their promotion or sensitive assignment. Using its intelligence files and access to the files of other industrial and commercial companies, the counterespionage effort should be able to identify risky applicants, promotion candidates, and persons considered for sensitive assignments. Armed with this intelligence, the personnel departments must refuse to consider individuals deemed vulnerable. The urgency of this coordination with personnel is illustrated by a few of the thousands of cases where insiders should never have been employed and where they have been the keys to successful industrial espionage:

- A deputy medical examiner in a large West Coast city had been on the coroner's staff for three and one-half years when it was discovered that he was never a physician, although he had been passing as such for twenty-five years.
- An employee of a paint company engaged in research and development of new paint formulas was discharged for absenteeism. He promptly stole the coded formulas of these new products and offered them in decoded form to a rival company.
- An employee of the 3M Company who had access to company secrets received a job offer with a rival company at a much higher salary, with the understanding he would turn over the secret formulas and processes of 3M to the competitor. He turned over ten key formulas. He then resigned from 3M, explaining that he was going to work for a company not in the same business as 3M.
- Two engineers at a major aviation company in the Northeast played key roles in the design and development of a complex integrated aircraft weapons monitor and control system. They resigned and went to work for a competing company. Within a few months, the latter company had developed a similar weapons system based on pirated secret data.
- The manager of marketing publications for a new division of Exxon that had developed highly successful office equipment resigned and a day later sent a letter to the vice-president of marketing operations at IBM offering to sell some top-secret Exxon documents for $100,000.
- An industrial spy reported that on one occasion when he attempted to bribe a janitor to turn over scrap to him, he found he was too late. Another spy had already made an arrangement with the janitor for the material.
- A former radar project engineer with an American aircraft company turned over information concerning defense missiles and other secret weaponry worth hundreds of millions of dollars to a Polish intelligence agent in the employ of the U.S.S.R.

The contribution of counterintelligence to the continuous screening of insiders can be of inestimable importance. Because the corruptive tactics of spy masters, terrorists, and organized crime are so effective, personnel profiles must be continually updated. Those employees we would ordinarily least suspect may have been compromised. Counterintelligence needs to be ever vigilant. People change. Their needs vary over time. The enemy operates on the cynical premise that every man and woman has his or her price. Human nature may be noble but it is, also, too often corruptible. As we noted in the famous Abscam case, even trusted senators and congressmen—sworn servants of the public—succumbed to greed.

ASSIST INVESTIGATION AND DEVELOPMENT OF EVIDENCE

It is one thing to develop intelligence that causes us to suspect a person or group of persons of being industrial spies. It is quite another matter to develop sufficient evidence to make an arrest or to dismiss an employee. Counterintelligence is available to assist in the investigation of suspected spies, agents, and their dupes. Once counterintelligence has identified a suspect and has documented its basis for such suspicion, the investigative process takes over. The investigation may be conducted by the industrial counterintelligence unit itself, or it may call on federal, state, or local law enforcement agencies for assistance.

Once particular targets of the investigation have been selected, specific investigative methods may be employed to develop evidence. The vast potentials of the unit will be focused on the task of proving the guilt or innocence of the suspect(s). Through the use of their investigative talents, field agents will concentrate on supplying evidence or providing leads that others may use for analysis.

In cases where espionage agents have been exposed, arrested, and unmasked, it has been a product of the painstaking work of the counterintelligence effort that provided the capability. Recent disclosures of treachery by trusted employees in the intelligence services themselves give added cause for concern about the integrity of employees generally. The need for counterintelligence of the highest order is demonstrated by such cases as these:

- Sir Anthony Blunt, curator of Queen Elizabeth's art collection, was exposed in 1979 as the mysterious fourth man in the Soviet spy ring that included Guy Burgess, Donald Mclean, and Kim Philby.
- Geoffrey Arthur Prime, who was employed as a translator of Russian by British Intelligence, was exposed by American counterintelligence officials, in October 1982. They alleged that he supplied Moscow with a stream of highly sensitive information about American and British interception of Soviet communications while he was employed at Britain's main electronic intelligence center in Cheltenham from 1968 to 1977.

- Hugh Hambleton, a professor at the Laval University in Quebec, who formerly worked in the economic section of the North Atlantic Treaty Organization (NATO), was recently convicted of giving NATO secrets to the Russians.

If Soviet moles are able to infiltrate the vaunted British intelligence services, how very vulnerable must be private industry to espionage! How important it is that we support industrial counterintelligence in its efforts to investigate suspects and, when appropriate, to bring them to trial.

In the 1982 case of Hitachi and Mitsubishi espionage directed at IBM, it was IBM's counterintelligence effort that supplied the leads and the evidence upon which the arrests of Japanese executives were based. This was a case of competitive industrial espionage by rivals of IBM whose companies are based in a friendly foreign nation. This same type of espionage could very well have been perpetrated by an unfriendly nation. A spy ring was involved that surely would have no scruples about selling information to the highest bidder. It should also be noted that Tokyo is suspected of being an international clearing house for the products of industrial espionage, particularly in the areas of advanced electronics and high technology. Except for the excellent use of sophisticated industrial counterintelligence, IBM would surely have suffered gravely, but beyond that our nation's many electronic businesses would have been placed in jeopardy. Indeed, our nation itself and our defense posture may have been dealt a very severe blow.

It is difficult to separate out the consequences of industrial espionage. The losers may not be limited to a particular business or a particular segment of industry; the losers may be the nation itself and its citizens. Industrial counterintelligence may not scare a Kim Philby, Guy Burgess, Donald Maclean, or Geoffrey Prime. However, recognizing the thrust of the Soviet's intensified drive to steal vital Western technology, industrial counterintelligence is a national source of the highest order. We in industry can do our stockholders a favor while we serve our country.

ASSESSMENT OF COUNTERMEASURES

Assessment of the need for countermeasures is less difficult than the assessment of particular, specialized, tailored countermeasures for individual industries. Foreign intelligence and espionage activities within the United States are at their highest levels since the Cold War began. Any enterprise working at or near the state of the art is a potential target for foreign technology transfer by political adversaries or economic competitors.

Targeting by foreign interests of technological information is a potent threat to proprietary data. Much information is not protected by federal counterintelligence yet is enormously vital to the survival of a company or an industry. This is the principal concern of industrial counterintelligence. However, efforts should not be limited to areas with special attraction for enemy nations. The theft of trade secrets and other proprietary information from whatever source damages the companies involved as well as the international economic posture of the United States.

In attempting to assess appropriate countermeasures to cope with industrial espionage, we must rely on industrial counterintelligence. One of the steps that will greatly assist in coping with industrial espionage is to set up a consciousness raising training program for security personnel and all other employees of our facility. Counterintelligence should be everybody's business, and perforce counterintelligence awareness education and training should be directed at all employees.[1] Training should include information and facility security, as well as the dissemination of threat information. Security consciousness at all levels of the organization is an essential first step toward implementing effective countermeasures.

Although there may be many important aspects to strictly technical intelligence collection by espionage agents, the threat of data collection by humans remains a major concern of counterintelligence. In any particular facility or industrial field, there are bound to be specific problems. However, the modus operandi is likely to be more or less constant. In some cases strictly technical espionage will be a major concern, but in all cases human spies will present the greatest challenge. Technical espionage can be attacked with technical countermeasures. Counterintelligence should identify the technical threats. Countermeasures then become primarily a matter of adequate technical resources.

When it comes to threats based on data collection by humans, counterintelligence assessment may be more complex and less consistent in terms of accuracy. Obviously, therefore, the assessment of countermeasures to combat human spies requires counterintelligence of the highest order. Culprits are usually thought to be loyal employees; they are often the least suspect because of their impeccable

---

[1] Nancy L. Barnes and John T. Miller, "Counterintelligence—Everybody's Business," *Security Management* (August 1981):107–111.

backgrounds and credentials. Yet these improbable traitors are discovered, if discovered at all, by counterintelligence that has the support of all connected with the facility.

The threat from insiders is real. It has been discovered that the pattern is for trusted employees to advance up the organizational ladder and ultimately to acquire access to sensitive information. At this point in their careers something happens. Perhaps they are compromised in some fashion, or coerced, or cultivated (seduced) by spy masters. In case after case where arrests have been made, it is indicated that the primary and dominant motivation is money. Spies, or potential spies, have information of monetary value. This is the challenge presented to counterintelligence.

If decision making is based on sound intelligence, we may have confidence that:

- Potential spies have been tentatively identified.
- Continuous early warning systems are in place to assess the threat of espionage.
- Vigilant security measures are ready to alert intelligence of suspicious activity.
- Surveillance of employees is maintained on a random and discreet basis.
- Liaison with other facilities, with the police, federal agencies, and the community has been established for information exchange.
- Undercover operations continuously monitor all personnel and evaluate possible disloyalty.
- Inventory of all sensitive sources of data, devices, processes, formulas, and trade secrets in effect is continuous.
- If espionage does occur, it will be detected and immediately investigated.

Counterintelligence must assess the amount and degree to which resources should be applied to each countermeasure. Decision makers have to be convinced of the threat and the need to expend resources to combat it. Counterintelligence can provide decision makers with reasoned assessments of the vulnerability, probability, and criticality of the danger faced by the facility. Countermeasures need to be cost-effective and within the realm of the possible.

GUIDE TO PREVENTIVE AND PROTECTIVE PRIORITIES

Our emphasis in the previous section on the threat of human spies, particularly insiders, was not meant to minimize the importance of general security measures. On the contrary, the discussion was based on the assumption that strict security was operational:

- Fencing, personal identification systems, guards, alarms, and other measures of access control were in place.
- Restricted areas were provided and controlled.
- Locks, safes, and vaults were available and used.
- Procedural and personnel security was of high quality and alert to the threat of espionage.
- Special attention was accorded to communication devices, computers, and associated technologies.
- Continuous sweeping for bugs and line checks for wire or induction tapping were conducted.
- All employees, visitors, vendors, and maintenance personnel were checked out on a continuous basis.
- Waste materials were pulverized, crushed, or otherwise rendered nonsensitive.
- Accident, fire, disaster control, and health programs were up to standard.
- Human and mechanical errors were backstopped by fail-safe provisions.
- Unethical practices were forbidden.
- Attention was paid to executive protection.
- The threats of terrorism and organized crime were recognized and dealt with.

All of these aspects of viable security programs, and even additional types of prevention and protection for specific facilities, need to be part of the total counterintelligence effort. Security efforts are expensive and must be evaluated in terms of their contributions to the counterintelligence effort. Perhaps all of those listed need to be implemented in some fashion; however, in most private security environments, there will never be sufficient resources to provide the ultimate defense in all categories of physical, personnel, and procedural security. Therefore counterintelligence must provide guidance to the decision makers concerning preventive and protective priorities. Such guidance may be on a strategic and/or tactical basis.

If counterintelligence has established that there is a likelihood of a penetration of the facility's outer defenses, but it is not necessarily imminent, the guidance may be strategic. It might recommend that fences be kept in repair, that razor-ribbon helical topping be added, that there be an increase of protective lighting, that continuous guard patrol be maintained, and fence alarms should be installed.

On the other hand, if counterintelligence has established that an attempt is about to be made to kidnap the president of the company, the guidance would be tactical (or operational) to meet the immediate need by providing protection to the threatened executive. Residential security systems should be quickly installed. Routes to and from the office should be varied, and a surveillance protection vehicle should continuously be tracking the executive's car. Perhaps a bulletproof vehicle could be bought or rented. Special bodyguards would be assigned on a twenty-four hour basis. In the event that these protections frustrate the plans of the kidnappers, it is possible that they may turn to the executive's spouse and children; thus family members may need equivalent protection.

Counterintelligence assists in establishing preventive and protective priorities based on the nature of the perceived threat. The threat may be more or less serious. It may be more or less immediate. It may be one that can be handled by facility security acting alone. It may be a threat that requires assistance from public authorities or from cooperating security directors in response to mutual aid agreements.

Counterintelligence determines the priorities and recommends to decision makers realistic responses to the specific threats anticipated on a strategic or a tactical basis. Without such guidance, unrealistic and wasted effort may ensue, and top management may lose confidence in the security operation.

DECISION MAKING ON SECURITY MEASURES

Aside from general guidance for preventive and protective priorities, counterintelligence should be of assistance in the security decision-making process. It should, by virtue of its attention to the nature of actual or potential threats, be able to provide advice regarding types and degrees of security prevention and protection. Counterintelligence is aware of the technology that espionage agents may have available and the likelihood of its use. Counterintelligence is also aware of the techniques employed to manipulate insiders and to penetrate physical, personnel, and procedural barriers. Using this knowledge, counterintelligence can provide facilities with sophisticated recommendations for security measures. These recommendations might relate to the following:

- Operations research applications.
- Compartmentation of all critical business functions.

- Proper security classification of operational data, places, and objects.
- Determination of who has a right to know and a need to know.
- Degree of screening of personnel needed.
- Measures to increase information security.
- Devices to provide communication and computer security.
- Quality of physical security required.
- State of the art in all aspects of security.
- Recommended liaisons with other data sources for mutual prevention and protection.

Operations research applications of counterintelligence might involve advice concerning seemingly mundane preventive and protective measures, such as how to forestall patent infringements, avoid legal entanglements, and provide necessary protections for trade secrets. Or it might be more sophisticated measures involving foreign espionage, activities of terrorists, or the inroads of organized crime. In each case, counterintelligence can provide to decision makers the information they need to take appropriate action and also provide them with advice as to the operations, applications, and methods best suited to achieve security in these areas.

If the judgment of decision makers is based on sound counter-intelligence, it may be that various critical industrial functions will be compartmentalized; that is, the functions will be segmented so that the penetration of one function will not result in the destruc-tion of the entire operation. It is somewhat like a warship. Enemy action may blow a hole in the side of the ship, but that area, being compartmentalized, will immediately be sealed off. Thus, even several hits may be sustained without the ship being sunk. Segmentation and compartmentalization may go beyond secured physical locations and the subdivision of sensitive processes; it may also relate to the protection of information. Various individuals may be made privy to only a part or a segment of the entire amount of the information needed to compromise the entire operation. Only one or two most trusted persons will have the entire picture.

Excessive security classification can be a costly mistake for several reasons. It may cause unnecessary delays in processing because of the requirements of clearances. If some things are obviously exces-sively classified, people may lose respect for the entire classification system. Special and costly security measures may be instituted without justification. On the other hand, where a very sensitive matter is underclassified or not classified at all, the spies will have ample opportunity. A realistic balance can be struck only if responsible counterintelligence is available.

It is essential that only those who have both the right to know and the need to know should have access to classified information, places, and things. Operational personnel may best be evaluated for such access where management has obtained individual clearances through counterintelligence. Such clearances should be revised on a continuous basis to ensure that the person involved is currently entitled to the access he or she seeks. Interaction by administrators and managers with counterintelligence will be helpful in determining the need to know of such persons, as well as their right to know.

The counterintelligence capability should be of inestimable assistance to the personnel department. There is always a question as to what extent personnel hired, promoted, or assigned to sensitive positions need to be screened. It would be desirable if all such persons were to receive a national agency check and a full and complete background investigation, including neighborhood checks, and so on. In the real world of business operations this is not done. The cost of such screening is deemed prohibitive and, in many instances, a waste of resources by business management.

Counterintelligence may advise as to what positions require that newly hired, promoted, or transferred persons should be fully checked out if they are to be assigned to sensitive positions. Similarly, counterintelligence may have obtained information concerning individuals that indicates potential problems. These persons must be thoroughly investigated and if the derogatory information proves to be correct or at least probably correct, the personnel department may be spared considerable embarrassment. The facility may have also been spared what might have been espionage. Thus intelligence detects subversion by knitting together small scraps of information to produce a basis for rational screening of personnel.

Counterintelligence may also advise as to potential threats to the security of information. In the light of this advice, security can be directed to address the actual threats, and resources will be applied where they are critically needed. Intelligence helps us to rifle in on our real problems rather than "shotgunning," and hoping that we may actually hit a target somewhere out there. The security of data is of such great importance that we cannot trust to blind intuition. We must be aided by counterintelligence.

Communication and computer security is essential for protection against industrial espionage. Many countermeasures can be employed against the interdiction of sensitive communications, some more expensive and exotic than others. Management must be aware of the latest developments in this field and have solid advice as to the best and most cost-effective devices available. Counterintelligence should be aware of the capabilities of actual and potential spies and therefore the extent of the effort needed to block competitive and/or foreign espionage attempts to penetrate communications. Some phases of communications are almost impossible to protect from sophisticated compromise unless secret codes are used. For example, the telephone and telephonic communications are very vulnerable.

Also vulnerable are computers and their operations. Many major computer crimes are currently being perpetrated; million-dollar thefts are commonplace. If common (or even uncommon) thieves can compromise computer systems, how much greater is the threat from sophisticated spymasters and espionage agents! We need every possible device and security procedure that will help to control the potential loss of sensitive data and information. Counterintelligence can help design appropriate measures to prevent penetration and compromise.

Physical security is expensive. High-quality physical security is much more costly than basic traditional security. It is important to know how much of a company's resources should be allocated to, say, perimeter security. If intelligence indicates that an industrial facility is likely to be infiltrated from without by persons or groups bent on burglary, looting, sabotage, theft of trade secrets, or other subversion, it would be justified in using a large amount of total resources for the physical security of the perimeter. On the other hand, if intelligence advises that outsiders are a lesser threat than insiders, we would want to direct resources accordingly. This is not to say that we should ignore the need for a comprehensive, balanced security effort. Rather there is a need to provide priorities based on a sound assessment of the nature of the threat. That assessment must be based on counterintelligence research.

Counterintelligence should be aware of the state of the art of espionage and counterintelligence and thereby assist security operations in ensuring that measures taken to defeat the spies are equal to the challenge. Intelligence will also help a company to keep abreast of the latest developments affecting every aspect of physical, personnel, and procedural security operations and methods.

Intelligence should be tapped for advice as to appropriate liaisons security ought to cultivate with federal, state, and local agencies. To what extent should information be shared with these agencies? To what degree can they be expected to provide mutual aid in preventive and protective endeavors? Advice is also needed as to maintaining liaison with other industrial and commercial facilities. Since many of these companies will be noncompetitors, there would seem to be no reason to avoid security liaison for general prevention and protection purposes. Whether these facilities are in fact competitors or have strong attachments of one kind or another with competing companies needs to be checked out by counterintelligence.

Indeed, as has been demonstrated by these examples of the use of counterintelligence for security management decision making, it is an unfortunate company that does not maintain a competent operational counterintelligence component.

AID TO RISK MANAGEMENT AND LEGAL TACTICS

To some extent the depredations of competitive industrial espionage may be compensated for by insurance or by civil court actions for damages. But insurance may be expensive and at best probably will not cover the full impact of the loss of trade secrets or other sensitive materials. If the espionage is detected and investigation reveals that its source is a competitor, suit may be brought for a large monetary recovery. If, however, the espionage is directed by a foreign competitor, substantial recovery will be unlikely. If it is directed by a foreign power, recovery is all but impossible. In any event, even in the case of domestic competitors the total actual damages are seldom compensated through legal processes.

An example of the inadequacy of recovery in damages is the Mitsubishi Plastic Industries case. The Celanese Plastics Co. of South Carolina sued Mitsubishi for having purloined through bribery technical trade secrets related to the Celanese filmmaking process. The suit was brought in federal court under the federal racketeering law. Charges were dropped by the court against Mitsubishi and three of their Japanese employees in the settling of the case. Mitsubishi was fined $50,000 and forfeited an additional $250,000 after pleading no contest to the federal racketeering charges. Thus for only $300,000 Mitsubishi acquired trade secrets worth millions from Celanese Plastics.

Neither insurance nor legal action is a sufficient shield against industrial espionage. This is not to say that risk management in a broader sense than mere insurance and legal tactics that are proactive instead of reactive are of little value in combating industrial espionage. Coordinated with counterintelligence, risk management and legal tactics may be very effective in combating espionage.

Intelligence may serve to assist insurance purchases and direct resources discreetly. Counterintelligence and risk management should be bedfellows for cost-effective insurance protection.

Two of the legal tactics that may be used on a proactive basis are contractual restrictions dealing with patents and trade secrets as a condition of employment and publication of procedures and distribution of a manual.

Employees in the United States are very mobile, making the safeguarding of trade secrets exceptionally difficult. Contractual limitations may be useful in this regard. The contract may limit the use and disclosure of trade secrets during current employment and any future employments and/or provide restraints against future activities of employees after they have terminated. The basic problem of such agreement arises from the right of a former employee to seek gainful employment that may involve prior experience. As a result, some of these agreements have not held up in court challenges. One of the best ways to ensure the legal viability of secrecy or nondisclosure agreements and noncompetitive covenants is to demonstrate that counterintelligence indicated the need for such affirmative legal steps in the particular case(s) in which they were used.

The use of intelligence in both risk management and legal tactics for the combating of industrial espionage is essential to the cost-effectiveness of insurance decisions and the design of lawful restraints on disclosure. Proactive legal tactics are also required to counter the operations of intelligence-identified spies and to bring them to justice. Intelligence will guide these enforcement efforts and help to ensure their success.

Counterintelligence has many uses that could be considered strictly in-house. Our intelligence is developed by us and used by us for many of the purposes mentioned in this chapter. This is fine as far as it goes; the problem is that it does not go far enough. There is a hidden challenge in the production of counterintelligence. That is the rational, highly protected, and sophisticated sharing of our intelligence with appropriate others.

If we do not share with counterparts and they do not share with us, our common goals will be frustrated. We will each be starting from scratch; we will be duplicating a hundred, or possibly a thousand, times efforts that could be shared for the benefit of all.

It is always difficult to consider disseminating the intelligence that has been so carefully developed and compiled, sometimes at great expense and at great risk. Among government agencies at all levels, there has always been a problem of intelligence sharing. State and local agencies frequently complain that federal agencies share information obtained from them but refuse to reciprocate. They call intelligence exchange with some agencies a one-way street. The authors can attest to personal experiences that tend to substantiate these complaints. However, these same state and local agencies that complain about federal agencies are reluctant to share their intelligence with other state and local agencies.

With many agencies and/or industries cooperating and coordinating intelligence, a far more effective counterintelligence effort at much less cost could be mounted. While the U.S. government and private industry are developing intelligence either in parallel or even at cross purposes, the KGB is optimizing its espionage resources. By avoiding duplication of effort and ensuring that appropriate information is available to all as needed, the KGB apparatus is overwhelming. In the strictly competitive espionage area, the situation is no different. Cooperation and coordination in the application of counterintelligence are negligible. There is no united front against spies and spy masters. Agents of foreign powers, agents of foreign competitors, and agents of rogue domestic competitors find defenses weak and scattered. No wonder they score so many touchdowns. No wonder our hard-won technological superiority is an open sieve, and foreign technology transfer is such a scandal.

The day of holding our intelligence so close to the vest that it smothers us should soon be over. If it is not over soon it may be all over for us. Is it too much to expect that we should have some faith in our fellow Americans? Should we not trust our own business colleagues, at least those who are not in a competing industry? Counterintelligence should be able to advise which agencies and industrial firms could be worked with on a mutual aid basis. This does not mean that we are about to share trade secrets. What we need to share is intelligence concerning espionage threats, from whatever source.

Can information sharing be controlled? Not many years ago, there was virtually no sharing of organized crime intelligence in the law enforcement field. Every federal, state, and major local agency had its own organized crime intelligence unit. Its files were kept isolated and inviolate, often not made available even to members of the same department, despite the need to have access by various interdepartmental peers and colleagues. Share these gems of intelligence with other departments or agencies—never!

When this situation was examined on a statewide basis, it was found that there was overlapping and duplication, incorrect assumptions based on purely local information, absence in one file of critical data held by another agency in the same locality, limited scope and myopic analysis, poor analysis and nonoperational file content, inaccurate data bases, and no national or statewide perspective

What was discovered in this research undoubtedly would be found at least to some extent by any study of industrial counterintelligence files today. The need for controlled information sharing and mutual aid is critical. Intelligence should be shared with colleagues and with public agencies. One of the most important uses of counterintelligence capability is to use data in trade for additional data in the possession of appropriate others. Without mutual aid and controlled information sharing, the counterintelligence effort is bound to be suboptimal.

Many security directors fear that by opening up files to others, they will lose control of their intelligence. This is a totally unwarranted assumption if prior to any dissemination of intelligence the following factors are analyzed and evaluated:

- Nature of the information to be shared.
- Source of the information.
- Classification of the information.
- Reliability of the recipient.
- Prohibition on third-party access.
- Reason for recipient's request.
- Use to which recipient intends to put data.
- Need to know and right to know.
- Previous sharing and exchange experience.

The decision as to whether to share will be based on a variety of factors. There is obviously no place in any information sharing system for the disclosure of proprietary information. There is so much else that needs to be shared. The threat of industrial espionage is a real and present danger. If we were faced by physical attack or enemy action, we would rally around. But here we are faced by something far more insidious and threatening: an invisible enemy ready to compromise employees and destroy the industry. It is time that those who are threatened organize a counterattack. The most potent weapon to use in combating industrial espionage is a viable counterintelligence capability, one that has brought together the best information and analysis.

ORGANIZED CRIME AND TERRORISTS

We have already discussed many of the uses of intelligence. It is not, however, the position of the authors that these are the only uses of counterintelligence. We are sure that conscientious developers of intelligence applications will find other uses in addition to those we have suggested. However, those presented here are uses that may be employed by security directors and managers in virtually any aspect of private security. We now turn to the use of intelligence for combating the special threats of organized crime and terrorism. It may be revealing to consider the experience of one of the authors in his efforts to encourage the development of computerized organized crime intelligence systems in the field of law enforcement. As director and founder of the New York State Identification and Intelligence System (NYSIIS), the co-author used computerization as a tool to achieve statewide sharing of organized crime intelligence and to achieve more sophisticated methods of combating organized crime. There may well be some parallels between the attitude of some police agencies and police chiefs toward organized crime intelligence and the attitudes of some in industry toward counterintelligence. This will not be a true paradigm but it may illuminate some dark corners of our security operations aimed at coping with industrial espionage involving organized crimes.

For many years in law enforcement, basically four strategies were employed in combating organized crime:

1. Attrition: Arrests of individual suspects. Except for limited increased organized crime overhead expenses, this did little or no harm to the organization.
2. Exposure: Sensational hearings conducted on a sporadic basis by politically ambitious prosecutors or commissions. Instead of hurting organized crime, these exposés may add to the subjects' reputations and serve to put victims in fear without the need to engage in violence.
3. Harassment: Use of vagrancy arrests, close surveillance, and other techniques of questionable legality. They produce undesirable public relations and demean the process of justice.
4. The ostrich practice: Ignore organized crime and deny its existence. This obviously gives aid and comfort to the enemy.

Despite the application of these strategies, organized crime has continued to thrive and expand. The New York State Identification and Intelligence System (NYSIIS), recognizing the inadequacy of past practices, developed five additional potential strategies:

1. Subversion: Tactical actions calculated to breed internal dissension or to create distrust and suspicion.
2. Alienation: Means devised to demonstrate and emphasize the disadvantages of membership in organized crime.
3. Disruption: Concentrated efforts to disrupt or dislocate organized crime activities, thereby reducing return on investments or increasing the cost of doing business.
4. Penetration: Efforts to buy information or informants or to penetrate organized crime with law enforcement representatives. (This calls for close liaison, coordination, and cooperation with law enforcement.)
5. Blocking: Use of public education to assist concerned persons to confine or eliminate further organized crime activities in their fields of interest.

The importance of these strategies lies in the fact that when they are properly used in a legal and ethical manner, they may enable us to counter the threat of organized crime.

All of these new strategies may be best employed in a multi-strategy approach that is capable of a flexible, imaginative attack based on a repertoire of possible strategies. Such an approach has been working well in the public law enforcement effort against organized crime, and it may be applicable to some degree in defenses against organized crime's involvement in industrial espionage. Not all counter-measures have to be passive and reactive; perhaps the best defense is a determined offense. Using counterintelligence capability and a pro-active security operation, we may gain the initiative and mount a successful offensive against organized crime. Some of the strategies developed by NYSIIS may serve well in using counterintelligence resources to combat industrial espionage.

We have much to fear from organized crime. Any strategy (or strategies) that will help us utilize our intelligence effectively will surely be useful. Organized crime operates in a shadowy world providing many services to the highest bidder. In reference to its impact on industrial espionage, we need to reckon with the fact that organized crime affects industry in the following ways:

- Fencing operations (trade secrets for sale).
- Infiltration of security guard unions.
- Compromising of sensitive personnel.
- Movement into more sophisticated and less obvious criminal enterprises.
- Potential threat of violence, blackmail, extortion, and financing of espionage operations.

The fencing of stolen high-technology data or devices is highly profitable for organized criminals. They have international contacts and are willing to sell to the highest bidder.

In order to consolidate the position of organized crime in dealing with private security, strong initiatives have been mounted to gain control of guard unions. A number of unions, including the Allied International Union of Security Guards and Special Police, and the Federation of Special Police and Law Enforcement Officers, are controlled by convicted racketeers as of 1983.

Organized crime has a long history of effective efforts at compromising and corrupting its victims. As personnel become privy to sensitive materials, they become potential targets for corrupters, who know how to trap victims through usurious loans, gratuitous payments of goods and services, embarrassing sexual and other exotic and erotic pictures and recordings, and so on.

Organized crime infiltrates any area where substantial profits may be acquired through illegal operations. As racketeers have become more sophisticated some eschew the more coarse and common types of enterprise such as gambling, drugs, and vice and target less obvious criminal enterprises such as industrial espionage.

The genius of organized crime operations is that all understand that whatever goes down, the activity is never too far from violence. Thus they are able to make offers that cannot be refused even if they are involved in the financing, fencing, or conduct of espionage, or other sophisticated types of criminal activity. Violence, blackmail, extortion, kidnapping, and all those other neat things lie just below the surface of their dealings. And those who get caught in the web know this only too well.

Intelligence can also pinpoint the possibility of *terrorist* activity targeted to defeat the success of our industrial economy. Counterintelligence should make security operations aware of the identity of terrorists, their modus operandi, and the need for executive protection.

International terrorism has shown an alarming increase in recent years. Although the vast majority of terroristic attacks have been overseas, domestically the United States has not totally escaped such violence. Also, American diplomats and business executives comprise the largest national target group for international terrorism, and this trend shows no sign of abating. Understandably, there is a growing concern for the safety of Americans both at home and abroad. Business men and women and industrial leaders are attractive targets. It is the responsibility of counterintelligence to give them advice and counsel as to the degree and nature of any risks.

The tactic of disinformation is being widely used against the United States by communist countries. They promulgate lies, propaganda, and false documents and then commit such violent acts as bombings, murder, kidnapping, and sabotage. Corporations, particularly those with multinational interests are rightly concerned. Intelligence can help to pinpoint vulnerable areas in advance and reinforce those areas with greater security resources. Intelligence should also develop specific procedures for dealing with terrorist attack on facilities and executives. It needs to develop policies for kidnappings, bomb threats, extortion attempts, and so on. Intelligence may reveal the need to consider kidnap and ransom insurance, at least for executives who travel internationally.

Thus, a very significant employment of counterintelligence is in combating domestic and/or international terrorism. Once again we see the relevance of this scourge to the security of American business and industry and to the continued survival of our most important executives.

Executive protection requires extensive planning and often the installation of expensive security procedures and practices, including the use of bodyguards. The security director, guided by counterintelligence, must develop plans, supervise their execution, and update them on a continuous basis. The plans should take into account the particular executive's role. If he or she travels overseas, a different plan may be developed for travel purposes than the plan used while he or she is in the United States.

There is a special need to protect executives while they are in transit. Seventy percent of all successful executive kidnappings have taken place while the victim was in transit, in most cases while he or she was driving. Home security and family education are key ingredients. Whatever else may or may not be done, the counterintelligence unit also has a responsibility.

GRAY MARKETS AND SPY GANGS

On June 22, 1982, two engineers from Hitachi, Ltd. walked into the offices of Glenmar Associates and spoke to the owner, whom they knew by the name of Alex Harrison. Harrison showed them the secret information he had obtained from IBM in accordance with prior agreements. The Hitachi engineers produced a receipt that demonstrated $495,000 had been wired to Harrison's bank account that day. At this point, Harrison produced credentials identifying himself as an FBI agent and arrested the two Japanese.

The espionage was part of Operation Pengem. An FBI sting operation, it was dubbed Pengem, short for Penetrate Gray Electronics Markets. IBM counterintelligence had developed evidence that Hitachi had acquired stolen IBM documents, and in August 1981, IBM learned that Hitachi was looking for more secret data. It launched an investigation and confirmed the intelligence. IBM then went to the FBI, which agreed to help with the case. This example is a classic case of the use of counterintelligence by a private company to protect its own proprietary information and to expose the operations of a gray market actively engaged in the transfer of U.S. technology to the U.S.S.R. and its satellites.

The scope of the lucrative gray market can be assessed by the fact that in 1983 there were fifty technology-theft investigations underway across the country, half of them considered major cases. There is a KGB presence and a Japanese presence wherever there is a concentration of scientific and technological research and development. Although industrial counterintelligence must deal with some of the world's best spy masters, industry is on its own. Industrial espionage, as in the IBM case, will be countered by industrial intelligence if it is to be done at all. Thus one of the significant uses and roles of counterintelligence is to tackle the gray market.

How does the gray market operate? Consider the case of John Henry Jackson, also known as One-Eyed Jack. Jackson has been depicted as a kingpin in the electronics underground. A current case against him in 1983 alleges that he organized and led a crime gang that stole 10,000 memory chips from Intel Corporation. He also is alleged to have remarketed 100,000 or so similar products, most of which were stolen. These silicon chips stolen from Intel were worth $100 each, a sizable loss of assets. But over and above the economic trauma is the fact that these computer chips have a broad application—from video arcade games to fighter-aircraft guidance systems.

The gray market has grown into a vast underworld distribution network for electronic components and computer chips. Not all that is marketed is stolen; some of the goods are surplus and factory rejects. The market has spawned spy gangs both foreign and domestic that are ready to sell to the highest bidder. It is called a gray market only because some of its dealings are within the fringes of the law. To a large extent, however, it has become a true black market serving questionable domestic and foreign competitors and hostile nations.

In the Intel case, the stolen chips were removed from a fenced storage room protected by alarms, twenty-four hour security guards, an employee badge system, visitor and after-hours sign-in logs, security audits, spot checks, and closed-circuit television. All of these good physical security devices were negated by the simple device of having an Intel security guard as an accomplice. Allegedly this guard carried the chips out of the storage area in garbage bags and on his person. This follows the usual pattern, since some 90 percent of all such thefts occur during the shipping and storing of chips. It is also a classical pattern in that the spy gangs recruit insiders to do the real dirty work. Intel has now augmented its counterintelligence and carefully monitors the local gray market.

There is no industry-wide effort to fight the gray market. As a result, each industry is not only receiving little, if any, help from public security agencies, but individual companies are getting no support from the counterintelligence capabilities of friendly domestic industries. The gray market is organized; legitimate industry is in disarray. The parallel between the successes of industrial espionage and the thriving business of organized crime is striking. In both instances an organized (but illegal) operation is winning over a disorganized (but legal) adversary. The answer is clear: we need counterintelligence of the highest order and cooperation and coordination of an even higher order. Gray markets and spy gangs can be defeated through counterintelligence intelligently used.

SUMMARY

Intelligence and its special application as counterintelligence as applied to cope with industrial espionage, organized crime, and terrorism has been the purpose of this chapter. The end product of counterintelligence is not always pretty. The finest hour of counterintelligence is when it prevents and protects its clients from falling into the toils of the corrupters and the spymasters. Without the ready alert of our intelligence to forewarn of grave danger even the best of us may succumb.

The intelligence product can be of great help in the identification of the threats we face. Counterintelligence can provide us with the big picture of the type of threats we need to address. It can also indicate to us what segments or specific parts of our businesses are most vulnerable. Thus, counterintelligence serves as an early warning system and enables us to do intelligence target hardening.

Counterintelligence is a strong ally of the personnel department and it is urgent that security and personnel be fully coordinated. Counterintelligence contributes to the continuous screening of insiders.

Countermeasures to cope with the ever-increasing threat of industrial espionage must be based on sound counterintelligence evaluations. We need to be concerned about espionage agents collecting information both by technical devices and by human beings.

Assessments and continuous assistance by counterintelligence may be employed to provide us with guidance to preventive and protective priorities.

Counterintelligence should be able to provide advice for management decision making as to the needed types of, and degrees of, security. We would expect recommendations for sophisticated but realistic security measures. Indeed, by better identifying the nature of the threat, counterintelligence may prove to be a profit center by providing security with truly cost-effective alternatives.

Coordinated with counterintelligence, risk management and legal tactics may be very effective techniques. Legal tactics so guided may be cost effective also. Proactive legal tactics may be used (as indicated by intelligence) to guide enforcement action against spies.

There is a hidden challenge in the production of intelligence: the discreet sharing of our intelligence with appropriate others. Information sharing can be controlled. Intelligence can be coordinated for the best interests of all.

Closely allied with the threat of espionage are the threats of organized crime and terrorism. These are also subject to the effective use and application of counterintelligence. Counterintelligence should make our security operations aware of the identity of terrorists, their modus operandi, and the need for executive protection. The security director, guided by counterintelligence, must develop plans, supervise their execution, and update them on a continuous basis.

Intelligence has alerted us to the development of gray markets and organized espionage gangs dealing in foreign and domestic technology transfer. When it comes to industrial espionage, much is left to private security counterintelligence. Spy gangs can be defeated through organized industrial counterintelligence intelligently employed and deployed.

New threats, new circumstances, developing methodologies, advances in technology, and so on will generate new needs, new uses, and new demands on our counterintelligence capability. It must be kept in trim to meet and combat industrial espionage.

IV. ESPIONAGE COUNTERMEASURES

12. Facility Security

The hole and the patch should be commensurate. —Thomas Jefferson

GENERAL PRINCIPLES

In dealing with industrial espionage in the United States, facility security is the exclusive responsibility of the legal form of ownership. Where the federal government is involved through grants or direct contracts, some assistance is provided by the cognizant department. Thus the DoD issues security guidelines of the most stringent nature. In some cases where the individual state is involved, some guidelines may also issue. For the most part, however, the private owner alone must cope with industrial espionage. It is essential that the owner seek a competent security director and provide adequate resources for the security department.

Security must be realistic, management oriented, and cost-effective. The security director must have the ability to assess risks and vulnerabilities and prescribe reasonable remedies that will meet the threat. Excessive amounts of security may be counterproductive and even clue industrial espionage agents to the fact that there are valuable research information, advanced processes, trade secrets, or other confidential data worth stealing. This is not to say that the security director should mute requests for personnel and resources; rather, the security director should be zealous but not overzealous, anticipate potential problems but not be overwhelmed by them. He or she should have a clear concept of the threat, its nature, and its likely targets. He or she should assess, evaluate, and draw rational conclusions based on evidence disclosed through surveys and inspections and on careful analysis of intelligence reports.

Information can be kept confidential and secret if access is limited. Generally, classified data, restricted areas, and so on should be accessible only to those who have the right to know and the need to know the data or have the right and the need to enter the restricted areas. The fewer people who have access and the fewer people who are aware of confidential and secret resources, the better for security. The fact that such resources are present should be concealed, for a breach of security has occurred when it becomes generally known that a target exists.

Facility security measures should be designed so that they give early warning of penetration or loss. Early warnings may be generated through facility intelligence or through alarm systems, audits, inventories, observations, and so on. Although it is essential to have the ultimate defense, or the strongest barrier, closest to the target, adequate physical defenses from the perimeter inward are essential. The concepts of early warning, combined with defense in depth, should point the way to quality security for the facility. The effect of fences, walls, doors, barred windows, and so on is primarily a delaying tactic, which needs to be backed up by rapid response from security personnel. In the absence of such immediate backup, no serious defense in depth has been provided. Such support should be alerted by some form of an alarm system along the fence line, on doors and windows, inside buildings, on the targets themselves, or within the restricted areas containing the targets.

It is most important that responsibility and/or guilt can be pinpointed to a limited number of individuals. The responsible persons have to account as best they can for any penetration or loss. While they themselves may be innocent, if they were assigned responsibility, they may be held accountable to assist in the investigation. Their knowledge of the persons, places, and things that may be involved should assist in resolving the case. If there has been collusion among two or more of the responsible persons, they will realize that their collusion rests on a fragile base since they are being held responsible in any event. This may result in one or another informing on the conspirators.

Perhaps the most important principle is to ensure that employees at all levels are security conscious and aware of such threats as may be within their purview. Employees who understand the need for security will cooperate with the security department. Executives will assist by showing their own regard and budgetary support for the security department; rank-and-file employees will serve as additional eyes and ears for the security director. The director and the security department in turn must create confidence and goodwill through their professional skills and competence and through their attitudes and dedication.

ILLEGAL ACCESS

An industrial spy who is an outsider—one not on the target company's payroll or not otherwise authorized to enter through the outer and inner defenses—must obtain access to the facility. The spy may need to penetrate the outer defenses to gain access to the specific objective of the espionage. The first line of defense is the protection of the perimeter. For this purpose, physical barriers are usually considered to be effective in deterring or delaying intrusion. The most common type of perimeter barrier is the fence unless the facility building itself occupies the entire plot. In this case the outer walls of the building are the perimeter and must be protected accordingly.

Perimeter Protection

A minimum height of at least eight feet is considered a basic requirement for a security perimeter fence. Usually this means seven feet of chain-link steel wire topped by one foot of tautly strung barbed wire. In many cases, the barbed wire is strung on V-shaped angled bars, or the fence may be topped by a concertina type of steel wire studded with razor-sharp blades. Since all fences are primarily used to delay the intruder, the perimeter must be alarmed so that there may be immediate guard response to attempts to penetrate the perimeter.

To the extent that building walls may be part or all of the perimeter, or the building walls are the second line of defense within a protected perimeter, they also need to be fitted with alarms. Buildings are vulnerable, primarily because of doors, windows, skylights, and other openings. These parts of the building are most in need of some form of counterpenetration alarm. In addition, skylights and windows require iron or steel bars and/or heavy steel mesh on all openings larger than ninety-six square inches if that opening is less than eighteen feet from the ground or less than fourteen feet from structures outside the building. Since most building break-ins are through windows, it may be desirable to paint the insides of windows so that thieves and spies do not readily become aware of the contents or of the activities of personnel within the building.

Generally security efforts avoid potentially lethal methods, even though they might ensure a high degree of security, so it is not surprising that some people are also opposed to the use of guard dogs in perimeter protection and/or sentry dogs on guard patrol. Nevertheless, guard and sentry dogs can be used very effectively in certain situations. Doberman pinschers, if properly controlled, can serve the dual purpose of sounding an alarm and capturing anyone who may have breached the perimeter. Sentry dogs, usually german shepherds, can make their rounds with security guards, increasing the effectiveness of the guards due to the dogs' keen sense of hearing and smell.

Perimeter protection is augmented by the use of a protective lighting system. Although the lighting itself is not a physical barrier, it increases the effectiveness of fences and patrolling security guards. Four basic types of fixtures are useful for perimeter protection:

1. Floodlights, which produce a beam of light.
2. Streetlights, which produce a low intensity and diffused illumination.
3. Fresnel units, which produce wide horizontal beams.
4. Searchlights, which produce a highly focused beam, which may be aimed in various directions.

Some or all of these may be used, depending on the requirements of a specific facility.

Protective Alarms

Protective alarms are a necessary component of both the outer and inner defenses. This discussion of alarms bridges the conceptual distinction between perimeter and interior physical security. Both the exterior gates and the fencing should be equipped with effective alarm systems. Fence alarms may use seismic sensors placed underground along the fence line and able to detect footsteps or vehicular pressure. Sonic alarms depend on noise for activation of the system, and vibration detectors are highly sensitive to the movement of the objects to which they are attached. Both may be used for fence protection. Laser beams have proved to be particularly dependable in outside locations, such as along a fence line. The fence gates may be protected by a host of sensing devices similar to those used in buildings to protect doors and other openings. They might include all of the sensors that could be used for fencing alarms, as well as the following:

1. Metal tape or wire having a continuous current system that will sound the alarm if ruptured.
2. Magnetic contacts on doors and other openings that sound an alarm when the magnetic field is broken.
3. Photoelectric systems using beams of invisible light as sensors have the capability of bending around corners and curves (by the use of mirrors) and thus may have special utility in some installations.
4. Motion detection alarms that depend on ultrasonic or radio frequency waves sensing any deviance in wave patterns caused by an intruder
5. Pressure sensors that may be concealed under a mat or a carpet.
6. Capacitance alarms that may be used for metal containers that are not grounded.
7. Closed circuit television, which may be used as an automatic alarm system as well as a surveillance system.

Parking Areas

Parking areas may be located inside the protected perimeter or outside it. In either case protection against industrial espionage will be facilitated by fencing the area. A fenced car park will allow for controlled entry and egress, so that unauthorized vehicles will be excluded and unusual activity of any kind relative to authorized motor vehicles may be better detected. If the parking area is outside the perimeter, fencing should help to reduce the number of vehicles that are stolen, broken into, or vandalized. If the fenced parking area is within the perimeter, control over access to the parked vehicles may prevent employees from secreting documents, materials, formulas, or other objects of espionage in their cars. Thus, from the standpoint of providing employees with less vulnerable parking areas and thereby increasing morale and from the viewpoint of discouraging the ready transport of the products of espionage, fenced parking areas are a wise investment.

Inner Defenses

Except for specially protected spaces such as interior parking areas, outdoor transformers, and yard storage areas, the facility buildings themselves comprise the main component of the second line of defense against illegal access. In this connection, the concept of defensible space is important:

1. Avoid creating blind areas with landscaping or building design.
2. Avoid low and unreinforced windows.
3. Windows should be made of unbreakable materials.
4. Avoid excess entrances and exits.
5. Use steel-reinforced roofing grids where necessary.
6. Use locking devices that guarantee their cylinders are designed so they cannot be picked.
7. Use locks designed to frustrate sawing or cutting with a bolt cutter and that can withstand pounding with a heavy hammer.
8. Where feasible, use time locks and locks activated by complex combinations, card keys, or coded pushbuttons or that are computer controlled using fingerprints, voiceprints, or hand-geometry technology.
9. Use appropriate security lighting for spaces within the perimeter and for the buildings themselves.
10. Use appropriate alarm systems.

The third line of defense comprises restricted areas and security devices inside the facility buildings themselves. Since in most cases it is impractical to give ultimate security attention to the entire facility, it is good practice to give priority to more sensitive areas within the plant. Areas that need special protection against industrial espionage, sabotage, or theft should be designated restricted locations, and only those persons who have the right to enter and the need to enter should be allowed access. Persons within such areas should display distinctive badges that verify their authorization to be present.

An effective method of controlling such badges is through a badge exchange system. The authorized person exchanges his or her regular facility badge for a different badge on entering the restricted area through the control desk. When leaving the restricted area, the person surrenders the special badge and retrieves the original badge he or she had surrendered on entry. If the facility has a very special secret area within the restricted area to which access is severely limited, a second badge exchange process may be indicated. The authorized person would surrender the restricted area badge at the secret-area control desk and pick up another badge verifying authorization to be present in this highly restricted area. When leaving this area, the person would surrender this ultimate badge and pick up his or her restricted-area badget, which is again surrendered on leaving the restricted area.

Locks, safes, and vaults are essential components of inner defenses. Locks have two basic functions: they provide a psychological deterrent and increase delay for intruders.

It is questionable whether any locking system will deter a professional spy or thief since there are so many ways such a person may achieve access by circumventing lock and key systems. The professional may pick the lock or use special devices to pull or rip out the entire cylinder. He or she may spring the door, peel the jamb, saw the bolt, remove door hinges, or simply obtain a copy of the key through failure of the key control system. An example of such a system failure is the inability of motels and hotels to account for room keys. Three types of keyless locks currently are being employed to overcome the limitations of keying systems: cipher-coded pushbutton locks; card entry systems (badges may be used for this purpose); and various electronic locks, some with computer assistance, that may grant access based on personal appearance, hand geometry, or some other characteristic.

Important as locking systems may be for the prevention of industrial espionage, a determined professional spy may be able to defeat any system. The greatest advantages are the delay factor and also the fact that some evidence may be left at the scene confirming a break-in.

A variety of safes are available for the storage of industrial espionage targets. Many of these targets are documents containing information on such matters as:

1. New financing and capital investments.
2. Planned mergers, acquisitions, or organizational changes.
3. Production costs.
4. New processing techniques or products.
5. Marketing methods and market area tests.
6. Customer lists, price lists, and advertising plans.
7. Numbers and quality of research staff.
8. Research findings, development, and pilot testing.
9. Trademarks and patents.
10. Lawsuits.
11. Regulatory agency violations.

Because the industrial spy probably wants such information, the safe should be burglar resistant. The possibility of fire should not be overlooked; therefore the room should have sprinklers. Perhaps an espionage agent failed to steal or photograph target documents; he or she may decide to set a fire to destroy the documents sought. Thus it is desirable to have duplicate documents at a remote site under the same strict security as is maintained at the principal location.

Vaults are basically large safes, but they project the image of being much more secure than safes. Walk-in strong rooms with time locks, multiple dial combination locks, steel bars, and foot-thick steel doors are impressive. If the entire strong room (including the floor and ceiling) is encased in steel plates, the vault will surely be a very secure storage space. Indeed, for purposes of fire security, a portion of the vault could be designed as a fire-resistant enclosure. Unfortunately, in many instances, the vault is not actually as secure as it appears to be, for penetration is sometimes effected through the vault floor, ceiling, or side walls.

SPECIAL SECURITY MEASURES

A number of special security measures need to be tailored to individual industrial espionage security threats. Some examples show particular espionage circumstances that indicate the need for special security measures.

1. Car manufacturers, somewhat like dress designers, invest large sums in tooling and design changes on new car models, and this information is very sensitive. As a counterintelligence technique, some companies are reported to prepare elaborate decoy models in an effort to confuse industrial spies.
2. Chemical research theft presents special problems. One espionage agent gained access to Merck & Co.'s research files over a period of several months prior to the announcement by Merck that it had developed a drug effective against a deadly poultry parasite. At about the same time the agent, Robert Aries, was ready to claim he had developed a drug that was equally effective. An investigation by the Merck security organization established that the data had been stolen from their subsidiary's files, and Merck filed suit against Aries for $7.8 million. In the meantime, it was also discovered that Aries had stolen industrial secrets from two other major U.S. companies.
3. The Concorde Jet was the target of an East German network of espionage agents who sought to pirate technical information that would cut costs for the U.S.S.R., which had also embarked on the development of its own supersonic transport. An East German hydraulics engineer was arrested in Paris carrying microfilm disguised as candy. He was on his way to

southwestern France to establish a front for stealing additional secret plans of the British-French Concorde from Sud-Aviation in Toulouse. Before being arrested, the engineer had already stolen many of the plans that he typically converted to microfilm. In some cases they were stuffed into tubes of toothpaste and dropped off for Soviet couriers in toilets on the Ostend to Warsaw express train. The Soviet supersonic aircraft was tested several months before the Concorde as a result of this industrial espionage.

It should be understood that the cases that have been made public by court action, arrests, and so on are only the tip of the iceberg. Industrial spies and counterspies play very hard ball. A poignant illustration of this is actually a follow-up of the Concorde spy scandal. At the 1973 Paris air show a Soviet TU 144 being displayed there crashed after trying to copy a sophisticated maneuver by the Concorde. The activities of the deputy air attaché to the Russian embassy in Paris indicate that the crash may have been due to an espionage failure. According to author Peter Hamilton,[1]

> French sources said at the time that [the deputy air attaché] had picked up a spare part from the Concorde's complex fuel distribution system in the display stand at the Paris International Air Show some days before the crash. At the time the part was incorrectly described in reports as a gyroscope. In fact it was a piece of delicate equipment which controlled the fuel distribution, and it was known that the Russians had had particular trouble with this system.
>
> Fuel aboard Concorde is stored in three tanks; one in each wing and one in the center of the fusilage. A special mechanism causes the fuel to move backward when the plane's nose is down and forward when the plane is climbing; to the left when the plane banks right and to the right when it banks left.
>
> It is believed that the TU 144 disintegrated when it tried to copy Concorde's "on/off" landing technique, in which it swooped down to the runway, brushed its wheels along the tarmac for a few yards and then soared up in a steep banking climb. This put the fuel distribution system through its toughest paces, and it is possible the TU 144 had not tried it before. Possibly the Russians felt that unless the TU 144 copied Concorde their aircraft would look second best and it must therefore try.
>
> The day after the crash Colonel Mironkine was ordered to leave Paris.

---

[1] Peter Hamilton, *Espionage, Terrorism and Subversion in an Industrial Society* (Leatherhead, Surrey, England: Peter A. Heims, Ltd., 1979), p. 64.

GUARD FORCES

Any facility that may be the target of industrial espionage must have a guard force. Despite the many technical tools available, only human beings have the ability to distinguish friend from foe and can make decisions to arrest or not to arrest. There are so many variables involved in security operations that the human brain is required to cope with them all. Computers may be programmed in remarkable ways and, together with robots, they may replace many guards assigned to routine tasks. We have not yet, however, arrived at that point in scientific development where we can rely on computer directed robots to actually perform the arrest process, or to decide when to shoot, or not to shoot, in resisting an intruder's attack.

Guards must be selected carefully and trained well. Unfortunately all too often guards are hired at minimum wage levels and are given little, if any, formal training. The first major government-funded study of the security industry, known as the Rand Reports, issued in 1972, severely criticized the quality of guard personnel and the lack of training that was provided them.[2] Guards are often inadequately supervised, undependable employees, inadequately investigated prior to hire, prone to misuse authority, and inadequately trained even when armed.

In dealing with guard forces, it is of some consequence for the security director to decide whether to hire guard personnel (proprietary) or to contract with an agency that supplies guards as needed for a fixed fee. There are advantages and disadvantages to both. The advantages of contract guard services, in theory, are:

1. The security director can get rid of individual contract guards easily.
2. The director has flexibility in contracting for more or fewer guards as needed.
3. Absentees may be replaced readily.
4. Administrative chores such as hiring, supervision, guard training, uniforming, and so on are taken care of.
5. Generally contract guards cost less and are most often nonunion.
6. Contract guards are likely to be more objective since they are not personally as close to the other facility employees as proprietary guards would be.

---

[2] J.S. Kakalik and Sorrel Wildhorn, *The Private Police Industry: Its Nature and Extent*, R-870/DOJ (Washington, D.C.: Government Printing Office, 1972), vol. 2. (Little has changed since this report was released.)

7. The contract guard service may be able to provide specialists and equipment as needed for a variety of nonroutine operations.

But there are disadvantages to contract guard services as well:

1. High turnover of personnel leading to shortages of guards.
2. Moonlighting (because of low salaries, guards may take other jobs or, alternatively, public police and others may moonlight as guards).
3. Lack of commitment to the facility.
4. Lax hiring practices and poor or nonexistent training.
5. Liability problems. Unless there are special provisions in the contract, the user of contract guards is not held harmless in the event of liability for the acts of contract guards. Such provisions may be an added cost of some considerable amount.

Proprietary guards have these advantages, in theory:

1. Loyalty to the employing facility.
2. Incentive; there may be greater promotion possibilities in the security department or elsewhere in the organization.
3. Less turnover and familiarity with the facility.
4. Augmentation of facility image.
5. More direct control and communication and better liaison with local law enforcement.

The disadvantages of proprietary guards should also be considered:

1. May become unionized and have a conflict of interest in handling strikes.
2. An excess of fraternization, causing loss of effectiveness, or collusion.
3. Expense, particularly because of fringe benefits.
4. Personnel problems (it may be hard to replace absent personnel, to fire incompetents, to lay off excess guards, or to expand the number of personnel as needs change).
5. Administrative burdens assumed by the personnel director and the security manager.

The security director should be aware of all of these advantages and disadvantages, many of which become more realistic when applied to a particular situation. For example, the ability to increase or decrease the number of guards without layoffs or emergency hiring may be appealing to industries with seasonal variations or cyclical patterns of expanding and contracting business activity. There is also much to recommend hiring a basic proprietary guard force supplemented by contract guards.

As guards and contract guard services increase in numbers, it is essential that their quantity be matched with quality. Aside from hiring practices, quality is likely to be a reflection of training requirements and government regulations. Training requirements have been recommended by the National Advisory Committee on Criminal Justice Standards and Goals.[3] The Private Security Task Force has set forth a minimum of eight hours preassignment training to be followed up by a recommended minimum of thirty-two hours of basic training to be completed over a three-month time period, with a maximum of sixteen hours of on-the-job training included in the thirty-two hours. The task force also recommended that all armed guards be required to complete successfully a twenty-four-hour firearms course with annual requalification. Government regulation is a far more controversial area; however, the task force recommended that regulation of the private security industry be performed at the state level, with consideration for uniformity and reciprocity among all states. It further recommended that licensing should be required to engage in the business of providing guard or patrol services and that "every person who is employed to perform functions of an investigator or detective, guard or watchman, armored car personnel or armed courier, alarm system installer or servicer, or alarm respondent should be registered with the [state] private security regulatory board."[4]

The security director of a facility that is a probable target of industrial espionage should try to have an exemplary guard force which will reflect credit on the company and the security department. Whether he or she decides on a proprietary or contractual guard force, or some combination of both, it is critical that the minimum standards set forth by the Private Security Task Force be met or exceeded. If there is state regulation, licensing, and/or registration, these procedures should be strictly complied with. Since industrial espionage has been so successful in the past, we must assume that our mettle will be tested in the future (at an accelerated rate) and we must not be found wanting. If our facility is penetrated by a spy or spies we will be held

---

[3] National Advisory Committee on Criminal Justice Standards and Goals, *Private Security: Report of the Task Force on Private Security* (Washington, D.C.: Government Printing Office, 1976), pp. 99–109.

[4] Ibid., pp. 282, 298, 317.

accountable. Our care in conducting guard operations may well help to prevent or minimize the catastrophe. In all cases we should be in a defensible position and be able to demonstrate at least minimum compliance with the above recommendations.

INFORMATION SOURCE PROTECTION

Although every security director would like unlimited resources and be able to strive toward the ideal of 100 percent security, that is unlikely. The director will have to make choices:

1. How best to assign available resources in order to optimize the utility of available resources in achieving security goals.
2. Critical review of goals to be certain that they are rational, realistic, and possible to achieve.
3. Assessment of threats based on a thorough understanding, shared with top management, of the cost-effectiveness of providing protection to a variety of potential targets.
4. Appreciation of the nuances of affording effective protection to a variety of information sources, recognizing what is possible.
5. Sophisticated analysis of useful lists of information sources and methods of espionage leading to meaningful decision making about the approach to take.

Such lists may be drawn up by the security director or found in the literature. Following is a list we have found very helpful in conceptualizing the ranking of various types of information about competitors available to all, or unavailable without some form of espionage effort. We commend the classification of information from or about competitors developed by Worth Wade:

1. Published material, and public documents such as court records.
2. Disclosures made by competitor's employees, and obtained without subterfuge.
3. Market surveys and consultant's reports.
4. Financial reports, and brokers' research surveys.
5. Trade fairs, exhibits, and competitor's brochures.
6. Analysis of competitor's products.
7. Reports of your salesmen and purchasing agents.
8. Legitimate employment interviews with people who worked for competitor.
9. Camouflaged questioning and "drawing out" of competitor's employees at technical meetings.

10. Direct observation under secret conditions.
11. False job interviews with competitor's employee (i.e., where there is no real intent to hire).
12. False negotiations with competitor for license.
13. Hiring a professional investigator to obtain a specific piece of information.
14. Hiring an employee away from the competitor, to get specific know-how.
15. Trespassing on competitor's property.
16. Bribing competitor's supplier or employee.
17. "Planting" your agent on competitor's payroll.
18. Eavesdropping on competitors (e.g., via wire-tapping).
19. Theft of drawings, samples, documents and similar property.
20. Blackmail and extortion.[5]

The Wade list begins with legal and ethical information sources, and, as one follows down the list, the sources and methods used become increasingly unethical and illegal. The Wade system can be helpful for facility security if it is used as a scale for counterintelligence efforts. Security must decide at what point in this chart to draw the line. Are we going to prepare our defenses for every tactic from 9–20, or will we draw the line at another point in the sequence? Where the line is drawn will have enormous consequences in terms of defining security needs. There are budget implications, commitment requirements, and cost-effectiveness concerns wrapped up in the decision as to what the stand should be. Theoretically, of course, we should not tolerate any industrial espionage against our own targets. Are we willing to pay the price for the degree of facility security required to defeat all industrial espionage? Is there a calculated risk factor that should be considered? All of the answers are dependent on the fundamental variable of where to draw the line.

LEGAL SECURITY

In efforts to cope with the various aspects of industrial espionage, the prophylactic aspects of the law should not be overlooked. The actual physical or electronic theft of information or material may result in criminal sanctions. Although an employee may have been suborned by an espionage agent, he or she may balk at actually turning over classified documents, etc., when informed of the criminal penalties involved. Some employees, on realizing the enormity of their actions and the potential punishment, may, out of fear of legal sanctions, renounce the plot and testify against the espionage agent. Certainly if it were not for the fact that both fines and imprisonment await

---

[5] Excerpted by special permission from *Chemical Engineering* (May 23, 1966) © (1966) by McGraw-Hill Inc., New York, N.Y. 10020.

the industrial spy who is caught, there would be even more espionage than now exists. The boom in industrial espionage makes us wonder if the penalties are not as severe as they should be, but some legal sanctions are far better than none at all.

All legal means must be used in the fight against industrial espionage. One of these means is to draw up agreements for the protection of sensitive information with facility employees, contractors, consultants, vendors, and others who have legitimate access to the information. These agreements may take several forms: pledges of secrecy and nondisclosure; covenants not to engage in competitive business or work for a competitor for a specified period of time or within a specified geographical region; and agreements to turn over to the employer inventions or discoveries developed during the term of employment.

These contracts are legal documents; the security director should not attempt to negotiate them on his or her own initiative. The role of the security director would be to convince top management of the need for such agreements and their role in the protection of trade secrets. The actual design of the covenants should be worked out with the personnel director and the company counsel.

The covenants serve many purposes. They are admissible evidence against any person who was a party to them if such person is in violation. They also have a psychological impact on the signatories, who become more fully aware of the need to protect against disclosure. Any disclosure, however effected, might reflect on those who have become responsible for nondisclosure. Noncompetitive covenants also should help to prevent false offering of a higher-paying job to an employee who may possess sensitive information. Agreements to assign patents and inventions to the employer should assist in frustrating espionage agents who want to offer large sums of money or other consideration for such patents and inventions.

Another aspect of legal security for the prevention of espionage in the industrial sector is the responsibility of the security director to join with colleagues in other facilities to influence legislation that will assist in the clearance of employees, in the surveillance of suspects, and in strengthening penal sanctions against industrial espionage. Security directors need to make chief executive officers aware of the imperatives of dealing with this phenonemon. The support of the legal community needs to be encouraged.

PERSONNEL SECURITY

In many cases, the ultimate success of the industrial spy is based more on the ability of the agent to turn employees than on sophisticated penetration of the facility. Given that the vast majority of employees did not seek employment with premeditated designs on sensitive information or with the intent of becoming a spy, we must deal with personnel security from the standpoint of what has happened to the offender to make him or her disloyal. This is not to say that some current employees of a facility were not actually deep-cover spies before employment but rather to say that we must recognize that concerns should be broader than concern about applicant screening procedures alone.

Applicant Screening

A personal history questionnaire is usually the first step in the screening process. This should be followed by verification of responses and, if necessary, a full background check. In all cases there should be a probationary period to allow for immediate and uncomplicated dismissal of persons who may be suspected of being security risks even though they passed the initial screening process. A similar screening procedure should be conducted when employees are promoted or otherwise assigned to sensitive duties.

Employee Education

In order to frustrate the efforts of industrial spies, companies should provide an education and training program in security matters. Employees should understand the industrial espionage prevention program. Continuous, intensive, and constantly reinforced indoctrination stress the need for protection of company secrets in order to secure the survival of the facility and the individual's job. At the same time, the extreme penalties that await disloyal employees who become traitors need emphasis. The security director should spark the thrust to motivate all employees to be alert to any attempts at penetration. All media sources should be employed in this educational endeavor, including posters, company newsletters, lectures, and even local press and radio.

Security Classification

Personnel in high security areas where the greatest damage could be inflicted by industrial spies should be given appropriate clearances, requiring special efforts to ensure the individual's loyalty to the company and to the country. The restricted areas should be classified, as well as the trade secrets and sensitive documents housed in these areas. Only those who have been appropriately cleared should be allowed access to these classified places and things and even then only on a need-to-know basis.

Personnel Supervision

The security director must maintain line supervision over his or her own department personnel. The security personnel responsibility extends to all insiders, from the boardroom to the factory floor, and it includes vendors, consultants, contractors, maintenance workers, and authorized visitors—all who are legitimately within the perimeters of the facility. The security director has functional authority over all insiders. Usually the higher up one is in the organization, the more one is privy to sensitive information and therefore the more likely to be the target of industrial espionage. The supervision of the security director must be pervasive.

Integrity Investigations

The security director cannot rely on past clearances or background investigations. People change and sometimes turn almost overnight. Constant vigilance is necessary. The security director must take a proactive, preventive posture.

Any derogatory leads should be followed up immediately. He or she should take full advantage of intelligence information from whatever source and conduct continuous assessments of the integrity of personnel with access to information that may be targeted by industrial espionage agents. If clandestine tactics are indicated, they should be used with considerable secrecy, discretion, and finesse for fear of union or individual or group employee objections. Among the possible methods that could be used by the security director to conduct integrity investigations are the following:

1. Background investigation update.
2. Use of polygraph and/or psychological stress evaluator.
3. Financial questionnaires.
4. Undercover (even deep cover) detectives.
5. Physical or electronic surveillance.
6. Rotation of employees on promotion and/or routinely.

7. Maintenance of surveillance over trash disposal.
8. Liaison with local, state, and federal agencies.

Discipline of Personnel

Discipline is critical to the maintenance of morale and integrity. If employees are flaunting security regulations and procedures, morale will plummet and the stage will be set for successful penetration. If discipline is positive, fair, and reasonable, it should increase morale and respect for security regulations. Security procedures are not always so easy to comply with, and honest, dedicated employees feel they are justified in their sacrifices if those who breach security are dealt with summarily. Strict discipline must be maintained throughout the facility, yet nowhere is the need for the highest degree of discipline more important than among the members of the security department itself. A failure by the security director to recognize that he or she and the entire security force are operating in a fishbowl can be fatal to the continued success of the espionage prevention program.

MUTUAL AID

The best efforts to defeat industrial espionage may founder because of inadequate attention to the community and the environment. We need answers to a variety of questions:

- Are some employees showing sudden signs of wealth?
- Are some employees leading double lives and escorting flashy members of the same or opposite sex?
- Are there locations where employees go to get drugs or other illicit merchandise?
- What are the general reputations in the community of employees assigned to sensitive duties?
- Have any suspicious strangers been seen around?

Continuous information from loyal employees and concerned members of the community can be vital to early warning and proactive prevention. Coordination with other security directors and local police can provide information on one's own employees. Some of the information, added to other data, may fill in the profile of either a deep cover plant in one's midst or an employee, or group of employees, who are being cultivated or have already been compromised. In any case, we need to share information and share in the information of others on a mutual aid basis. We cannot defeat an organized and determined enemy unless we are also organized and, hopefully, even more dedicated.

SUMMARY

This chapter dealt with the general principles of facility security. It is particularly urgent for private owners to seek a competent security director and provide adequate resources for their security department.

There needs to be a clear concept of the nature of the threat in the particular environment. Facility security measures should be so designed that they give early warning of penetration or loss. Concepts of early warning when combined with defense in depth should point the way to quality security. It is essential that there be responsibility and accountability pinpointed to a limited number of individuals for proper asset protection and loss investigation. Employees at all levels must be aware of the threats that may be within their purview.

Illegal access was discussed in reference to perimeter protection, protective lighting, and alarm systems. Inner defenses and the postulates of defensible space were outlined in reference to facility buildings. The third line of defense comprises restricted areas and security devices inside the facility buildings themselves. It is usually impractical to give ultimate security attention to the entire facility; priority should be assigned to more sensitive areas within the plant.

Special security measures often need to be tailored to individual industrial espionage security threats. The scope of the threats is such that we can never be sure what special problems we will next encounter. We must not overlook the fact that we only hear about the cases that have been discovered (many of the most successful espionage cases are never discovered). Also, industrial espionage cases that have been discovered are often not publicly revealed.

Despite sophisticated security technology, guard forces are still needed because of the importance of human judgment. Contract guard services and proprietary guards both have advantages and disadvantages. Whatever type of guard is used, minimum training standards have been recommended by the National Advisory Commission on Standards and Goals.

Security departments always have limited resources to work with and must understand that achieving 100 percent security is impossible. The challenge for the security director is to establish priorities and maximize available resources through wise decision making.

The security director should use the prophylactic aspects of the law. The threat of criminal sanctions may well inhibit employee theft of protected information. It may also cause employees who have already turned to renounce the conspiracy and assist security in repulsing the efforts of spy masters and foreign agents. Other legal tactics include the drawing up of agreements for the protection of sensitive information with facility employees, contractors, consultants, vendors, and others who need legitimate access to such information. These agreements include nondisclosure and noncompetitive covenants and promises to turn over to the employer inventions developed during employment.

We should also seek to influence legislation and all members of the legal community to aid all security directors in their counter-intelligence efforts.

The imperatives of personnel security were detailed, including applicant screening, employee education and training, security classifications, supervision, integrity investigations, and discipline of personnel.

The best efforts of security directors to cope with industrial espionage may founder because of inadequate attention to the community and the environment. Citizen informants and feedback from loyal employees and concerned members of the community are vital for early warning and proactive prevention. Security must also maintain a dialogue with other security directors, local police, and government employees.

13. Electronic Security

I regret often that I have spoken, never that I have been silent. —Cyrus

In many of the previous chapters, we have discussed various aspects of electronic security. We have not, however, gone into any depth concerning the electronic espionage techniques and equipment available; nor have we gone into any depth in our discussions of electronic counterintelligence techniques and equipment. This chapter's objective is to put it all together so the impact of electronic security in this era of industrial espionage may be understood in full perspective and in all of its ramifications.

ELECTRONIC ESPIONAGE

In order to provide effective defenses against electronic espionage it is essential that we have as much knowledge as possible about the nature of the threats we may have to cope with. Perhaps the best way to defeat the spy is to be as knowledgeable as he is about his own tradecraft and then, thinking like a spy ourselves, anticipate the kinds of espionage that might be used to compromise our own security. It has been said by Herchell Britton, Executive Vice-President of Burns International Security Services, *Forbes Magazine*, and many other authorities that America has become a soft target for industrial espionage. If America is a soft target generally, it is an even more mushy target for spies who employ the latest state-of-the-art electronic espionage. There are special industrial espionage schools in Japan; Switzerland; and most European Communist countries, notably East Germany. In addition, the KGB has a major training institution in Russia. To what extent are industrial espionage centers available in this country? To a very limited extent, and mostly for the training of government agents who may become involved in industrial espionage only because of the government contracts held by some private industrial facilities.

As far as academic involvement and fundamental research is concerned, it is virtually nonexistent. Aside from a course being taught at Northeastern University College of Criminal Justice by one of the co-authors, the authors have been unable to identify another academic offering in this entire country. There is a shocking lack of American academic literature, circa 1983. A prior U.S. text by the famous authors Timothy J. Walsh and Richard J. Healy titled *Protecting Your Business Against Espionage* (New York: Amacom Division of A.M.A., 1973), was found to be out of print. It is the authors' fond hope that this text will help stimulate academic courses in this critical area, and some basic academic research as well.

Another disturbing aspect of this abnormal reaction is the attitude of many industrialists and businessmen. They are aware of the ravages of espionage but they feel helpless to combat it. Many of the more realistic and progressive entrepreneurs, however, have upgraded their security staffs. Some have hired special consultant firms that offer counterespionage expertise and actually perform necessary sweeps of offices, conference rooms, and restricted areas to cope with ever-present threats of electronic espionage.

ELECTRONIC INSTRUMENTATION

Some of the most dangerous instruments known to man are not necessarily nuclear or neutron bombs or the other lethal equipment and hardware of shooting wars. Electronic instruments are deadly in the traditional geographical kill and maim struggles of armed forces to acquire or defend land areas, and they are equally lethal in the new battlegrounds of economic warfare. We speak of the electronic signal, message, and information instruments used for communications in shooting wars and in times of so-called peace. These instruments are very dangerous because they are so readily used for proactive espionage and so effectively adapted by spies for passive espionage. These are the armaments of electronic espionage.

Electronic Audio Systems

Sound systems generally are composed of a microphone, an amplifier, and a reproducer. The microphone converts sound waves into electrical energy; it picks up these sound vibrations by the use of a diaphragm within the instrument itself. The amplifier magnifies the electrical impulses picked up by the microphone so that they may be sufficiently strong to be audible. Reproducers then convert these electrical energies back into sound waves that may be heard by the human ear.

In terms of espionage, microphones are the most critical ingredient of audio surveillance for they may be used in such a fashion that the victim is not aware of their presence on a person, in a place, or attached to an object. Among other places a microphone may be secreted is in a room on the undersides of various items of furniture or even on draperies. If the room microphone requires wiring, the wiring is usually carefully hidden or disguised and run out of the room by the shortest possible route. When it is not feasible to use a microphone covertly within a room, the spy may use contact units such as the suction cup and the steel spike. These are generally used on windows and doors or by boring a hole through a common wall up to the point of, but not penetrating, the interior wall. In the latter case, the steel spike microphone would most likely be used. The windows, doors, and walls of the room itself may serve as vibrating diaphragms for the contact microphone. In-room speakers may be converted into microphones.

The espionage agent may also use directional microphones in order to pick up sounds at some distance. Thus the spy may be able to overhear a conversation at a remote table in a crowded restaurant or eavesdrop on the voices of subjects from a window across an alley or street. There are basically three distinct types of directional microphones: the parabolic microphone and the so-called rifle or shotgun and the machine gun microphones. The parabolic microphone uses a dish that focuses sound waves on the center-mounted microphone and amplifier. The rifle or shotgun microphone uses a single tube with the microphone at one end; it is aimed at the targeted sounds. The machine gun directional microphone consists of a bundle of long metal tubes of small diameter with the microphone at the inboard end; it is also aimed at the sound source.

Other specialized contact microphones are the electronic stethoscope and the keyhole and tube microphones. The former is employed as a doctor uses a stethoscope but against thin walls or doors as opposed to a human chest. The latter are microphones with long hollow tubes, flexible or rigid, that can be run through cracks and keyholes or mounted inside walls (or on the other side of walls) with only a pinhole in the wall itself.

Wireless microphones or miniaturized transmitters operate in a manner similar to a walkie-talkie transceiver with the transmit button secured in the on position. They are available and in use in micro-miniaturized form that may be readily concealed almost anywhere.

They may also be concealed in a person's food and be ingested. There have been reports of the use of these tiny transmitters attached to postage stamps or buried inside martini olives. Usually these bugs operate on miniature batteries, which have a limited life span. In some cases, the bug may attach to a present power source. It could be attached to wall sockets tying into existing power sources, or it could be dropped into a telephone handset and operate indefinitely off the low-voltage power always present in the telephone line. Some of these transmitters may be such tiny chips that four of them could fit on top of a dime. Just as transistors made current miniature surveillance bugs a reality, we may look forward to an entire new generation of passive surveillance devices using laser beams. It is said that laser beams will soon be able to read some conversations through closed windows at a distance of more than a mile.

An espionage agent will require some form of remote control over the bug's on-off position, particularly where he or she is dealing with microminiaturized transmitters that have limited life spans because of the tiny batteries. The spy may also want to be able to cease bug transmissions when the target is about to have a sweep done of the premises where the bugs are installed. Normally electronic sweeps will not pick up dead or nonoperating transmitters. To the extent that remote control is used or other units that are sound activated are employed, there can be a much longer life span of the clandestine installation. Furthermore, the spy can secrete the bug when access is available and start transmissions at a later selected time.

Although bugging is illegal in most states, it is generally widespread in industrial espionage. Even some licensed private detectives will do a bugging job for the espionage agent and spy. Bugs are openly advertised for sale under the rubric of personal baby sitters, burglar alarms, guitar amplifiers, wireless microphones, and counterespionage devices. A 1971 survey of commonly available eavesdropping devices revealed that an entire spectrum of surveillance devices is readily available on the open market and that they do present a security hazard.[1] Samuel Daskam, who conducted the survey, concluded that the threat of the 1968 Omnibus Crime Control and Safe Streets Act (Public Law 90–351), which outlawed electronic eavesdropping, has not been realized. He further concluded that even a bigger threat is the mass producer making legitimate consumer items because these are sold through many outlets at low cost.

A product schedule from a manufacturer of countersurveillance and surveillance electronics contains some interesting items:

---

[1] F.G. Mason Engineering, Inc., 1700 Post Road, Fairfield, CT 06430.

- Voice actuator
- Wearable tailing transmitter
- Vehicle surveillance system
- Stethoscope amplifier assembly
- Stethoscope
- Flexible tube microphone
- Miniature contact microphone
- Rigid tube microphone
- Auto transmitter
- Body transmitter
- Fountain pen microphone
- Drop-in transmitter
- Harmonica transmitter
- Automatic telephone line intercept

The reader's attention is invited to the Electronic Surveillance Glossary to be found at the end of this book.

Another aspect of electronic audio systems is the use of tape recorders. Tape recorders bridge the gap between surveillance devices that are basically independent of the telephone and those types of industrial espionage techniques that are telephone dependent or telephone related. Tape recorders are used for both types of electronic surveillance. Tape recorders most often are magnetic tape devices that may be activated manually, electronically, or by voice. They have the ability to erase their own tape for reuse or for the destruction of surveillance evidence. In the course of electronic espionage, a variety of recorders may be used:

1. Relatively large high-fidelity tape recorders with multihour recording capabilities.
2. Self-activating recorders triggered into on-off positions by remote control, voice activation, or other electronic switching devices.
3. Miniature tape recorders that can be concealed on the person for surreptitious recording of conversations where the subject is near or face to face.
4. Tailored recorders that may be used in connection with microphonic, telephonic, or radio-surveillance operations. These may be large, medium, small, or miniaturized to suit the circumstances of the particular espionage effort. They may be combined with amplifiers and with devices that will screen out irrelevant noises from the original microphonic sound pickup, particularly useful in connection with long-range directional microphonic surveillance.

Telephone Systems

Few people in industry understand how dangerous a telephone can be; they speak over the phone as though they were speaking face to face with the other party in a debugged private office. The fact is that anyone talking on a telephone is talking to the world and should say nothing confidential. There are so many vulnerable locations and easy tap-in points in the system that it is virtually impossible to prevent spies from eavesdropping. Many of these tap-in points may not even require a trespass, and almost all of the taps are difficult to discover.

A number of telephone bugs are readily available on the open market and many are openly advertised under various caveats such as "for law enforcement use only," "this unit may be used only for recording one's own telephone conversations and it is illegal to use it in any other manner," "this unit is not offered for sale as a surveillance device, and in most states it is illegal to use it for such purposes," and so on. These devices do have some legitimate uses, but their ready availability for industrial espionage poses a security threat.

Among the devices available are the following:

1. Tiny telephone transmitter: A complete, self-energized, solid-state, miniature transmitter.
2. Conference telephone broadcaster: Self-energizing and polarity free (this device is easily installed at a point remote from the telephone instrument itself).
3. Automatic recorder switch: Alligator clips that may be attached to telephone wires anywhere along the telephone line.
4. Room/telephone transmitters.
5. Terminal block transmitters.
6. Drop-in transmitters.
7. Harmonica transmitters.
8. Automatic telephone line intercepts.
9. Dial longlines tone generators.

Adding to the surveillance problem of telephonic communications are the hundreds of thousands of telephone company employees who have either authorization or the capability of overhearing traffic. Undoubtedly some are serving the purposes of espionage agents. All they need is a handset and access to the pairs and cables or the telephone line itself. Also central telephone offices routinely monitor and record traffic. Seventy percent of all long-distance calls are transmitted by microwave radio, which can be readily intercepted. Recently AT&T has been allowed to use its resources for computer transmissions, electronic funds transfer, and other special functions, providing more reason for industrial espionage agents to cultivate telephone company employees.

There are two categories of telephone surveillances: direct and indirect. The former is most often used and poses no difficulties for the spy in most cases. The indirect tap usually involves induction coil pickups, which can be purchased in radio and electronic stores inexpensively. Ordinarily they must be physically attached to the phone or secreted near the handset with a small direct-coupled amplifier to add volume to the signals. The induction unit can be easily disguised and readily hidden. It is also feasible to use a more powerful induction tap in the vicinity of the telephone land lines; with a strong amplifier attached, there will invariably be good reception. Another type of indirect wiretaps are wireless radio taps, which will transmit messages that can be picked up by any properly tuned VHF or FM radio receiver. A combination of the inductive pickup and a radio transmitter provides espionage agents a covert package that draws no current from the telephone lines and is detectable only by radio transmitter detectors.

A common FM radio tap of which millions have been sold, known as the drop-in, may be installed in seconds by replacing the microphone capsule in the handset with a capsule wireless monitoring apparatus that is indistinguishable from the regular capsule except that a tiny screw head may be visible through one of the holes on the top. (The screw is a frequency adjuster.) These devices are very inexpensive, run indefinitely on the telephone current, and are activated only when the receiver is taken off the hook.

Optical Systems

Optical systems offer a host of sophisticated surveillance techniques that pose a threat to industrial security. In some cases, they can be combined with audio surveillance systems to create a remarkably effective espionage tool. For example, combining high-powered telescopes (particularly those that use light amplification or infrared light, for low light level or dark night vision capability) with long-range directional microphones, the spy may see, hear, and photograph targets night or day from a safe distance. Even without benefit of audio, the high-powered telescope and camera can be useful for photographing papers, processes, documents, and graphics that can be viewed through a window. Miniature cameras can be concealed in cigarette packages, compacts, pens, and other common paraphernalia to be used for clandestine photographs. One of the principal tenets of successful industrial espionage is to obtain the targeted information without the subject's being aware of the fact that it has been purloined. Using hidden cameras means that the actual documents may be replaced in the files still intact.

Optical systems may be combined with computer technology to monitor the movements of targeted vehicles. The automatic license plate scanning system (ALPS) can read license plates on passing vehicles and instantly check them with a computer list of targeted cars and trucks. Thus the spy can log and clock the movements of rolling stock.

Snooperscopes can aid in taking pictures that may be used to blackmail employees into cooperating with the industrial espionage agent. Motion pictures are particularly useful in this regard. They may also be used to film target processes that would not be as meaningful if captured in only a series of still photographs. In terms of identifying persons who are maintaining low profiles or are dissimulating their identity, motion pictures may be much more effective than stills because they may capture mannerisms, walking gait, habitual movements, or other peculiarities. Optical systems, especially tailored for a particular mission or off the shelf for general surveillance, are part of the spy's armory and they are particularly effective when combined with electronic wizardry.

Code Systems

Espionage agents must be able to break codes—unscramble scrambled electronic messages—or have access to such capabilities. Although industrial espionage has not dealt with codes to any great extent in the past—certainly not to the extent employed for political and military counterintelligence—more and more utilization of codes has become a factor in business and industrial communication. The vulnerability of telephone transmissions, computer linkages, and remote computer access terminals—indeed all kinds of verbal and written communication—has stimulated the use of coded messages. Security directors often recommend automatic scramblers for radio and landline transmissions and coded signals for classified data. These precautions make the spy's employment of electronic surveillance more difficult and help to harden the target. Although the espionage agent ultimately may be able to break the code or have it broken, there will be at least some delay and the spy may turn to less difficult penetrations. Also if codes are changed on a frequent basis, by the time the spy has broken a particular code it may be superseded.

Spies have traditionally avoided plain-language messages for fear of interception and subsequent disclosure. They have used dead drops and safe houses for the delivery and transmission of the fruits of their espionage. Likewise, they have transmitted and received operational information in a form that is not readily intelligible. Since one-time codes may be the spy's preferred mode of encryption, these messages are virtually impossible to decode. Thus the spy is likely to be deeply engrossed in protecting his cover and will be jealously guarding his own avenues of communication, while at the same time taking full advantage of the naïvete of targeted business and industrial executives. The industrial espionage agent is often a master of his or her tradecraft, whereas the leaders of business and industry are only beginning to realize the criticality of electronic counterintelligence in our current state of economic warfare.

Espionage Armament

In the United States, we have been led to believe there is little actual violence associated with industrial espionage. This is not to say that spies are likely to be less violent when they are involved in one or another type of espionage. Whether there is a political, military, or industrial target, spies will do what they have to do to carry out their missions. If this involves violence, either carried out directly or through a surrogate, the industrial espionage agent will not flinch. Spies who have been trained and indoctrinated may stimulate violent confrontations, encourage terrorist attacks, or actually suborn assassination. If their objectives can best be met by immoral means, they are usually quite prepared to commit murder, kidnapping, brutal assaults, torture, rape, arson, or whatever type of blackmail, extortion, or other corruption will achieve their goals.

With espionage agents, the end justifies the means, and they usually have available to them the necessary electronic weaponry, including remote-control bombs, hired mechanics with electronic sniperscopes, and professional goons with walkie-talkies and other electronic aids. They also have access to false identification papers of all kinds in order to provide cover for themselves and their operatives. It all adds up to a powerful covert force ready to corrupt, to compromise, to blackmail, and to shed blood when necessary, using the very latest advances in electronics to aid their clandestine operations.

Computer Espionage

Electronic espionage uses computers for research and intelligence purposes and for operational purposes to assist in penetrating target computer systems. Also computers are used by the target business or industry for storing, processing, and disseminating sensitive data and information sought by industrial espionage agents.

An example of the use of computers themselves as tools for penetrating computerized information is a case involving two competing computer facilities that operated as service bureaus. One of the service bureaus had developed a proprietary program for handling client data that was regarded as confidential and very valuable. It was selling its services to clients on the basis of the program, which allowed it to optimize its time-sharing schedule. An employee of the competing computer facility ferreted out the secret telephone number used by the regular clients of the first bureau's computer to key in an assigned user code. He was able to use his own computer to gain computer access to the target program, and the second company planned to steal the first bureau's proprietary programs to use it themselves to improve their own time-sharing operations.

Examples of the penetration of targeted computer systems by the many other resources and methods available for such espionage are legion. There are at least three areas of vulnerability:

1. The computer itself, its programs and programmers, its operators, its location, its input-output peripherals, and its storage areas.
2. The dissemination procedures and their supporting hardware and personnel involved. This includes electronic transmission to remote terminals and/or actual manual delivery of computer output.
3. The remote terminals themselves, the recipients of computer data at those terminal, and/or the recipient of manual delivery of the printouts.

In the first instance, the corruptive and coercive talents of the espionage agent may be employed to corrupt programmers, operators, and guardians of storage areas. If the computer location is not properly secured, it may be penetrated by the spy. In the event that the agent has provided a deep cover spy, he or she may be a programmer, operator, or other authorized user of the computer facility.

In the second case, the spy could employ bugging and wiretapping techniques at any point along the electronic transmission system.

Computers use electromagnetic energy in the high end of the radio-frequency spectrum; as a result, random radiations are created near the equipment and along the transmission lines. If the target data and information are sent by courier, he or she could become the target of the spy's blandishments or threats.

Third, at the remote terminal we would have a situation similar to that at the originating computer facility in terms of vulnerability to espionage. If retransmission is allowed either by further computer linkage, hand delivery, or otherwise, all of the techniques used in the first and second situations are again repeated. The computer spy is most likely to be a computer specialist. Such espionage calls for considerable skill; however, if it is done expertly, it will be almost impossible to detect.

Just as computer espionage calls for highly skilled operatives, so does computer counterespionage require even more finely trained, more imaginative, and more keenly intelligent personnel in order to defeat the industrial espionage agent.

ELECTRONIC COUNTERINTELLIGENCE

We have discussed espionage first and have dealt with it at great length because we believe that one must fully comprehend the nature and dimensions of the threat. We are not suggesting, however, that the best defense in these cases is a good offense and that the best counterintelligence strategy is to use the same tactics as the opposition. Rather, we need to be able to think like a spy and to have a full understanding of the best defenses and the priorities of protection, but that does not imply that we have to act like a spy or be a spy. It may take a thief to catch a thief, but an honest detective who thinks like a thief can be far more effective than one who may have become a thief himself, for the latter never knows when the axe may fall. Let us look now at the various categories of counterintelligence in their electronic manifestations.

Countering Espionage in Electronic Audio Systems

Aside from good physical and personnel security systems, the first step in dealing with electronic audio system espionage is to conduct an electronic sweep and a thorough physical search of target areas. In terms of electronic audio systems, there are three elements to the sweep: checking for microphone transmissions, detecting semiconductors, and making a physical search.

The first category may be identified by a spectrum analyser to locate transmissions or metal detector to locate microphones or wiring. The detector cannot be relied on completely because the bug may be constructed of a material that it would not regularly pick up. The debugger will also employ radio-detection equipment to determine if there are any radio transmitter bugs. If, however, the bug's transmitter has been switched off or the bug is dead, there will be no detection. For the second category, a sophisticated device is the nonlinear junction detector. These are expensive, costing about $18,000 in 1983, but they are effective. The instrument was developed under government contract and only recently has been declassified. It is a microwave transceiver that detects the presence and existence of semiconductors. Since semiconductors are the essential elements of modern electronic circuits, this instrument can detect clandestine transmitters, tape recorders, amplified microphones, voice-actuated switches, and other electronic circuits. Even if the circuit containing the semiconductors is off or broken at the time of the sweep, the semiconductors will be detected. Depending upon the medium, the unit can see anywhere from three inches to six feet into an object.[3] However, a pneumatic tube connected to a pin hole will not be detected.

It is essential in all cases that the counterintelligence effort include a comprehensive physical search. This might include taking up carpets, removing moldings, removing gratings, pulling furniture apart, unscrewing fixtures, taking down pictures, tracing all wires, lifting sills, and even boring into paneling, ceilings, or walls. Obviously this search can be upsetting to the business involved, and the industrialist may try to have the work done on a weekend. This solution would be fine except that many of the transmitting devices may be turned off at that time and the traditional radio-detection equipment would not be effective. If a physical search is conducted using the nonlinear junction detector, it is not unlikely that live or dead bugs and even tape recorders will be discovered, particularly if the premises searched are executive offices or boardrooms where sensitive information may be discussed.

A sensible precaution is to assume that any room may be bugged and be guided accordingly. Some very scrupulous persons will discuss sensitive matters only while facing out an open window. This may not be bug-proof, particularly if that tactic is regularly used, for the miniaturized transmitter may be secreted in the window casement. It may be wise, however, to hold very sensitive conversations and meetings in places other than the company's executive offices or the facility's

---

[3] Kevin D. Murray, "The Corporate Counterspy," *Security Management* (April 1981):49, 50.

boardroom. Organized crime principals sometimes meet on the upper selling floors of a randomly selected large department store to discuss conspiratorial matters, or they may meet in a randomly selected restaurant and sit near the juke box where they feel they can talk without fear of being overheard. Such precautions may seem excessive to most business executives; however, if the information to be discussed is highly secret, it would be foolish to risk disclosure by meeting in any location that may be bugged. One technique is to switch the announced location of a conversation or conference at the last minute to foil the spy's plans by the element of surprise. Closing open windows may help defeat directional microphones of the parabolic or shotgun variety.

The telephone is always suspect because of its many vulnerabilities, some of which are difficult to detect. Two types of measures should be employed to detect telephone eavesdropping. The first responds to the fact that the telephone instrument itself may be the location, and even the source of power, for an electronic audio transmitter. This espionage technique might employ the drop-in microphone transmitter, or it may use induction coil pickups. Since these taps are very much the equivalent of the electronic audiosystems already discussed, the same counterintelligence tactics will apply, especially the physical search of the telephone itself and its immediate environs.

The second type of tactic to defeat telephonic espionage calls for sophisticated countermeasures. It is not easy to detect a telephone tap and often even more difficult to locate the tap, despite the fact it is known that the lines are in fact tapped.

Some frequently advertised, sometimes effective devices for detecting wiretaps include the following:[4]

1. Telephone analyzer. This system can perform a series of tests that aid in determining the electrical characteristics of an unknown in a circuit and gives a clue to the circuit's identity;
2. Digital volt-ohm meter. This is very helpful when obtaining voltage and current readings at telephone terminations and when checking to see if wires in the ceiling are hot.
3. High-gain audio amplifier. This amplifier is used to determine if audio information is being transmitted over a pair of wires.

"There is a plethora of 'counterspy' equipment on the market today. It ranges from worthwhile to worthless, most of it in the latter

---

[4] Ibid., pp. 50–53.

category. Public ignorance and a love affair with fancy knobs and dials have allowed this proliferation of products."[5]

There is a great deal of wiretapping in the industrial environment. Electronic espionage is big business, and wiretapping is one of the simplest and most difficult to defeat tools of the espionage agent. Absolute telephone privacy does not exist. Detection of taps by instrumentation is relatively unreliable, particularly since certain types of taps and bugs do not change the electrical characteristics of telephone lines at all. Security may have done an exhaustive sweep, including a physical search of the lines, and shortly after this time-consuming and expensive sweep has been completed, a new tap may be installed. There is no such thing as a tap-free phone, and we should be guided accordingly. This is not to say that we should fail to try to identify and locate taps, for even if we have not prevented the tap, we can become aware that we have been had.

A case in point is the Hazel Bishop wiretapping. Hazel Bishop, the cosmetic firm, reportedly lost $30 million as a result of a competitor's wiretapping. Another among the thousands of known cases concerns the Amphenol Corporation situation. While the company was engaged in merger and acquisition negotiations, the chairman became suspicious that information about the company was being obtained by outsiders. An investigation disclosed that a listening device was attached to a telephone in the chairman's home.

Countermeasures against Optical Espionage

One of the simplest and most effective methods to counter optical surveillance is to direct a very bright light, possibly a mirror to redirect the sun, at the source of the optical surveillance. This may damage the spy's sight and can mask out any pictures that are being taken by telescopic or other types of cameras. In this regard one can readily imagine the devastating defense that a properly directed laser beam could be—at least one blind spy per surveillance. Optical devices being developed that are designed to see through dense foliage or even walls will aid in uncovering the spy conducting a surveillance.

On a less sophisticated level, many optical surveillance systems may be neutralized by simple, sound physical security measures. Placing restricted areas in central locations, plus painting or otherwise shielding windows, will help to defeat long-range optical surveillance systems. Even the employment of automatic optical readers can

---

[5] Ibid., p. 53.

be defeated by shielding the target legends (or license plate numbers) where optical readers are suspected. In reference to vehicle license plates, additional or spurious plates may be used to confuse and confound the spy.

Optical espionage may also be countered by the use of traditional methods including use of decoys, camouflage, disguises, jamming the optical system by electronic countermeasures if it is electronic dependent, and shielding of the objects of optical surveillance by proper storage procedures and curtaining off of sensitive operational areas.

Code Counterespionage

Spies use codes, and they have available the same types of electronic scramblers that industry may use. Counterintelligence efforts must be as zealous as those of the spies themselves in trying to break through the barriers of protected communication. If we can decode industrial espionage communications, we may discover where the dead drops are located, where safe houses exist, and indeed the identity of some of the agents. If our piercing of the veil of secrecy enables us to discover their plans, all our efforts will be amply rewarded. If in the course of our efforts we actually identify one of their agents who is undercover or is a deep cover spy, we will have achieved the ultimate in successful counterintelligence. Thus, it is essential that security directors have the resources to intercept and decode the communications of the industrial espionage network, even as that network tries to intercept and decode (if we are sufficiently alert to code our messages in the first place) our communications. Just as spies are masters of their tradecraft, we need to become masters in counterintelligence.

Industry also needs to develop its own coding systems. A number of very complicated codes can be generated on a random basis by computers. Electronics can be used to scramble electronically transmitted messages and unscramble the same at the point of destination. Perhaps the most secure of all codes is the so-called one-time pad. This pad provides the code of the day or a code for each separate message. The recipient of the messages has the same pad.

Any code can be broken if enough time is allowed for cryptoanalysis. Computers can expedite the breaking of codes. When the one-time pad is used, no matter how rapid the cryptoanalysis, it will not let anyone catch up with the next message since that will be in a new code. A great deal can be learned from military and political counterintelligence in reference to cryptography. In this connection, the data encryption standard (DES) developed by the National Bureau of Standards is a computerized process available to business.

Countering Espionage Armament

Espionage agents will stop at nothing to carry out their missions. In addition to eavesdropping, they may use corruption, blackmail, extortion, and/or various kinds of physical violence, including torture, rape, arson, brutal assault, kidnapping, and even murder. Industrial society must recognize the amorality (or immorality) of the spy. As we have said previously they are masters of their tradecraft and know how to use silencers on their weapons, how to use electronics to set off explosives from a remote location, how to use sniperscopes (and snooperscopes in the dark), how to use electronic vehicle surveillance systems and tailing transmitters, how to kidnap, how to torture, and how to kill.

Our first reaction is to think in terms of executive protection, which is certainly an appropriate area for countermeasures. In addition, however, we should think about scientists and others who may also have access to, or knowledge of, target information. We should also be concerned with the safety of rank and file employees. The espionage agent may attack by force or corruption the highly placed and the less highly placed. Creating some form of chaos at the facility, or inducing fear of bodily harm among employees, can create the proper climate for the spy to flourish and achieve his or her goals.

Countermeasures against Computer Espionage

Much of the defense against computer spies is good routine physical and personnel security practice. Sensitive inputs need to be classified and handled accordingly. They need to be protected from disclosure and be transmitted and stored in a secure environment. Accountability for all classified input is essential. The computer room itself should be restricted at all times, and admittance by systems analysts and programmers should be forbidden or strictly controlled. There is little need today for programmers to enter the computer installation itself since there are remote visual display units available for any legitimate purpose.

It may be desirable or necessary to sweep the computer installation itself for bugs or taps. It may also be wise, if sufficiently sensitive programs are to be run, to screen the computer center electronically to prevent electromagnetic radiations. Cables leaving the installation need to be filtered to remove their radiations. Rooms may be screened by copper-wire mesh or sprayed aluminum.

Auditing and inventory procedures should be strict and continuous, and care must be taken not to destroy audit trails. Computers are vulnerable to erasure, and it is possible to lose records irretrieveably if there has been no provision for either tape or hard-copy backup. The spy or saboteur can cause havoc by compromising or sabotaging computer records, so a set of backup records should be maintained at another location. Wherever sensitive records are stored outside the computer facility, they should be accorded the same high degree of security protection they were provided in the computer room itself.

Remote-terminal access devices present additional vulnerabilities from unauthorized users, switching errors sending sensitive data to a terminal not cleared for same, or actual program or base data modification during remote access to permit future unauthorized retrieval or to cover up prior manipulations. The use of scramblers may be helpful, and it is perhaps wise to have control of the cryptography separate from the computer itself and unavailable to the computer center or terminal operators.

There are many vulnerabilities in computer security. In 1982, another devastating vulnerability was discovered. According to Donn Parker of SRI International, of Menlo Park, California:

> We have just discovered a very serious vulnerability—a trap door in existing computer systems. The weakness is extremely widespread and it essentially means that all the systems that we thought were relatively secure—are wide open.
>
> Three weeks ago we would have said, "Well these systems are pretty secure." Today we're saying if you know about this trap door, their security is zero.[6]

Much of the reported computer crime has been lightly dismissed by the public. Even though it is obviously epidemic and amounts to about one-half million dollars of theft per shot, little concern seems to be forthcoming. We should, therefore, brace ourselves for the future. Experts foresee grave portents for espionage in their scenarios of tomorrow. For the most part, these thefts are the result of poor security plus the failure of the computer industry to take a strong stand against the theft of industrial secrets. These threats, and the security that has been unavailable to counter these threats, have placed the computer industry in jeopardy and have attracted espionage agents in droves. As a result there may be more foreign agents in Silicon Valley than there are in East and West Berlin. It is said that industrial espionage is far more extensive than anybody had ever realized due to

---

[6] Bill Lauren," Computer Crime," *Penthouse* (June 1982):109, 110, 178.

the diabolically clever tradecraft that leaves no "fingerprints" to give a clue that information theft had ever occurred.

CONCLUSION

The reality and vast dimension of industrial espionage in our nation today has yet to be fully comprehended by our citizenry.

One must recognize that the industrial spy has the initiative. He or she may strike anywhere and at any time; all that the security forces can do is be prepared as well as possible to meet the attack. This preventive and protective role should be viewed as proactive and systems oriented. A piecemeal, uncoordinated approach will never suffice. We need to organize a rational, coherent, counterattack that takes full advantage of the resources of the world of electronics. We need to be convinced that for every electronic offensive there has to be an electronic counteroffensive, if we but have the wisdom to see that the system is set up and survives.

SUMMARY

This chapter examined the implications of electronic security. Effective countermeasures are suggested in the light of the electronic expertise of industrial espionage agents.

Spies have available to them numerous resources and tactics. Those include various types of microphones and tape recorders. The use of lasers and other state-of-the-art technologies will expand these potentials in the future. We noted that electronic bugs are illegal in most states, yet, their instrumentations appear to be freely advertised and readily purchased on the open market.

An exceedingly important vulnerability that needs to be protected against is the transmission of data by landline or microwave. The telephone is particularly vulnerable because technological surveillance of it is almost impossible to detect. It was noted that 70 percent of all long-distance calls are transmitted by microwave radio, which can be readily intercepted.

Optical surveillance has become sophisticated, and such systems pose a distinct threat to industrial security. In some cases, they can be combined with audio surveillance systems to create a most effective espionage tool. High-powered telescopes that may be used in the dark or at low light levels can be coupled with long-range directional microphones so that the spy may see, hear, and photograph targets night or day from a safe distance. Miniaturized cameras can be concealed in such common items as cigarette packages, compacts, and pens. Hidden cameras assist the spy in obtaining targeted information without the subject's being aware of the fact.

Espionage agents have elaborate resources for breaking all kinds of codes, including scrambled electronic messages. The use of scramblers and other coding devices, however, helps to harden the target, if only because the spy is delayed while trying to solve the encryption. Spies themselves of course, use codes.

Computer espionage involves the new technology in a variety of ways: to penetrate target computer systems, to store and generate intelligence, to eavesdrop on disseminations of data, and to compromise remote terminals. Such espionage calls for considerable skill; counterintelligence requires even greater computer skills.

Generally electronic counterintelligence can be effective without using the same methods and resources as do spies. But security must think like a spy to develop its defenses. Security needs to sweep for microphonic transmissions, semiconductors, and suspicious physical objects. The telephone is always suspect because of its many vulnerabilities and the fact that it may, in itself, be the location and even the source of power for an electronic audio transmitter.

Countermeasures against computer espionage include good routine physical and personnel security practices. Auditing and inventory procedures should be continuous and audit trails preserved. The problems of collusion between programmers and operators, remote terminal vulnerabilities, and trap doors in existing computer systems are very real. Computer crime and lax security have contributed to the epidemic of foreign technology transfer. The fact that the spy's tradecraft in this area leaves no "fingerprints" makes it impossible to estimate the extent of such activity.

14. Surveillance Sensitivity

The mouse that hath but one hole is quickly taken. —Herbert

Few people recognize all that is going on around them. Instead, most of us concentrate on inner thoughts while automatically traveling frequently used paths. Intent on solving pressing problems or dwelling on pain or pleasure, victims rarely recognize when they are being watched. To some extent, we all are creatures of habit and cannot hope to escape observation by those intent on following and recording our movements and words. And yet there would be little terrorism, espionage, or crime success without those facts provided by successful reconnaissance and surveillance.

The purpose of this chapter is to create an awareness of surveillance methods and techniques. Another benefit of this chapter results from clear delineation of those habits that make surveillance easy for the espionage agent. Practical exercises designed to increase surveillance sensitivity are presented.

Surveillance is a tool or method. It may be defined as very careful observation and the subsequent recording of specific information for later use. Surveillance data are used to make plans for a variety of nasty activities, including espionage, terrorism, and other crimes. Surveillance is also a tool of police, counterintelligence agents, security personnel, and hobbyists.

Bird-watchers in particular practice many surveillance activities, including patient visual observation from concealment, optical surveillance using binoculars and telescopes, and placement of eavesdropping equipment to film birds and to record their calls. Bird-watchers' observations are used to produce reports that help others locate hard-to-find species. Records of nesting places and bird habits make future outings pleasurable. No harm comes to birds as a result of such surveillance.

Surveillance practiced in connection with industrial espionage, however, usually results in severe harm to the object of observation or his or her employer. Terrorists use surveillance to plan for assassination, kidnapping, and other crimes. Spies use surveillance to plan an individual's compromise. Data theft, and facility penetration result from prior surveillance. Organized crime, intent on extortion or business takeover, conducts surveillance to assist these activities. Surveillance is a preliminary activity that makes many crimes more likely of success. Surveillance also reduces the risk for the terrorist, spy, or other criminal in regard to apprehension and punishment.

The well-trained soldier, skilled in combat, may abandon surveillance sensitivity and ambush awareness in civilized surroundings, with disastrous results. A U.S. Army officer was living in Tehran, Iran, with his family before the shah was deposed. Each morning he left his house punctually and walked to a nearby corner where he waited to be picked up by an embassy vehicle. The officer never looked behind as he walked to the corner. His wife alerted him to reports of strangers hanging around the neighborhood, but he ignored the warning. Surveillance continued almost openly and on foot. He did not recognize it. Captured documents showed that terrorists could hardly believe his carelessness. Finally, after weeks of surveillance, two terrorists pushing a motorcycle shot him in the face one morning as he walked from his house.

Business and personal risk can be reduced through a practical understanding of surveillance itself and the ways of surveillance sensitivity. Surveillance can be avoided with effort. Surveillance can be recognized with knowledge. Seldom, outside of Hollywood and television scripts, however, does the intended victim realize that surveillance has taken place, let alone that it is in progress. Failure to avoid or recognize surveillance allows criminals to construct operational plans. Unsuccessful or unproductive surveillance usually makes the spy, terrorist, or other criminal choose another, easier, target. That fact provides a powerful incentive for security personnel and all executives to become surveillance sensitive.

The average home owner has learned about the advantages of dead-bolt locks, the dangers of keys left in a car or under the mat, and to use timers on home lights in an effort to reduce the risk of burglary. These measures presume the burglar will conduct a short surveillance or reconnaissance before acting. But executives seldom give a thought to being recognized or followed by espionage agents bent on surveillance as a preliminary to other criminal activity. It took a major educational effort to make home owners conscious of burglars' methods. There must be a similar educational campaign to alert executives about espionage and, especially, about surveillance as a preliminary to espionage and covert action.

CATEGORIES OF SURVEILLANCE

Local surveillance operates around a fixed location. Surveillance agents are placed to observe the general activity at a location or to observe the local routine of a specific individual or individuals. Typical local surveillance takes place at a business, factory, route point, residence, or institution. This category of surveillance is hard to recognize whether the surveillance is external or internal. Spies carrying out external surveillance exhibit little movement and are often placed in concealed locations such as a rented office, home, apartment, or in a semi-concealed location such as a specially constructed surveillance vehicle. Internal surveillance involves the use of an agent-in-place who masks the surveillance by pretending to carry out only the normal activities of an employee, visitor, customer, repairman, or public official.

Transportation surveillance takes place when espionage agents follow the movements and activities of cargo sent by truck, rail, barge, aircraft, or ship. Both external and internal agents may be used. External surveillance must follow along as the cargo moves; internal surveillance is possible when an agent has found a way to ride along with the cargo. Cover activities for internal surveillance are similar to all agent-in-place roles. They include the employee, public official, a person needing a ride, and so forth.

Personal surveillance is usually a combination of local and transportation surveillance. An agent may succeed in becoming the victim's chauffeur, maid, houseboy, or other servant. The agent may be spying willingly or unwillingly. That makes no difference to the victim. Surveillance vehicles or rented locations may be used as local surveillance sites near the victim's home or office. Pedestrian or vehicular tails are used to follow the victim's movements. This type of surveillance often involves several people or even several teams of people, as well as various vehicles to reduce the chance that the targeted individual or security detail will spot surveillance movements.

Electronic and optical eavesdropping can involve the constant attention of espionage agents in order to monitor the eavesdropping results. Eavesdropping devices may be automatic, requiring periodic changes of batteries, tapes, or film. In the case of radio-frequency transmission of closed circuit television picture or sound, using house or vehicle current for energy, there may be no need for any agent to touch the equipment after installation has taken place. Electronic eavesdropping includes telephone monitoring, conversation monitoring, and vehicle monitoring.

Cameras used to record activities in a particular location or the activities of an individual are of many types. The 35mm camera with a telephoto lens and motor-driven film advancement is a favorite surveillance tool. Closed-circuit television offers many surveillance opportunities, especially since technology now offers miniaturization and pinhole lenses. Motion picture cameras are frequently used to record a victim's gestures and movements for later positive identification.

Telephone-answering arrangements, whether through an answering service or use of an answering machine, offer a good opportunity for electronic surveillance. Espionage agents may cultivate employees at an answering service for information on the victim's messages, contacts, movements, and plans. Answering machines that allow remote retrieval are dangerous in respect to surveillance since anyone can buy a tone generator of the same make as the answering machine. Some machines allow up to thirty-two code combinations; however, it is doubtful that many customers alter the factory setting. An espionage agent can easily determine the make and model of an answering machine and buy a tone generator in order to retrieve messages regularly without anyone's becoming aware of this information theft.

Pretext telephone calls for surveillance purposes can involve the home, hotel, or office. The spy calls using a suitable pretext and requests information about an organization or an individual. The calls may be directed to the targeted individual's location or to neighbors or nearby businesses. The cross-directories sold by the telephone company and city directories are often used to locate neighbors of the victim. Callers can claim to be representatives of a credit bureau needing information in regard to a line of credit or specific purchase. The travel agency pretext of confirming reservations is used often. The executive-recruiting pretext is one of the best ways to elicit information directly from an intended victim. Almost everyone is flattered to be considered for a position offering more responsibility, salary, and benefits. "Give me your travel schedule for the next few weeks so we can follow up on this offer," is almost sure to be answered in considerable detail.

Another successful telephone surveillance technique involves the use of references on the almost sure bet that they will not be checked by the victim. The very mention of these names will most likely unlock the victim's tongue. The caller claims to have called because so-and-so suggested they meet. The purpose stated often reflects a knowledge of the victim's interests. No meeting is desired, merely knowledge of the victim's whereabouts on particular days.

Corporate and personal messages move by many means through various channels. All messages are subject to interception for surveillance purposes. Mail is easily opened, read, copied, and resealed. Secretaries and mailroom personnel as well as personal servants have ample opportunity to delay mail and pass it on to an agent skilled in surreptitious opening techniques. Teletype messages are vulnerable to interception, as are in-house memoranda and verbal messages.

Desks and file cabinets, both at home and in the office, are fertile resources for the surveillance agent or a proxy. Desk calendars are often annotated. Secretaries customarily keep their boss's appointment diary in or on their desks. Telephone number files are rich sources of contacts. These individuals may be later interviewed in an effort to learn the victim's habits and plans.

The target of the surveillance often makes everything easy for the espionage agent by publicly informing his or her secretary or family of daily plans and routes. Other obvious tipoffs result from conspicuous transfer of clothing to be cleaned, mowers to be repaired, or an overnight bag to the victim's vehicle.

CRITICAL JUNCTURES

There are many times and places when surveillance is particularly dangerous to the potential espionage victim. Surveillance at these critical junctures may expose a vulnerability so attractive that immediate action, in the form of kidnapping or assassination, will go forward. Another type of critical juncture is represented by situations during which the potential victim becomes careless, with no thought of danger to come later as the result of careless utterance.

Travel often becomes a critical juncture in this regard. The traveler may not know the area and so ventures out at a time of day when local authorities offer minimum police protection. Or the traveler may indiscreetly ask for advice on gambling, prostitution, drugs, or other illegal activity normally under the control of organized crime. These groups sometimes work on the behalf of terrorists.

Most people are aware of what we call the bus syndrome. People traveling a long way by public transportation often talk indiscreetly to strangers sitting in an adjacent seat. Similar dialogues occur between strangers who meet at a bar or social function some distance from home.

Competitors bent on industrial espionage know that those attending trade shows as working exhibitors spend long hours in the hall. When the exhibit closes for the evening, exhibitors often go to the hotel bar or restaurants with new companions or on the recommendations of strangers.

Another example of critical juncture results from habit patterns. Who has not driven to or from work on automatic pilot? Somehow we arrived but cannot remember details of the too-familiar journey. Accustomed ruts take us to stores, restaurants, movies, and homes of friends usually by the same route. We congratulate ourselves upon finding our parking spot free at various locations. Our alarm clocks wake us at the same time each working day. We go through our washing up, eat the usual breakfast or skip it as usual, then exit the door promptly at the same time. The car is parked overnight in the same place. Espionage agents thrive on routines because they make planning of criminal acts easy.

Once in the office we glance at our desk calendar that shows golf at the club Wednesday afternoon, as usual, with the regular foursome and lunch at that good ethnic restaurant, as usual, on Thursday. Almost every day holds a routine event for most of us. Human nature likes routine and often resents change, however minor. This tendency is obvious in exaggerated cases but unnoticed in ourselves. With some people you can tell the time of day according to where they are and even the day itself by their tie or dress. The more habits or patterns that exist the easier it is to be victimized. But we love our habits, don't we?

Jogging is perhaps the worst possible habit for those chosen as surveillance targets by terrorists. Joggers like early morning hours when most others are asleep or still at home. The reason for choosing such times is understandable. Joggers often choose bright, conspicuous clothing that is ridiculous to everyone but friends and family—and to surveillance agents whose job is made easier.

One of the coauthors learned an early lesson about noting surveillance. My partner and I entered an Italian restaurant late in the evening after conducting a surveillance ourselves. We sat opposite one another at a rear table. "Don't turn around," my partner, Dave, said. "Don't look over your shoulder. We are being followed."

"How do you know?" I countered.

"A young fellow rushed in the door after us. I saw him just as I sat down. He was looking everywhere. After noticing us he sat down at a table near the entrance. He'll order coffee, pay in advance, and wait for us. Let's enjoy our dinner while he sweats and then set a trap."

After a luxurious meal, we got up and walked out, looking neither left nor right, discussing sports avidly. Once outside, as agreed, I sprinted to our car to make ready to follow the surveillance agent while Dave ambushed him by simply standing still just outside the restaurant door.

The surveillance agent inside gave us twenty seconds, then burst outside, only to be flustered at the sight of Dave, standing calmly and facing the restaurant entrance. The agent halted momentarily, then ran past to his own car. He rapidly departed the scene, but I had been ready and followed the agent long enough to get his car's license plate number. We already had his description. I went back to the restaurant and retrieved my partner.

Yes, we found out who it was. The young amateur was an agent in training with a national agency. He had been assigned to put us under surveillance as a good test of his abilities. He just was not good enough to beat Dave.

Travel in a foreign country is another critical juncture. There is often jet lag, culture shock, unfamiliar currency, and usually an unfamiliar language. Drivers may be driving on the left. Banks do not keep American hours. The food may be too bland, too spicy, or too oily. Naturally, these small differences and inconveniences cause confusion to the visitor. Given sufficient time and the proper attitude, jet lag vanishes and the differences become enjoyable or outright fun. In the meantime, the visitor is particularly vulnerable to espionage and susceptible to surveillance. This is especially the case if the visitor does not understand the language or has an indifferent interpreter.

There is a tendency for foreign hosts to show the American visitor a good time and first class treatment. Both of these generous acts make the groggy guest practically glow in the dark to surveillance agents. Itineraries frequently are made out far in advance in correspondence between the home office and the foreign subsidiary or other overseas connection. Naturally, the itineraries see wide circulation.

SPECIAL CASE: TERRORIST SURVEILLANCE

International terrorists strike at buildings, places, or things and take hostages to ensure safe return to their sanctuary. Not all hostages survive. A casing team is sent from sanctuary to the target area to perform reconnaissance and surveillance. It returns home. A support team goes in, locates supplies, caches them, and returns to sanctuary. The hit team enters the target country less than twenty-four hours before the strike in order to thwart any checking by public authorities. Because the casing team stays such a short while, it is almost impossible to spot this type of surveillance. This is not personal surveillance but rather local. Surveillance sensitivity must be replaced with common sense. Targets must avoid being in the wrong place at the wrong time. This is where strategic and tactical intelligence can help.

National or internal terrorists operate in one country. They can afford to take considerable time in conducting surveillance and otherwise preparing for a hit. Internal terrorists strike usually at human targets; they are thus the most dangerous of terrorists. Their standard practice involves witting or unwitting cooperation by an employee in regard to the victim's habits and schedules. Their surveillance is very loose; it is usually detected only after the hit. Surveillance sensitivity, then, must apply to both local and personal concerns, with special emphasis on routes to and from work. Terrorists prefer to strike along such a route.

Females dominate some terrorist groups and comprise the majority in others. They are to be considered very likely choices for surveillance duties and other active missions such as maiming (knee-capping), assassination, and kidnapping. Potential victims must watch out for females in the late teens to middle thirties. (Some Italian businessmen, concerned about terrorist surveillance, have chosen to hire only older secretaries. These were felt less likely to be susceptible to the overtures of terrorists.)

SURVEILLANCE FUNDAMENTALS

To become surveillance sensitive, it is first necessary to learn the fundamentals of surveillance:

- Know the subject and his or her habits.
- Know the areas likely to be visited.
- Be inconspicuous according to the surroundings.
- Be prepared to break off surveillance.
- Be resourceful and be equipped for contingencies.

A background investigation of the victim coupled with interviews of neighbors and friends, using suitable pretexts, prepares the agent for surveillance activity. Agents use newspaper files, company newsletters, and other public information sources. They check court records to determine property and residences owned, scan motor vehicle records to locate vehicle and license numbers assigned, enlarge telephoto pictures to show details, and use motion pictures to reveal habits, distinctive gait, and various angles of view.

The information assembled should include the victim's residence, locker and other storage facility, vacation home, recreational vehicle, company car, and personal vehicle. Habits to be ascertained, if possible before initiating surveillance, include driving routes to and from the office and other regular stops, such as shopping areas, bars, spas, clubs, recreational sites, and the homes of friends and relatives.

An area reconnaissance will prevent confusion when following the subject. Ideally the surveillance agents should be familiar with all areas where the subject is likely to go. Familiarity is accomplished by a reconnaissance at a time the subject is known to be elsewhere. Agents often procure maps and aerial photos. In the case of buildings, blueprints may have been filed. Those are public information and easy to obtain.

Surveillance agents are seldom worried that they will be spotted by the victim they follow. More dangerous are the police and naturally suspicious individuals. The latter are found in every neighborhood and in every office. They pride themselves on the ability to be in the know before anyone else. Sometimes called busybodies, they are the dread of all surveillance agents, public as well as private.

Inconspicuousness is fostered by the choice of agents considering physical type, dress, vehicle, education and cultural habits. The use of a surveillance vehicle eliminates several of these problems. The habit of customizing vans with mirrored windows has been a great help to surveillance agents who can rest comfortably in an air-conditioned or heated van while spying, taking pictures, or monitoring eavesdropping devices. Another boon to surveillance agents is the now-familiar vehicle headrest, which serves to hide the heads of surveillance agents. Recreational vehicles have been a blessing.

An example of conspicuousness during surveillance is presented. Take the case of the red Corvette, not necessarily the best choice for surveillance. A part-time private investigator, a former state policeman who should have known better, decided to use his red Corvette convertible for surveillance. He was assigned the task of following a clothing delivery driver on scheduled rounds in the Baltimore, Maryland, area. Soon after the surveillance began, the delivery driver was seen to abandon his route. The Corvette followed the truck. To the agent's surprise, they wound up at a police station. The delivery driver had spotted the Corvette, particularly noteworthy since one headlight was frozen open and the other frozen closed. Fearing a hijacking attempt, he drove to the nearest police station to report the suspicious vehicle that had been following him for the past hour. (Of course, the part-time private investigator had a number of excuses for his difficulties. He was, nevertheless, fired.)

Long-range surveillance is often preferred because it puts the maximum distance between the agent and the subject. Short-range surveillance becomes obvious quickly and is used only by the amateur or the police when desiring to intimidate a criminal. The break-off rule requires agents to cease surveillance immediately if they even suspect that the object of the surveillance is becoming suspicious.

Because a surveillance may lead to an environment other than expected, it is necessary to carry clothing that will allow inconspicuousness. For example, the surveillance may lead to a golf course, where normal business attire is very much out of place. A sports shirt and golf cap provide reasonable emergency disguise in such a situation. Agents should take food and beverages, spare film and cassettes, change for turnpike and telephone, and blankets in addition to various changes of clothing. A ground cloth and insect repellant can be useful, as is a portable toilet. Some agents can use makeup and carry a makeup kit along with their various clothing changes. Vehicles used for surveillance should be equippped with cutoff switches to alter light patterns front and rear for night work. Many other ideas will occur to the imaginative agent. A couple of empty peach baskets or a few fishing rods in the rear seat of a sedan turn a surveillance vehicle into a family car. Baby things, such as diapers, are also used as props for a camouflaged surveillance vehicle.

RECOGNIZING SURVEILLANCE

Surveillance agents often have difficulty distinguishing vehicles they wish to follow at night. For this reason, they use a number of methods to make the followed vehicle conspicuous. Part of surveillance sensitivity involves inspecting vehicles to see if they have been marked in some way.

Since surveillance usually follows rather than precedes its quarry, alterations to the victim's vehicle are at the rear. Tail lights must be inspected because a lens may have been broken to display a white bulb light in contrast to the colored lens intact on the other tail light. Both lights need to be verified operational because a bulb may have been removed or a dead bulb substituted so that the light pattern is altered. A different-colored bulb may have been substituted also. An inspection should be made for decals, especially the reflective type. Reflective tape is sometimes attached in an easy-to-recognize pattern. Crude attempts to mark the vehicle can involve the use of magnetic reflectors attached to a flat rear surface. Of course, none of this may be necessary if the owner or chauffeur has himself innocently attached reflective decals of one kind or another to reflect membership in an auto club or other organization. Such decals are sometimes displayed on rear windows to the delight of surveillance agents.

Less visible but of higher sophistication are mobile transmitters, called bumper beepers, that can be magnetically attached to the underside of a vehicle in seconds. These devices can be located by visual inspection of the underside of the vehicle. If a service station hydraulic lift is not available, there are several vehicle inspection mirrors that suit the purpose. Since a bomb may be disguised to look like a transmitter, it is best not to remove any suspicious object so attached. Prudence dictates calling the police bomb-disposal unit and making use of another vehicle in the meantime. (Peter Minogue, a defense driving instructor, has recommended the installation of high-intensity headlights in front and a set of concealed rear quartz lights fitted with 100 watt bulbs. This, he feels, will end both night-time pursuit and/or close surveillance.)

Repair personnel who appear at a home or office, especially for electrical or telephone maintenance, should be highly suspect; their purpose may include the installation or servicing of an eavesdropping device, camera, tape recorder, or microphone. Surveillance sensitivity suggests that all repair personnel be checked before allowing them access to any facility. This should be done by calling the number listed in the telephone directory, not the number they offer. A description of the serviceperson and vehicle should be secured. Any discrepancy is cause for concern. Even if the repairman is genuine, there is a possibility that greed or blackmail will influence his actions while on the premises. For this reason, all repair personnel should be accompanied by a knowledgeable, mature employee—not a young, temporary person whose knowledge and interest may be unequal to the task of monitoring the repair visit. Computer maintenance personnel fall into the same category. They should be monitored by a computer supervisor whose integrity has been verified.

Penetration attempts may be recognized by regular examination of all locks and hinge pins. Scratches may indicate attempts to overcome the lock or pin in order to secure unauthorized access to install eavesdropping devices. Windows should receive the same attention. All openings, including roof openings, skylights, and basement openings, are avenues for the surveillance agent who must penetrate the facility to steal data, place eavesdropping devices, or hide for other purposes, such as planting a bomb or committing assassination.

Recognizing what is out of place is an excellent way to recognize surveillance, but there is no way to define out of place. Operating in familiar surroundings or with familiar people, all of us can recognize things or people that do not fit in with that particular place, group, or situation. This instinct can be developed through practice and, especially, by active curiosity.

PSYCHOLOGICAL PREPARATION

This is truly a fishbowl society. Privacy is an illusion that can only be realized temporarily through luck, skill, or incredible expense. If we are lucky, no one cares enough to penetrate our privacy. If we are skillful, it becomes a low probability that we are vulnerable to surveillance. Only large corporations and governments can expend the time and money that real privacy demands. Radio-frequency shielded rooms, scanning equipment, high-grade scramblers, complete background investigations, instrumental detection of stress, and thorough twenty-four hour security are beyond the reach of most commercial interests. Even if privacy can be afforded, there is an image problem. Customers are not encouraged by a paramilitary, high-security commercial environment.

Retail electronic shops sell microphones, tape recorders, voice-activated switches, closed circuit television cameras and lenses, as well as component equipment, that can be used to construct and conceal eavesdropping devices. Parabolic (long-range) microphones are available from electronics mail-order firms. Anyone can buy a resistor, capacitor, and amplifier to bypass a telephone hook switch, creating a live microphone at each telephone receiver. If the telephone is multiline, a spare pair of wires will do as well when properly connected. Binoculars and telescopes are easy to procure. Night-vision devices, although expensive, enable anyone to become a surveillance agent after dark. Optical image enhancement can be used with or without cameras or rifles.

Modern technology has brought professional camera equipment to the masses. A wide array of lenses and films is easy to procure. Some of this film is so fast that pictures can be taken in what otherwise appears to be the dark.

Long-distance telephone calls are a matter of record to you, the telephone company, and customers of unscrupulous employees who sell your list. Among their customers are some banks, loan companies, private detective agencies, and others. Called telephone numbers can be matched with the names and addresses of those called even if their numbers are unlisted. Bill collectors call these lists *phone breaks.* While illegal, the use of phone breaks has spread nationwide, making everyone's telephone calls open to surveillance agents for a small fee.

Credit records that routinely list a person's real estate purchases, employment history, salary, and other sensitive information are available to anyone who is a member of a credit bureau. All businesses that extend retail credit, as well as lending institutions, and professionals may join the local credit bureau. Local credit bureaus can procure credit information nationwide as a result of their associate links. It is not hard to find someone subscribing to a credit bureau who will help a friend by checking on someone else. Everytime someone makes a credit transaction or applies for credit or a loan they diminish their possibilities of privacy and enhance the resources available for surveillance preparation by an espionage agent.

Paranoia Is Not All Bad

Becoming surveillance sensitive is simply becoming more alert to one's surroundings and the possible dangers. There are many advantages to alertness in addition to being able to notice acquaintances first. You will see that attractive person of the opposite sex before anyone else in your party. You will be able to see the check coming in a restaurant. Whether you turn toward or away from these opportunities is not important. That you enjoyed a choice is important.

Becoming surveillance sensitive will prevent those accidents where the victim is caught unaware. When the piano falls from a fifth floor loft, you will not be under it! When a speeding car jumps the curb and heads your way, you will be elsewhere.

There can be no doubt that awareness is a positive condition. The sedentary habits of the modern city dweller, dulled by crowded conditions, noise, and haste, reduce the awareness of many potential victims. Surveillance sensitivity involves methods to rekindle the desire to pay close attention to everything in the immediate environment. Wherever you are, be there!

Disguises

Simple disguises are best. Learn about disguises by trying them out on people who should recognize you. One of the coauthors had worked five months at an educational institution, always dressed in suit and tie. One Saturday, dressed casually in T-shirt and jeans, he entered the building with his key and walked down the hall toward his office. Another faculty member was in the hall. He spoke sharply: "What are you doing here?" and approached within two feet before he recognized the intruder. Clothing had proved an extremely effective disguise because it was out of character.

Glasses with plain lenses are an excellent disguise for the clear sighted and those who wear contact lenses. Frames should be selected for their attention-getting qualities.

Wigs are effective disguises for women. Men, however, seldom choose toupees or wigs that fail to attract attention to the wearer. Hats are better disguises for males. Hats are pejorative; that is, they place the wearer in a distinct category. A baseball cap with a dirty emblem works well unless that is the wearer's normal garb. Oversize clothing, not bright in hue, often succeeds in confusing the surveillance agent expecting someone of a certain weight and proportion. One member of the party, ideally a bodyguard, should be dressed better than the principal who is being protected to confuse watchers.

Douglas Macnair, a former colonel in the U.S. Army military police, is known by many as Blackstack Mac or Smokestack Mac. He determined that it was prudent to paint out the logos on marine oil tankers, reasoning that pirates and terrorists needing intelligence on ship movements would be stymied. His act made him a legend in the oil security field. So, things as well as people may be disguised.

Practical Exercises

People who suspect they may be attacked at any minute are usually alert to their surroundings. Adrenalin pumps, the heart beat increases, and muscles tense unless fatigue or injury makes such response impossible. But, no one can remain at such a state of readiness endlessly. Executive protection personnel, although highly trained, usually burn out in a year or two from constant strain. Therefore it is unrealistic to base surveillance sensitivity on combat reflexes. Alertness must be based on intellectual rather than emotional grounds.

Many readers are familiar with the routine alertness of aircraft pilots who easily spot another aircraft that appears as only a dot in the sky to others, provided they even see the dot. Hunters too are able to pick a quarry out of an admittedly distracting environment.

Both the pilot and hunter must be observant. They have learned what to ignore and what requires reaction. Their skills make the effort seem easy. In neither case does the skill arise from talent only. It is the result of patient and persistent practice. The pilot's eyes are never still. The hunter's eyes and ears stay alert. These are not really conscious efforts. Surveillance sensitivity can become a skill through practice.

Several surveillance sensitivity exercises are presented below. They are suitable for almost all ages and both sexes. These exercises are meant to stimulate awareness and the self-development of other, more sophisticated exercises.

MEMORY. We have all made observations that confirm our sometimes inaccurate memories. Where did we park our car? When is the birthday? What was I supposed to bring home? What is his name again? What was that answer supposed to be? A good memory has many advantages, including surveillance sensitivity. The more we remember, the easier it becomes to recognize new or out-of-place elements in our environments that could signal surveillance. Did I see that person before, perhaps, yesterday? Has someone rearranged my things? These are questions easily answered by the person with a good memory or who has practiced memory development.

It is not difficult to develop a better memory. Certain occupational groups, especially the police, seem to develop phenomenal memories in relation to past experiences having to do with their work. Interest always sharpens the memory.

There are several memory systems available. The methods of Harry Lorayne, available in book form, are recommended.[1] He has developed an easy, practical system for remembering faces, numbers, names, and large numbers of items. The advantages of a good memory are so many that it seems only common sense to learn a memory system.

Whatever memory system or nonsystem is preferred, these two memory exercises can increase surveillance sensitivity:

1. Place in your memory all of those people who seem to be hanging around in one locality or another that you frequent. Refer to those memories wherever you go. Determine if the same loafer is seen to appear in several geographical locations at the same time you are there. (If so, have someone investigate.) It is important to peg your memory with each person's prominent facial feature and dress.
2. Place in your memory all vehicles (license plates and occupants, too, if possible) that are driven or parked near your own. Check frequently to see if the same vehicles appear again and again as you travel or are parked nearby your destinations. Investigators can trace vehicle ownership through these remembered license numbers.

OBSERVATION. To see is not the same as to observe (notice). *Awareness* is a term related to observation. Awareness often comes slowly, if at all. The expression *last to know* is significant in that it supposes someone close to an event was unaware of its significance until too late. *Significance* is another word pertinent to observation skills. It is necessary first to see, second to observe, and third to judge the significance of an event. Action comes after an appreciation of an event's significance. Surveillance sensitivity leads nowhere without action to interrupt the surveillance. That action will not occur unless observation has taken place. Obliviousness is the enemy to observation.

Watch where you are going! Pay attention! Keep your mind on what you are doing. These platitudes have a modicum of common sense, indicating that a lack of awareness is all too common.

---

[1] *How to Develop a Super-Power Memory* (New York: New American Library, 1974), and *Secrets of Mind Power* (New York: New American Library, 1975).

Children in ghetto areas can spot a plain-clothes police officer because a belt-holstered pistol or revolver causes a pants leg to sag on the side where the weapon is holstered. These children are alert to strangers. Adults can do even better in observation if they are willing to practice.

The following two exercises are designed to help observation as an aid to surveillance sensitivity:

1. Film or arrange to have filmed activities in which a potential victim participates. Film this person's comings and goings at long range. Develop and study the films to locate possible surveillance agents or vehicles. Pick out surveillance sites that would have been optimal if surveillance had taken place. Explain the findings to the potential victim. Ask the person to be alert to such situations in traveling and to note them for later analysis.

2. Tell the potential victim that a friendly surveillance team has been put in the field to test his or her powers of observation. Do or do not actually field the team. You can be sure that the potential victim will be very observant. Debrief and go over all observations that he or she made. Be thorough because the potential victim, alert to the possibility of friendly surveillance, may actually spot hostile surveillance.

AVOIDANCE. There is little doubt that it is better to avoid surveillance than to fall victim to it. No matter how well developed the memory and observation skills, it is possible to fail to notice active surveillance efforts. For this reason, prudence dictates acting in such a way that surveillance becomes difficult. This difficulty will increase the possibility of mistakes on the part of the surveillance operatives. Such mistakes, captured by memory and observation, reveal the presence of surveillance and allow the victim the option of calling for help or taking refuge.

Some executives find avoidance exercises tedious because their routine becomes interrupted. These people do not understand the threats posed by surveillance. If they continue to resist surveillance sensitivity, a letter should be placed in their personnel file stating that noncooperation will be a factor considered in ransom negotiation.

Several avoidance exercises are offered as examples only. They may be used with or without disguise and/or makeup.

1. List all reasonable routes to and from locations to be visited. Employ a random number system to choose each route each

time a visit is to be made. Employ the random number system just before each departure. Route selection should include alternative building exits and entrances.

2. Announce business meetings or social gatherings. Then change the location at the last moment and move times up, if possible. The alternatives should be subjected to random number choice. Include the use of motor homes, easily rented, as mobile meeting sites that can be parked or driven or both.

3. Alternate every aspect of life that offers choice. Prepare a list of all activities and attempt to build alternatives into everything so that the habit of change becomes ingrained. Executive protection personnel are taught to expect the unexpected. The victim can become the hunter by choosing to create the unexpected, instead of falling victim to another's choices.

SUMMARY

Most people have neglected their abilities to note what and who are close at hand. Comfortable ruts are not the exception but the rule. Such habits increase the likelihood of successful surveillance followed by acts of espionage, terrorism, and other crimes.

Surveillance is done in many ways. Local surveillance observes a particular area or site. Transportation surveillance targets movement of cargo by any means. Personal surveillance follows a particular individual wherever that person goes. Electronic eavesdropping is another form of surveillance that can include cameras, closed circuit television, or microphones. Telephone answering is particularly prone to surveillance attempts. Pretext interviews and telephone calls are used by surveillance agents. Messages may be intercepted.

There are a number of critical junctures to beware of in surveillance sensitivity. They include travel and trade shows. But habit patterns remain the most dangerous periods for the potential victim.

Knowing the fundamentals can help prevent the success of surveillance. These include knowing the subjects and their habits; knowing where the subject is likely to go; keeping inconspicuous; being prepared to end the surveillance due to the subject's suspicion; being resourceful and able to adjust to changes during the surveillance period.

Surveillance attempts may be recognized sometimes by inspecting a vehicle at the rear and underneath. Unexpected visits of repair personnel need to be challenged. All such visitors need escorts. Desks, windows, file cabinets, and all means of entrance and exit must be examined for signs of forced or unauthorized entry.

Potential victims of surveillance need to realize that privacy today is only an illusion or very temporary situation at best. Modern technology has put electronic eavesdropping within reach of millions. High-speed film and night-vision devices make darkness a poor cover. Telephone records are not secure. Credit records are easily accessed.

Surveillance sensitivity implies becoming more alert. That has many benefits.

Disguises can help reduce the risk of positive identification, which must precede surveillance. The potential victim can be disguised, and/or a member of the protective team can be disguised to resemble the potential victim. Even ships, such as oil tankers, can be disguised.

Practical exercises must be based on intellectual, not emotional, grounds. Surveillance sensitivity is a skill based on memory, observation, and routine avoidance.

Electronic Surveillance Glossary

Active device (surveillance) A device that is transmitting, or is capable of transmitting, electronic intelligence.

Actuator A voltage or voice-sensing device normally used to turn on or off a transmitter or tape recorder.

Antenna That portion of a surveillance device or countermeasure receiver that radiates or receives radio signals.

Anti-bug A radio frequency or audio frequency generator that interferes with the operation of an electronic audio surveillance system.

Audio Sound waves audible to the human ear (up to 15 KHz).

Band A defined group of radio frequency waves.

Beeper A miniature transmitter usually employed for tailing or locating a suspect, package, or automobile.

Big ear A microphone that is extremely sensitive to audio frequencies arriving from one particular direction, while rejecting those arriving from other directions.

Black box A term used to describe a piece of electronic equipment whose characteristics are not generally known.

Body bug A microphone with a transmitter that is worn.

Body mike A microphone designed to be worn and connected to either a transmitter or a recorder.

Broad band A defined group of frequencies covering a large portion of the radio spectrum.

Bug Electronic audio surveillance device, which may be wired or wireless.

Bug detector A device used to signal the presence of a nearby radio frequency source.

Bugging The process of monitoring conversations by electronic means.

Bumper beeper *See* Beeper.

313

Carrier   Radio-frequency signal upon which intelligence is impressed.

Contact mike   Microphone that converts vibrations caused by sound impacting on a solid object to electrical energy.

Countermeasures   Defensive techniques designed to detect the use of electronic audio-surveillance devices.

Debugging   *See* Countermeasures.

Demodulation   The process of extracting audio information from radio-frequency signals.

Detection   The process of determining the presence of electronic signals.

DF   Direction finding.

Directional microphone   *See* Big ear.

Drop-in   A radio transmitter that has the appearance of a telephone mouthpiece element.

Eavesdropping   Secretly listening to or recording conversations; including both bugging and wiretapping.

Feedback   Squeal caused by the output of an amplifier feeding back to its input.

FM   A modulation technique in which the frequency of a device is moved up and down the spectrum.

Frequency   A precisely defined portion of the radio spectrum.

Harmonica bug   An audio amplifier connected to a telephone line through a tone-sensitive switch, which is activated by telephoning the monitored premises and sounding the coded tone. The called telephone does not ring and is held open so the caller can hear the conversation taking place in the vicinity of the microphone and amplifier.

Harmonics   Frequencies of exact integral multiples of a fundamental frequency.

Hot mike   An active microphone or one that can readily be made active. Also, the activation of a telephone element when the telephone is in the hung-up position.

Howler   *See* Screamer.

Inductive pickup   A transducer that functions by the principle of electromagnetic induction, rather than by direct connection to a circuit.

Infinity Transmitter   *See* Harmonica bug.

Jammer   *See* Anti-bug.

Keyhole microphone   A microphone connected to a slender tube, which is used to listen through small openings.

Monitoring   The act of listening-in (or supervising) on a line without causing interference.

Noise   A random signal generated over a wide spectrum, which can be either radio frequency, audio frequency, or both.

Non-linear junction detector   A recently declassified device that detects the presence of semiconductors.

Parabolic microphone   *See* Big ear.

Parallel RF tap Radio transmitter that is connected across a pair of telephone lines.

Parasite Radio transmitter that obtains power from the telephone line to which it is attached.

Passive device (surveillance) A device that is activated from a remote source.

Planting The process of placing a surveillance device.

Receiver (RF) A device that can monitor a defined group of radio frequencies.

Receiver (telephone) The earphone in a telephone handset.

Ringer Telephone bell and the electrical circuit that makes it work.

Scrambler A device that converts intelligible audio into unintelligible audio.

Screamer A radio-frequency detector fed to an audio amplifier, which causes uncontrolled feedback when positioned near a concealed transmitter.

Search The process of both physically and electronically looking for a surveillance device.

Series radio tap A radio transmitter that obtains power from the telephone line to which it is attached, in series with one wire.

Shotgun microphone *See* Big ear.

Snake microphone *See* Tube microphone.

Spike microphone A contact microphone affixed to a rod, or spike, usually passed through a wall to bear upon the inner wall of an adjoining room, thereby transmitting audio frequency vibrations to the microphone using the wall as a diaphragm.

Stethoscope A device used to listen through solid media.

Suction cup *See* Stethoscope.

Surveillance Secretly observing the behavior of another; includes both eavesdropping and visual surveillance.

Surveillance (AF) A process of monitoring audio information and passing these data through wires.

Surveillance (RF) A process of monitoring audio information and passing these data to a transmitter.

Tap A surveillance device used on a telephone.

Technical surveillance Any combination of bugging or wiretapping.

Telephone set A complete telephone, including handset, ringer, and all other associated parts located at a subscriber station, with the exception of protective equipment.

Terminal block The point at which individual telephone instruments are connected to the interior phone lines of a building.

Third wire tap Activating a telephone microphone by adding a third wire to the circuit, so the telephone microphone is active while the handset is hung up, thus bypassing the hookswitch. *See* Hot mike.

Tone   A precisely defined frequency in the audio spectrum.

Transmitter (telephone)   Mouthpiece microphone in the telephone handset.

Trigger transmitter   Device used to turn on and/or off a remotely located bug.

Tube microphone   A microphone with an integral rigid or flexible tube, which is the primary path to the microphone for sound waves.

Video   A radio frequency signal associated with a television picture.

Voice-actuated switch (VOX)   Switch that closes when audio frequency energy is impressed at its input.

Wireless microphone   A miniature, battery-powered radio transmitter.

Wireless tap   A radio transmitter connected to a telephone line by a matching network feeding its audio frequency input.

Wiretap   Any device employed to intercept any wired communication and the act of applying.

Bibliography

BOOKS

Aubrey, Arthur S., Jr., and Caputo, Rudolph R. *Criminal Interrogation.* Springfield, Ill.: Charles C Thomas Publisher, 1965.

Barron, John. *K.G.B.—The Secret Work of Soviet Secret Agents.* New York: Bantam Books, Inc., 1974.

Bergier, Jacques. *Secret Armies*: Trans. Harold J. Salemson. New York: Bobbs-Merrill Company, Inc., 1975.

Bottom, Norman R., and Kostanoski, John. *Security and Loss Control.* New York: Macmillan Publishing Co., 1983.

Calvocoressi, Peter. *Top Secret Ultra.* New York: Ballentine Books, 1980.

Carroll, John M. *Secrets of Electronic Espionage.* New York: E.P. Dutton & Co., Inc., 1966.

Carroll, John M. *Confidential Information Sources: Public and Private.* Woburn, Mass.: Butterworth Publishers, 1975.

Department of Justice (LEAA) *Basic Elements of Intelligence.* Washington, D.C.: U.S. Government Printing Office, 1976.

Dulles, Allan. *The Craft of Intelligence.* New York: Harper & Row, 1963.

Fain, Tyrus G.; Plant, Katherine C.; and Milloy, Ross. *The Intelligence Community: History, Organization and Issues.* New York: R.R. Bowker Company, 1977.

Gallati, Robert R.J. *Introduction to Private Security.* Englewood Cliffs, N.J.: Prentice-Hall Inc., 1983.

Halperin, Morton H., and Hoffman, Daniel. *Freedom Vs. National Security: Secrecy and Surveillance.* New York: Chelsea House Publishers, 1977.

Hamilton, Peter. *Espionage, Terrorism and Subversion in an Industrial Society.* Leatherhead, Surrey, England: Peter A. Heims LTD., 1979.

Heims, Peter A. *Countering Industrial Espionage.* Leatherhead, Surrey, England: 20th Century Security Education Ltd., 1982.

Hyde, H. Montgomery. *The Atom Bomb Spies*. New York: Ballantine Books, 1980.

Kakalik, J.S., and Wildhorn, Sorrel. *The Private Police Industry: Its Nature and Extent*, Vol. II, R–870/DOJ. Washington, D.C.: U.S. Government Printing Office, 1972.

Liddy, G. Gordon, *Will*. New York: St. Martin's Press, Inc., 1980.

Lieberstein, Stanley H., *Who Owns What Is In Your Head? Trade Secrets and the Mobile Employee*. New York: Hawthorn Books, Inc., 1979.

Myagkov, Aleksei. *Inside the KGB*. New York: Ballantine Books, 1976.

National Advisory Committee on Criminal Justice Standards and Goals. *Report of the Task Force on Organized Crime*. Washington, D.C.: U.S. Government Printing Office, 1976.

National Advisory Committee on Criminal Justice Standards and Goals. *Report of the Task Force on Private Security*. Washington, D.C.: U.S. Government Printing Office, 1976.

Page, Bruce; Leitch, David; and Knightley, Phillip. *The Philby Conspiracy*. New York: Ballantine Books, 1981.

Pennsylvania Crime Commission. *Health Care Fraud: A Rising Threat*. St. Davids, Pa.: Commonwealth of Pennsylvania, 1981.

Pennsylvania Crime Commission. *A Decade of Organized Crime*, 1980 Report. St. Davids, Pa.: Commonwealth of Pennsylvania, 1980.

Prawdin, Michael. *The Mongol Empire*. London: G. Allen Publisher, 1940.

President's Commission on Law Enforcement and Administration of Criminal Justice. *Challenge of Crime in a Free Society*. Washington, D.C.: U.S. Government Printing Office, 1967.

Smith, Joseph Burkholder. *Portrait of a Cold Warrior*. New York: Ballantine Books, 1976.

Smith, Paul I. Slee. *Industrial Intelligence and Espionage*. London: Business Books, Ltd., 1970.

Steven, Stewart. *The Spymasters of Israel*. New York: Ballantine Books, 1980.

Tyson, James L. *Target America: The Influence of Communist Propaganda on U.S. Media*. Chicago: Regency Gateway, 1981.

U.S. Department of Defense. DoD5220–22. *Industrial Security Manual for Safeguarding Classified Information*. Washington, D.C.: U.S. Government Printing Office, 1981.

Walsh, Timothy J., and Healy, Richard J. *Protecting Your Business Against Espionage*. New York: Amacom Division of American Management Association, 1973.

Wilensky, Harold L. *Organizational Intelligence*. New York: Basic Books, 1967.

Yardley, Herbert O. *The American Black Chamber.* New York: Ballantine Books, 1981.

PERIODICALS

Anderson, Edward J. "A Study of Industrial Espionage—Parts I and II," *Security Management* (January and March 1977).

Anonymous. "ASIS Speaks Out: "Theft and Subversion of U.S. High Technology," *Security Management* (July 1982):2.

_____. "Spy Given B1, 'Stealth' Data, CIA Says," *Boston Globe* April 29, 1982.

_____. "How Japan Will Finance Its Technology Strategy—the Business Intelligence Beehive." *Business Week*, no. 2718 (December 14, 1981):50-52.

_____. "It Pays to Shred for Security and Hinders Office Snoops," *Modern Office & Data Management* 18, no. 5 (June 1979):11-23.

_____. "The Business Stake in Soviet Snooping," *Business Week*, no. 2513 (December 12, 1977):57-58.

_____. "Modern Security in Industry," *International Criminal Police Review* 32, no. 311 (October 1977):242-246.

_____. "Security Through Snooping," *INFO Systems* 20, no. 9 (September 1973):84-85.

Barron, Cheryl. "The Security Risk," *Management Today* (August 1977):70, 72, 74-76.

Barnes, Nancy L., and Miller, John T. "Counterintelligence—Everybody's Business," *Security Management* (August 1981):107-111.

Blanchard, Robert "Open Season on Company Secrets," *International Management* (U.K.) 35, no. 2 (February 1980):34, 38-39.

Bottom, N.R., Jr. "Security Intelligence," *Security Management* (January 1979):18-33.

_____. "Is Someone Watching You?" *Professional Protection*, 3, no. 5, 8-12.

_____. "Loss Prevention Intelligence," *Professional Protection*, 4, no. 2, 28-31.

Bowen, William. "Who Owns What's In Your Head," *Fortune.* July 1964, p. 177.

Cleland, David I. "Competitive Business Intelligence Systems," *Business Horizons* 28, no. 6 (December 1975):19-28.

Collins, Craig M. "Use Advice from Clausewitz' Classic on War to Sharpen Industrial Competitive Intelligence Systems," *Marketing News* 14, no. 22 (May 1, 1981).

Dyer, J.D. "The Technical Security Survey," *Security Management* 25, no. 4 (April 1981):54-57.

Farrel, Jack W. "Information Security: More Than Money Alone," *Traffic Management* 17, no. 8 (August 1978):42–44.

Furash, Edward E. "Problems in Review—Industrial Espionage," *Harvard Business Review* (November–December 1959).

Glueck, William, et al. "Protecting Trade Secrets in the 70s," *California Management Review* 16, no. 1 (Fall 1973):34–39.

Heims, P.A. "Unethical, But Legal," *Security Management* (December 1981):10–15.

———. "Industrial Espionage and the Private Investigator," *Security World* 9, no. 10 (November 1972):34–39.

Hoyt, D.B. "Computer as a Target for the Industrial Spy," *Assets Protection* 1, no. 1 (Spring):41–47.

Hughey, Ann. "IBM Data Plot Tied to Hitachi and Mitsubishi" *The Wall Street Journal*, June 23, 1982.

———. "We Are a Soft Target," *Forbes* 126, no. 6 (September 1980): 42–44.

Kelly, C.M. "Domestic Industrial Espionage," *Security Management* (November 1975):8–10.

Kesney, Ed. "Shielded D.P. Rooms Combat Industrial Espionage," *Data Management* 19, no. 7 (July 1981):22–23.

Lauren, Bill. "Computer Crime," *Penthouse Magazine*, June 1982, pp. 109–110, 178.

Mann, Richard A. "Industrial Espionage Made Legal: The Freedom of Information Act," *Michigan Business Review* 31, no. 6 (November 1979):13–17.

Menkus, Belden. "Management's Responsiblities for Safeguarding Information," *Journal of Systems Management* 27, no. 12 (December 1976):32–38.

Mixson, Paul. "Loose Lips Sink Sales," *Sales and Marketing Management* 118, no. 2 (February 7, 1977):37–40.

Moskal, Brian S. "Sleuthing the Opposition—Does Anything Go?" *Industry Week* 195, no. 4 (November 21, 1977):52–57.

Murray, Kevin D. "The Corporate Counter Spy," *Security Management* (April 1981):48–53.

Nelson, S.D. and Wolff, G.R. "Tightening the White Collar—The Criminalization of Trade Secret Theft," *American Criminal Law Review* 14, no. 4 (Spring 1977).

Perham, John. "The Great Game of Corporate Espionage," *Dun's Review*, October 1970, p. 30.

Palisano, Peg. "Why You Should Be Bugged about Electronic Eavesdropping," *Occupational Hazards* 43, no. 3 (March 1981):80–83.

Pearce, F.T. "Business Intelligence Systems—The Need, Development, and Integration," *Industrial Marketing Management* 5, no. 2/3 (June 1976):115, 138.

Pemberton, A.B. "Protecting Business Intelligence," *Security Gazette* 16 no. 5 (May 1974):182–183.

Reid, John E. "Behavior Symptoms of Polygraph Subjects," *Polygraph* 2, no. 1 (March 1982):39–40.

Salmans, Sandra. "Looking Out for Product Poachers," *International Management* (U.K.) 34, no. 6 (June 1979):14, 16, 19.

Simpson, Chris. "What Are the Soviets Doing in the Silicon Valley," *Computer World* 15, no. 6 (February 9, 1981):1–8.

Smith, Richard Austin. "Business Espionage," *Fortune*, May 1976, pp. 118–194.

Tavernier, Gerald. "Is Your Company Worth A Visit," *International Management* 29, no. 6 (June 1974):24–28.

Unger, Harlow. "The Spies of Silicon Valley: How Industrial Espionage Is Hurting the Computer Business," *Canadian Business* 53, no. 12 (December 1980)

Velloci, T. "Can Business Collar White Collar Crime?" *Nation's Business*, November 1978, pp. 35–44.

Wall, Jerry L. "Probing Opinions," *Harvard Business Review* (November–December 1974):22–38, 162.

Ward, W. "Technical Surveillance—Some Basic Considerations," *Assets Production* 1, no. 1 (Spring 1975):35–39.

Webster, W.H. "Director's Message," *F.B.I. Bulletin*, August 1981.

_____. "Director's Message," *F.B.I. Bulletin*, September 1980.

_____. "New Decisions Alter F.B.I.'s Traditional Role," *Security Management* (November 1979):12–16.

Winklemann, R. "Countering Clandestine Surveillance—Industrial Espionage as a Real Threat Calling for Counter Measures" *Security Gazette* 20, no. 3 (March 1978):84–89.

Wood, Nat. "Security with No 'Strings Attached.'" *Security World* 16, no. 4 (April 1979).

Zais, Arnold M. "Financial Executive's Guide to Blocking Electronic Espionage," *Financial Executive* 49, no. 9.

Index